W9-AMO-382

THE MAN STAN: MUSIAL, THEN AND NOW . . .

THE MAN STAN: MUSIAL, THEN AND NOW . . .

As Told to Bob Broeg

The Bethany Press
St. Louis, Missouri

Library of Congress Catalogue Number
ISBN: 0-8272-2312-9 (paperback)
ISBN: 0-8272-2313-7 (cloth cover)

Cover art by Amadee of the Sports Department,
ST. LOUIS POST-DISPATCH
Photographs courtesy of ST. LOUIS POST-DISPATCH
and by Acme, World Wide and Westrich Photography Studios—
St. Louis

Printed in the United States of America

In 1964 President Lyndon Johnson named The Man as leader of the nation's Council on Physical Fitness.

The late President John F. Kennedy gave Musial a warm welcome at the 1962 Washington All-Star game.

Contents

Dedication

To those who have played the game
and to those who have watched it,
hopeful that others in the future
will enjoy playing baseball
as much as Stan Musial did, and
writing about it as Bob Broeg did.

Introduction

The Other Man's Look at 'The Man'

Any time it rained I knew I could get a good open-date story from my man, Stan Musial. And as one whose rainy days were brightened when traveling with "The Man" as a baseball writer, I'm happy that fortune and the good Lord have continued to shine on him since he laid down one of history's most productive bats.

I remember the steamy overcast day in August 1969, at scenic Cooperstown, N.Y., the picture postcard village that houses the Baseball Hall of Fame on Lake Otsego. Rain fell until just before Musial stepped up for induction and then the sun broke through the thick green trees of James Fenimore Cooper's Leatherstocking country.

Pat Dean, wife of the late, colorful Dizzy Dean and an outspoken woman, said with a smile, "It figured. The sun always shines on Stan the Man."

Pat Dean would be among the first to claim the saying that goes, "it couldn't happen to a nicer guy."

The most amazing thing about a man whose greatest playing field asset was his consistency, has been the consistency with which he has achieved, handled and lived with success. I never bothered to ask Stan his hat size, but I know it's the same now in wealthy middle age as it was when he was a poor immigrant's son trying to make good. He was then known to my old boss, J. Roy Stockton, and many others, as the "Donora Greyhound."

The nickname didn't stick, but, of course, Musial did, to break records, many of which fell before Henry Aaron's durability and ability. I was most impressed that he wound up with exactly the same number of hits on the road as in St. Louis, 1815 each. That was determined years ago by the late Hall of Fame historian Lee Allen, my predecessor as columnist for *The Sporting News.* I was also impressed that the Cardinals' versatile Number 6 became the only man ever to play 1000 games in each the infield and outfield.

The many managers for whom he played all left with the similarly expressed view that it had been a joy managing the superstar who needed no managing. With no display of temper or temperament, The Man played it the company way. If there ever was a better team man, I'd like to have met him.

For a player, the storybook climax to a storybook career would have been if the Cardinals had won the pennant and then if Musial had won the World Series in the near-miss season and his last year, 1963. They did win in '64, largely as a result of the Brinks' robbery of baseball in which general manager Bing Devine heisted Lou Brock from the Chicago Cubs. It was Musial's first year away and he again displayed the common touch of an uncommon man.

The Man was a proud person and a most confident hitter. He wouldn't even go along with good friend Joe Garagiola's gag that he would have had Stan "hitless" in a book inscription for Johnny Carson. And yet he was honest and humble, a star without a "first person complex."

"The Cardinals," Musial said flatly after his club won the 1964 pennant, their first in 18 years, "couldn't have won with me in left field."

Stan meant with an old Musial, of course, and not a Musial of earlier days. In all fairness, the fellow who played those last several seasons didn't run or field as fast as the Donora

Greyhound of earlier years.

Largely because of that so-so throwing arm, injured in the accident that left him a Class D pitcher with a perilous future in 1940, Musial was not a perfect player.

Not the best, but, as Dizzy Dean said, "He was amongst 'em."

He was, and is, just what former baseball commissioner Ford Frick said in pre-game ceremonies that September afternoon in 1963 when The Man bowed out his last two times up with basehits. Among remarks later inscribed on the base of the not too flattering statue of Musial outside Busch Memorial Stadium, Frick said:

"Here stands baseball's perfect warrior, here stands baseball's perfect knight . . . "

As a baseball general manager, Musial went one for one with a world championship in 1967. As a businessman, if he hasn't hit 1.000, he must be close to the lead in the Financial League. Stan might not have been the best or most attentive student ever to come out of Donora High School back in the hills of western Pennsylvania, but he became, over the years, a quick judge of the difference between a good deal and a bad one. He could make a fast study of a business ledger to determine the bottom-line potential.

Most recently he has turned over more and more authority to his late partner Biggie Garagnani's son, Jack, and his son Dick. In the meantime Stan and dear wife Lil, who has shared both lean years and sorrows with him, have enjoyed traveling.

Wisely, Musial turned down the chance to manage, contending—with some surprise to others—that he was afraid he would be too tough. He thought that as a former star he would expect too much from the young men who played for him. Besides, it would be foreign for the good-natured guy to crack the whip when he didn't really have to.

Stan felt strongly that his long-time road roommate and close friend, Red Schoendienst, the old master second baseman, would be low-keyed and successful. When Schoendienst took over in 1965 a job that had been a graveyard for managers, Stan put the eight-ball in the side pocket with a correct forecast.

"I see Red lasting a long time on the job, like Walter Alston with the Dodgers, because he's got good judgment and also the patience to be a good manager."

So while old roomie Red sat in the dugout for 12 years and frowned, "Stahsh" Musial has indulged himself as he had wanted during those years when he was one of the best—and certainly most disciplined—ball players. When he quit traveling as a performer, he said he wanted to do three things: go on a family picnic; see a Kentucky Derby; and take in the Indianapolis 500.

When Bold Forbes held off Honest Pleasure in a two-horse race to the wire in the 1976 Kentucky Derby, the Musials were excited boxseat spectators at Churchill Downs. And before Tony Hulman intones, "Gen-tle-men, start your en-gines," you can bet the loudest vroom-vroom that Stan will be at the famous old 500-mile brickyard the next time around. You can bet, too, all the little green apples God didn't make, that if Musial is there, it won't rain in Indianapolis.

It never rains on Stan the Man's parade.

I was amused when *Philadelphia Inquirer* columnist, Tom Fox, who accompanied the Musials to Europe in 1976 as guest of philanthropist-sportsman Ed Piszek, expressed amazement at the Man's musical talent.

From watching Stan play or dance to a Polish polka, listening to him manipulate a slide whistle in the Cardinals' clubhouse or keep time with coat-hangers on an aluminum clubhouse chair, I could have told friend Fox that this extraordinary fella had limitless capacity for entertainment besides hitting a round ball squarely with a round bat.

Why, back there shortly after World War II, at a time the "Third Man Theme" from an Orson Welles' spy thriller was popular background music, Stan toured West Germany to entertain occupational troops. One snowy night Musial sat down in a Bavarian bierstube at Garmisch-Partenkirchen, and learned, from an amused old German, how to play the difficult zither.

Philadelphia's Fox of the Fourth Estate wrote that he never expected to hear "The Red River Valley" played on a harmonica at midnight in Oslo, Norway. But there, slouched against the fender of a taxi outside the Oslo airport, was the virtuoso, Mr. Musial, rendering the country-western classic with all the mournful longing of a homesick cowpoke who had just ridden in from the range rather than flown in on a 747.

Musial can handle a harmonica the way he did opposing pitchers. He can, as Fox learned, also whistle so well that you'd swear you were listening to the flute in the Spirit of '76. And, wife Lil says, teasing, he spent more for the accordion he bought himself out of that first World Series check in 1942 than he did for the diamond ring he had promised Diamond Lil.

During a second visit to Poland, his father's homeland, in 1976, Musial was a smash hit, even with folks completely unaware he'd ever smashed a hit. At a Warsaw restaurant, Stan engaged in a harmonica-accordion duet with the house musician, and, Fox related with awe, he played for hours.

On another occasion, Musial played at the home of Czeslaw Petelski, a film maker, who reacted by offering Stan a role in a Polish movie, promising to film part of it in the United States.

"Aw, look, I'm no actor," said Musial, grinning that lopsided grin, "I'm just a cowboy."

See? Even when he's unbelievable, Stan the Man is believable. He is the most believable in commercials, as shown by an advertising survey recently taken in America. Why, the closest Stan ever came to a cow or being a "cowboy" was when he ate the bovine's male cousin at his own restaurant in St. Louis or when he eats today at one of his favorite gourmet dining places.

Life is just a bowl of berries for my man Stan. A bowl of berries, indeed, and none of them razzberries. Stanley Frank Musial, successful ball player-businessman, family man and friend, just goes through life smiling, shaking hands, laughing at his own jokes as well as yours, repeatedly saying, "S'wunnerful."

It is, too, the poor-boy-to-rich-man saga of Stan (Everybody's Man) Musial. S'wunnerful.

—Bob Broeg

1

THE MAN'S OWN STORY

And I thought I had seen baseball change!

I still believe I played in the most exciting era of big league baseball. I saw the game change from long train trips to short plane flights, from cabbage leaves under the cap in hot weather to air-conditioned dugouts.

But in the baker's-dozen seasons since my retiring from ball player to business executive, I've seen baseball tradition tossed off as easily as the players' time-honored custom of flinging their gloves onto the field near their positions. Remember when big leaguers did that and kids copied them—to the despair of parents putting out hard-earned dollars for leather gloves and mitts skinned and scarred prematurely into discard by harsh handling on concrete-hard diamonds?

In view of off-the-field and in-the-court activity since I bowed out with a couple of basehits at the end of the 1963 season, it's almost riciculous to try to remember the trivial things of the past. Like one time back before the early '50s. Luke Sewell, then managing Cincinnati, decided that if it made sense to drag an infield by groundskeepers before a game, to minimize the chance of bad hops, it was even more logical to tamp down and smooth the basepaths in the middle of a game.

If that new practice seemed sensible then, consider what it is like now that there are NO bad hops. Now there are lightning-like artificial-turf playing surfaces, the kind that can make a middle-aged codger drool because he didn't strike out often and hit sharp ground balls. Back then I always thought the secret of hitting was mental concentration, physical relaxation and avoiding hitting fly balls to center field, which was the deepest part of just about any ball park except Cincinnati's former old park, Crosley Field.

I saw dramatic changes in the 22 years I played, from the beginning in 1941 to the end in 1963. When I first joined the St. Louis Cardinals, night baseball was a seven-game-a-season novelty that, as envisioned by Cardinals' clubowner Sam Breadon, made every day Sunday at the box office. By the time I hung 'er up, they were playing night ball on Sunday in Texas, and later even at World Series games.

One-half a century's lack of progress in franchise shifts was ended in 1953 when, en route to Atlanta, the Boston Braves moved to Milwaukee. Westward expansion in 1958, plus the unconscionable abandonment of Brooklyn, and momentary loss of New York to the National League, soon brought Los Angeles and San Francisco into the big leagues. And that brought the airplane, a grateful change to a guy who never had learned to sleep or rest as well in a railroad Pullman as in a motionless hotel bed.

To my regret, the transportation trend took away those baseball bull-sessions which were so rewarding on long train rides. Some of the little ball players do get together now on shorter plane trips. But their conversations deal more with what astute Marvin Miller has wheedled, in fancier fringe benefits, than on how to hit an especially bothersome pitcher or how to defense an opposing player with a hot bat.

Understand, please, that I'm no fat cat living in the past and putting the knock on the present and future. I've been too lucky to ever rap anything about the game that made me a fortune and a reputation. I'm very pleased and flattered that a national advertising survey a couple of years ago labeled me as coming across in television commercials as "most trustworthy and likable."

The point is that for all my nice-guy reputation—which is really one of gratitude and appreciation for what life and baseball and, of course, a generous God have given me—I'm a guy who has as many opinions as the next fellow.

One of my opinions is that ball players did indeed merit the compromise of loosening the straps in that old career-long straitjacket, the reserve clause. Even though I was ultimately richly rewarded, and, even once given more money by Gussie Busch than I'd asked for, I still went through a couple of unpleasant moments early in my career. If I had had an opportunity to play out an option then, I would have been treated more fairly.

I wonder about fairness now, too, with the box-car size bidding for instant major league free agents. By 1977 it was already jeopardizing the financial structure of many, if not all, ballclubs.

I know that one of my famous left-field predecessors in St. Louis, Chick Hafey, never did get a decent contract. I know, too, that the super-star whose position I followed by scarcely a year, Joe Medwick of the old Gas House Gang, found himself in a constant demeaning salary wrangle with Branch Rickey and Sam Breadon.

Muscles Medwick didn't endear himself to the big boss the year Rickey passed the buck (but not the bucks). And Ducky-Wucky found himself fighting for a couple of thousand of dollars with the big boss, Breadon.

At one point, Breadon said it had resolved itself to a matter of principle—not principal—and that he'd just as soon "throw this $2000 out the window."

Undaunted, Medwick cracked, "Mr. Breadon, if you ever threw $2000 out a window, you'd still be holding on to the other end."

No wonder Muscles wound up traded to Brooklyn. After all, it was a better fate than had befallen Hafey, who, as defending National League batting champion, was dealt to Cincinnati in 1932. At that time Cincy, later a power, was the Siberia of baseball.

So, you see, I believe particularly in these changing times when everyone wants to do his own thing and so few want to be tied down to lifetime contracts.

I'm not going to snigger at individual salaries because, after all, I was paid $100,000 as far back as 1958. As I write this in a time of spiraling inflation, I see that my pay was worth at least twice as much more then than now. I'm aware, too, that as economists have told me, Babe Ruth's Depression salary of $80,-000 in 1930 was worth five times that much at the time of the nation's Bicentennial.

But players now forget that the fancy fringe benefits cost the owners, too. I refer to the generous life insurance, sick and maternity benefits and old-age comforts, not to mention heavily increased regular-season meal money and spring-training walking-around money, enough to enable a player to take his family to Florida or Arizona, at the ball club's expense.

As one who was there when the Cardinals' Marty Marion and old trainer, Doc Weaver, drew up the first pension plan idea 30 years ago, I've seen a paper-and-pencil notion become a reality. Such a reality that, as a 20-year man, I could have collected several hundred dollars a month at 50. And if I wait until I'm 65, I'll get nearly $25,000 a year pension.

Yes, baseball has come even farther than I have. Now there are new parks, more pleasant working and playing conditions. If the athletes don't price themselves and the clubs out of business by driving up tickets too high, there will continue to be more spectators, too. Baseball has NOT lost fans; football merely has closed the once-large gap.

I saluted expansion, but I hated to see other people crushed, as Brooklyn's were, when the borough moved its beloved Bums to Los Angeles after the 1957 season. I personally hated to see Ebbets Field go, because I hit so well there. But my favorite park still stands as the oldest in the National League—Chicago's Wrigley Field. I liked the Cubs' park best, I guess, because they play all day games.

In my mind, after the first year and first time the National League expanded, the growth, first to 10 teams and then to 12 clubs in each league, has watered down talent somewhat. Conversely, it has helped super-stars such as Henry Aaron stay on and feast longer on subpar pitching. And, just think, over in the American League a gaffer doesn't have to field any more. Ted Williams, you quit too soon.

Like my old road roommate, Red Schoendienst, a truly outstanding defensive player and good hitter who wore well as a manager, I'm not so certain that the fielders are better. But, as Red and Ted Williams both say, the gloves are larger and superior to the old ones, aiding fielding. The slider has helped pitchers, too, and cut down on batting averages.

I thought the larger, symmetrical, two-sport stadiums, becoming popular when I retired, would cut down on the long ball and bring back emphasis on the basehit and the stolen base. Indeed, in addition to rare ones such as record-breaker Lou Brock, basestealing has increased almost as much as I figured. Hitters don't study their art form sufficiently. Or they don't play the team game adequately, when they hit a ball behind the runner to move him up and minimize chances for the back-breaker: the double play.

As you can see, I am critical, but only mildly. As I said that delightful summer day in 1969 at Cooperstown, N.Y., when I was inducted into the baseball Hall of Fame: "Baseball was a great game, baseball is a great game and—if nobody kills it greedily—it WILL be a great game."

If ball players aren't figuratively as hungry or as eager as when I broke in, they are better-conditioned, physically stronger and, therefore, basically just about as good. Naturally, though, now the other sports pay well, too. And college and professional football and basketball have siphoned off some of our national pastime's potential talent.

I think I speak with some authority because I came up at the start of the '40s and played against men who had been prominent in the '20s and '30s. And I played long enough to finish against the stars of the '50s and early '60s, some of whom, such as Aaron, blossomed into record-breakers in the '70s.

I know I'll never be able to repay the game that took me from a $65-a-month Class D pitcher to such a pleasant life, including marriage to the high school sweetheart who stood in for me at my graduation. Lil and I also have a great son, Dick, three lovely daughters—Gerry, Janet and Jean—and six joyful grandchildren.

Dick, along with Jack Garagnani, the talented son of my late partner, Biggie, runs our very successful enterprises. These include the second Stan Musial and Biggie's restaurant in St. Louis, the Red Bird bowling alleys and three hotels—the Ivanhoe at Bal Harbour, Fla., the Clearwater Beach Hilton and our St. Louis Airport Hilton.

I'm president of the corporation and look over the books. I always watch that bottom line! I also make appearances for my people, as well as for the Cardinals, for whom I'm still senior vice-president. I like golfing in the 80s, and hunting, too, since farm-boy Schoendienst taught me you don't go bird-shooting wearing two-toned sports shoes. I especially enjoy the honor of membership on the 12-man Committee on Veterans that annually selects men for Hall of Fame induction at Cooperstown, where you'll always find me in early August.

I've dabbled in politics and had the pleasure of appointment by President Lyndon B. Johnson in 1964 to head the United States Council on Physical Fitness. I filled that post throughout LBJ's term in office. I believe the country and our young ones now are more conscious of physical fitness, not as I used to like to say, physical FATNESS.

I campaigned for President John F. Kennedy in 1960 and had a refreshing experience with him in Milwaukee. We'd met first outside the Schroeder Hotel where I was waiting for the team bus to take the ball club to County Stadium. At that time JFK was campaigning in the Wisconsin primary.

"You're Stan Musial, aren't you?" said the good-looking young man, extending his hand. "My name is Jack Kennedy. I'm glad to meet you."

Obviously I recognized the Senator from Massachusetts, who said, pleasantly, "They tell me you're too old to play ball and I'm too young to be President, but maybe we'll fool them."

Two summers later, the All-Star game was in Washington. I'd taken Lil with me and pried number two daughter Jan away from her pet horse for a sight-seeing trip in New York.

There, closing in on age 42, I hit four home runs in a row, three of them in one game. Janet, then 12, gravely told a St. Louis reporter she was relieved because she was afraid Daddy would strike out. Lil cried for joy. Twice before I'd hit three homers in a game and my pretty blonde wife, though a good fan, had missed both times.

Back in 1941, at Springfield, Missouri, she had been diapering our first-born, Dick, under the stands between innings every time I teed off. In 1954, the afternoon I hit five in a doubleheader against the Giants at St. Louis, Lil had stayed home because Jan, just a baby, was ill.

At Washington, friend Senator Stuart Symington arranged for a tour of the White House, including the President's private quarters. Just before the All-Star game in D.C.'s beautiful new stadium I was summoned to the Presidential box.

Mr. Kennedy shook hands and I reminded him of the amusing remark he had made about the relativity of our ages a couple of years earlier. He remembered, smiling.

"I guess, Mr. President, we fooled them, all right," I said.

In the sixth inning of the game, the late, great Fred Hutchinson, my old St. Louis boss, then managing Cincinnati, beckoned me to pinch-hit. The game was scoreless when I faced Camilo Pascual, Minnesota righthander, who had a good old-fashioned overhanded curve.

Mr. Kennedy leaned over to one of his staff and said, "I hope the old man gets a hit."

I lined a two-strike curve into a right field. As I trotted off for pinch-runner Maury Wills—who scored the run that was the springboard to a 3-1 National League victory—I received a warm reception, including applause from the Presidential box.

I couldn't help thinking to myself, "If only Lukasz Musial could see his son now . . . "

I was a poor boy who struck it rich in so many ways as a player through the wonders of baseball. And though I never professed to be a mental heavyweight, I had my own opinions. I liked to consider myself a team man first—and I was proud to be called "a star without a first-person complex." I often had as many opinions as players who sounded off. I just kept my likes and dislikes to myself.

Now, I'm willing to speak my piece. Sound off, that is, if not pop off.

I'd like to straighten out a few wrinkles just as I did fastballs, wrinkles in a legend that, I hope, will help many another young man follow the rainbow. As they say in the fairy tales, "Once upon a time . . . "

2

Donora

Donora, my home town, lies 28 miles south of Pittsburgh in western Pennsylvania's industrial Monongahela Valley. It nestles in a sharp elbow of the valley, on the western bank of a slow, silt-laden river that flows north.

In 1900 the blast furnaces came to Donora, and a year later the rod, wire, nail and galvanizing mills. In 1915 a zinc plant was built and the entire river bank was lined with giant smokestacks. From the river, the town crawls up a 400-foot rise, gradually at first, then more steeply, to reach the level of the surrounding hills. The yellow-brick streets and frame houses with their asphalt shingles are gray from years of smoke and grime that meant business to Donora.

To survive in this rugged climate, the inhabitants had to be rugged. Most were immigrants from Russia and Germany and Poland. Language difficulties compelled them to clan together, in their churches—their are six Roman Catholic parishes alone—or in the social clubs. Everyone worked in one of the three industries. That's how my parents met.

My mother, Mary Lancos, a hearty woman with a hearty laugh, was born in New York City, but her parents, immigrants from what is now Czechoslovakia, moved to Donora when she was small. Times were hard and Grandmother Lancos raised nine children and fed 16 boarders in a five-room house. At eight, Mary went out to work house-cleaning. As a teen-age girl she used to row her father across the Monongahela River in a skiff very early each day and row him back again in the evening. He worked in a coal mine four miles beyond the river. He walked there to spend 12 hours underground, for which he was paid 90 cents a day.

In 1910, when she was 14, my mother went to work in Donora's wire mill. There, while sorting nails and taking the "whiskers" off them, she saw a shy, little Pole named Lukasz Musial. He worked in the shipping department, handling hundred-pound bundles of wire, wrestling them into freight cars. Lukasz, born on a farm near Warsaw, had come alone to America. He had little education and knew no English, but my mother worked with Polish girls and had picked up enough of the language to understand him when they met at a dance. They were married before she was 18. My father brought home $11 every two weeks and they paid $4 a month rent.

The first four children in the Musial family were girls—Ida, Helen, Victoria and Rose—and my father was really longing for a boy by the time I came along on November 21, 1920. Father named me Stanislaus, though he always used the Polish nickname Stashu. My given name got changed to Stanley later, when I went to school. Pop was so delighted to have a son that he bragged that there certainly would be another and that I wouldn't be baptized until that brother was born. Brother Ed came along, all right, two years later. So my earliest distinction was toddling to my own christening at St. Mary's Polish Catholic church.

I was born on Sixth Street, near the center of town, but when I was about seven or eight we moved to Grandma Lancos' larger house, near the hilltop. By walking just a few feet from this house on Marelda Street, I could look down on the residential section, the distant ribbon of business houses, the switch engines darting between the smoke stacks and the barges moving slowly along the river. Across the Monongahela, the hills were completely bare, vegetation killed by the smoke and chemical fumes carried over from Donora by the prevailing west wind.

Today, its mills closed as obsolete, Donora is struggling harder for its existence than my parents had to struggle to raise six children in the Depression. I remember the strong smell of sulphur from the zinc works, but the zinc works are no more. One damp, windless day in October, 1948, those fumes from the smoke stacks filled the narrow valley with poisonous smog for four whole days. Twenty-one elderly residents of Donora died and nearly half the diminishing 12,000 population suffered in some degree. My father was one of those affected, and I brought him and my mother to St. Louis. Pop died two months later at 58.

I wish Pop could have lived to enjoy more of my success. I got a tremendous kick out of watching him shyly glow with pride over my baseball achievements. I'm especially glad he got to Florida for spring training that last year. Bob Hannegan, who just had become president of the Cardinals, treated the Polish immigrant as if he were Count Casimir Pulaski or Tadeusz Kosciuszko. I think Pop would have been glad to vote for Hannegan—twice—if the former Postmaster General had run for office. A year later, Bob was dead, too.

My mother soon decided to return to Donora, to her friends and the rest of our family. I built a home for her there, but I had to enlist neighbor spies to keep her from cutting grass or shoveling snow or other physical tasks she tackled well up into years. Mom died at 79 in 1975.

The other Musials all lived close by her, though our family thinned out alarmingly fast. My oldest sister, Mrs. Ida Daniels, died unexpectedly of a heart attack three weeks after my playing retirement in 1963. The second-oldest sister, Mrs. Helen Jones, who lived in Washington, Pennsylvania, where her husband managed a bowling alley, divorced and married our brother-in-law, Frank Daniels, now a retired crane operator in Pittsburgh.

My third sister, Mrs. Victoria Wagner, lived in Ambridge, Pennsylvania, married to a jeweler and had two sons. Dear Vickie died when I was off to Poland getting a national sports honor early in 1973. My other sister, Mrs. Rose Lang, whom we called "Red" as a girl, is married to a linotype operator in Pittsburgh. They have five boys.

Brother Ed—"Honey" ever since a neighbor began calling him that when he was a kid—was a pretty good hitter who played minor league baseball after nearly five years of military service in World War II. He lives in Monongahela, Pennsylvania, works as a machine operator for Westinghouse in Pittsburgh and has two girls and a boy.

Back in the '30s, we Musial kids had few of the advantages our children have today. Our father never earned more than $4 a day, and our mother usually hired out to help make ends meet. My sister Ida earned her first money at the age of eight when she scrubbed a neighbor's kitchen and bathroom floors. Her reward was a nickel for a movie.

They tell me I created an economic calamity as a toddler when I developed a taste for the canned condensed milk we used to sweeten coffee. The girls were warned to keep an eye on the milk so I wouldn't grab it off the table and drink it. I don't remember that or the technique they say I used for a time to avoid paddlings. I'd hold my breath and my parents would panic, afraid to spank me. That is, until Grandma Lancos took over. Stashu wouldn't hold his breath THAT long. Wham! You know, I heard my mother say how polite I was as a boy. I appreciate the compliment, but I think Mom forgot—or overlooked—how forcibly we were taught to respect our elders. I learned the meaning of discipline early. Not unkindly, either.

Mom was a marvel at making a little go a long way. Fresh milk and meat were too expensive. Every two weeks, she would buy a 50-pound sack of potatoes and a hundred-pound sack of flour, 25 pounds of sugar and 15 pounds of coffee. She baked bread in an outside oven, 10 loaves at a time. With eight hungry mouths, the bread would last just two days. We kids picked blackberries and elderberries for jelly.

Although I learned long before I became a restaurateur to appreciate a thick sirloin steak or succulent lobster, I'll never forget the "hunky" dishes Mom turned out, such as pierogi, halucki and kolatche. Kolatche is a kind of sweet roll, halucki the more familiar cabbage roll and pierogi a delicate combination of flour, potato and sugar folded into a thin turnover and baked. Mom's pierogies were a favorite whenever she visited one of the family or when one of us visited her.

Mom never failed in heat or snow to walk down the hill to the mill each morning, carrying my father his hot soup in a round lunch pail. He had a weak stomach and she felt he needed the warm lunch. And Pop would hold back a cookie or an apple so that he'd have something for me when I ran down to meet him after I heard the 5 o'clock whistle.

Although I worked at little odd jobs, I'm particularly grateful to my parents that I didn't have to work as much as many of my friends. I was able not only to play more, to develop my athletic talent, but also to become the only member of my family to finish high school.

The nice thing about having so many sisters was that they did most of the chores, except hauling in the coal from our private "mine." There was actually a pit in the back yard at 1139

Marelda. I'd crawl down it to get fuel for the kitchen stove. When Mom and the girls were working and I got home first, even after baseball or basketball practice, I'd have to warm the baked beans and slice the lunch meat for our supper.

We didn't have much except kindness. A family of eight—nine when Grandma Lancos was still living—squeezed into a small five-room house. There were times, Mom recalled, when Ed and I had to be sent to school in canvas-top sneakers because she couldn't afford shoes. But there never was a time when I didn't have a baseball. My mother made many for me out of a little bit of this and that, sewn together.

I don't know whether it is significant, but, searching my memory these many years later, I can't recall any toy before I received my first ball.

3

A Good Joe

I wanted to be a big league ball player from the time I was eight years old. A man named Joe Barbao helped me build the dream that came true. The Barbaos became our neighbors when we moved up the hill to grandma's house on Marelda Street. Joe was about 30, a pleasant blue-eyed Spaniard of part Belgian ancestry and a former minor league pitcher and outfielder. When I met him, he still was playing as a semi-pro in the Monongahela Valley even though he did hard, hot work as a short-shifter in the zinc mill.

A short-shifter put in only about three hours in the morning because of the intense heat, drawing the metal out of the furnaces and reloading honeycombed apertures for the zinc-cooking process. The faster a man worked, the sooner he escaped. So as a wide-eyed youngster, I first saw my neighbor loosening up his arm in Marelda Street for twilight and semi-pro games. Joe's brother caught him. I'd get my brother, Ed, and we'd play catch alongside the men. Joe used to watch us, tickled because both Musial boys were left handed. Soon Joe began to offer suggestions, and I'd ask questions. He loved to talk baseball and I loved to listen. He'd tell me stories about the big leaguers and their records. I began collecting penny baseball cards, a forerunner of the bubble-gum fad that became so big since World War II.

This was 1929. The Philadelphia Athletics were beginning a string of three pennants under Connie Mack, and my idol naturally—because I threw lefthanded—was one of the greatest of all southpaws, Lefty Grove. Later, as I began to pitch, my favorite was another classical lefthander, Carl Hubbell, but at the beginning it was Grove all the way, and I had more cards with his grizzled face than of any other player.

My parents, especially my mother, liked baseball, too. Mom would take us over to Palmer Park, a combination picnic grounds and baseball field, to watch the home-town team. Once when we were watching a game, John Mortak, Donora's great hero of the '20s, ran into a tree in the outfield and knocked himself out. Mom was the first to reach him.

Soon I began to play in pick-up games with other kids on a cow pasture or any bit of grass we could find. We played softball a good deal, too. Joe Barbao still calls it "depression" ball, but I'm not nearly so hard on the game. I don't think it will hurt a budding baseball player a bit. The point is to practice all the time, whether it's baseball or softball, if you're really as serious about ball-playing as I was. Before long, I was playing with the older boys, who put up with me, I guess, because I didn't foul up their fun. I have to give Joe Barbao credit for whatever skill and poise I had in those days. Many a night we'd sit looking at the town lights twinkling below while Joe talked baseball until the 9 o'clock mill whistle sounded curfew for us kids.

People tell me I was "frail and skinny" in my early teens, but I can't have been as frail as I seemed because I could hit and throw hard even then. And the fact that I was strong was my father's doing. He insisted that all of us—the girls, Ed and I—take part in gymnastics taught by the Polish Falcons, the club to which Pop belonged.

Three times a week, from the time I was nine or ten, we went to the Falcons. We'd march and drill and then work out on the apparatus and mats. We'd swing on the parallel bars, leap over the "horse" and do all the tumbling that helped me avoid injury in my playing career. In the spring our instructors took us outdoors to compete in track and field events with other towns. I can't say enough for the three body-building years I spent with the Falcons.

Although baseball equipment, and the money to buy it, was extremely scarce, we kids somehow managed to scrape together enough to field a team in an informal Donora junior city league when I was 14. The first clipping I've got from my boyhood shows that the Heslep All-Stars, as we called ourselves, walloped Cement City, 24-2. It was a case of the kids from the wrong side of the track walloping the rich ones, except that the rich kids weren't really so wealthy, either. In that game, the clipping shows, I batted fifth and had four hits, three of them doubles. I struck out 14 batters and walked two in a game that took FIVE HOURS.

I suppose most kids start out wanting to pitch. Seems to me that the hardest-throwing and best-coordinated usually pitch and hit clean-up. A lefthander, particularly, has limited opportunities. Only five of the nine positions are open to him—pitcher, first base and the three outfield spots—and many sound baseball men even frown on using a lefthanded-throwing player in left field.

Then, of course, in my case, there was my admiration for Joe Barbao, also a pitcher. Kids naturally tend to imitate their heroes. When Joe began to manage semi-pro teams in the Monongahela Valley, I was his bat boy. I managed to see that no pick-up game interfered with my job. Then one day something very exciting happened. Our team, the Donora Zincs, was playing at Monessen and our starting pitcher was cuffed hard and early. Barbao, who had pitched only the day before, called to me and said, "Stan, how would you like to pitch?"

Ever since a teacher forced me to write righthanded when I was a child, I've stammered when I was excited. This time I was speechless. I should have been scared because I was a kid of 15 who would be facing grown men, but I wasn't. Joe Barbao had seen me play in sandlot games against older boys, and I knew that he wouldn't let me pitch if he hadn't thought I was ready.

I stood only about 5-4 then and weighed less than 140 pounds, but I could throw hard and had a pretty good cunny-thumb curve that Joe himself had taught me. Like most lefthanders, I was wild enough to keep 'em loose at the plate. I pitched six innings and struck out 13.

That did it. I was "in."

Ironically, my pitching performance cost Joe Barbao his job as manager of the Zincs. Men who had grumbled when Joe put me in were glad to have me after I had proved myself, but they still were miffed at Barbao. He had used a player who was not a dues-

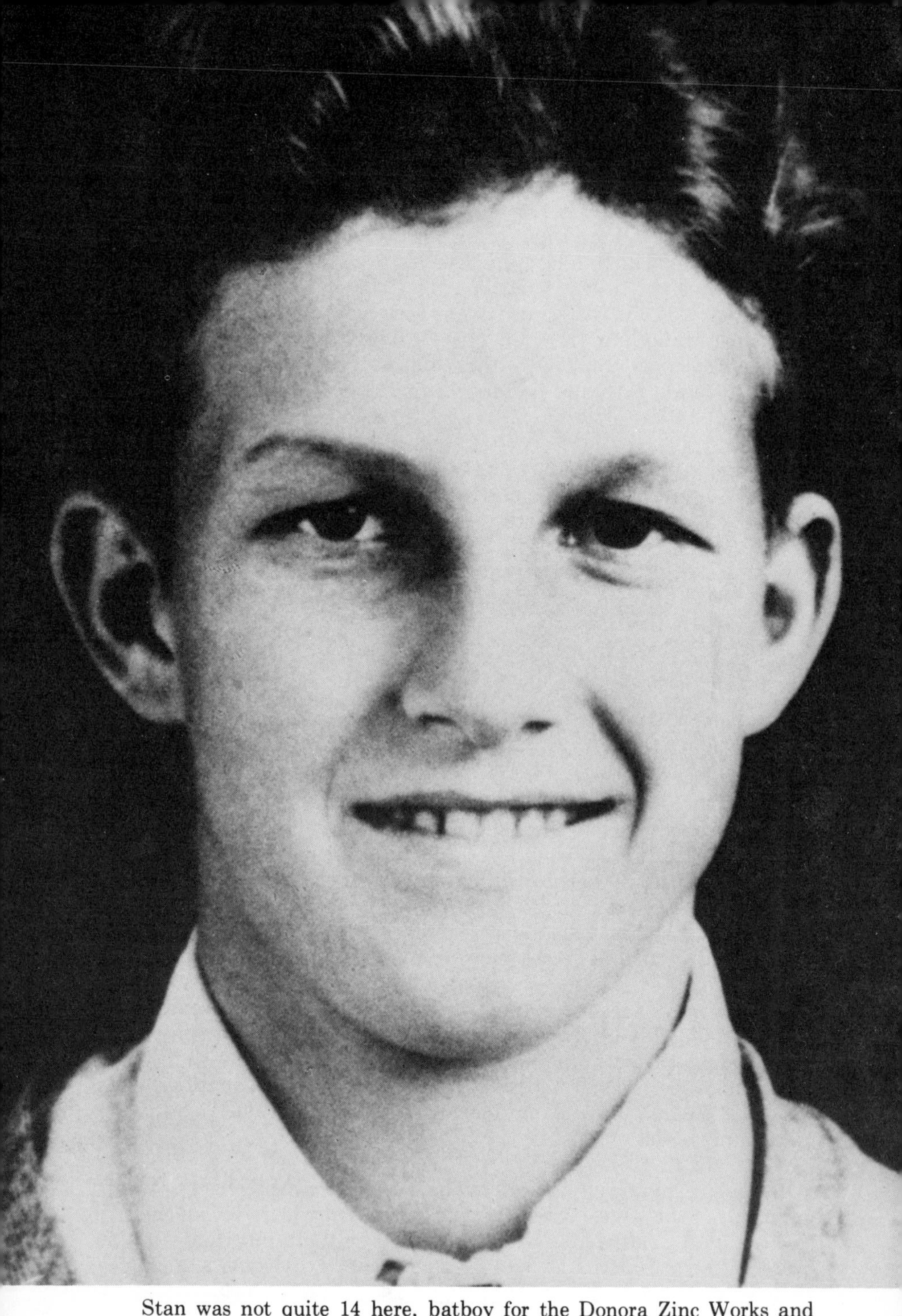

Stan was not quite 14 here, batboy for the Donora Zinc Works and pitching for kid teams back home.

paying member (two bits!) in the Donora Zinc Works A.A.

That chance to pitch for the Zincs came at a good time for me because the junior city league season was over. We had had a fine year and finished in first place, but I wasn't always so sure of myself playing with men's teams. Steve Koskoski, who replaced Barbao as manager for a time, remembers calling on me to pinch-hit one day. I was so nervous that I swallowed my gum—and struck out.

The Zincs played most of their home games at Americo Park down close to the river and north of the plant. Railroad tracks ran just beyond the first-base line and inner-city trolley tracks fringed left field, making it considerably shorter than right. That inviting topography taught me early what so many lefthanded hitters find most difficult—how to hit to left field.

When I pitched my first nine innings for the 1937 Zincs, I lost a 7-5 game to Fairhope, partly as a result of our team's four errors. A clipping from the Donora Herald shows I had pretty good control that day. I walked three, struck out one and tripled. Said the Herald solicitously:

"Musial is too small for steady playing now. He has a world of stuff and a brainy head, but overwork can harm a young player very easily."

Maybe, but I couldn't play enough to suit me. In 1937, I also played for the Eugene V. Jobes American Legion Post of Donora. The Legion's worthy junior baseball program has provided a springboard for many major leaguers, especially in areas like ours that didn't have high school baseball. At least not until my junior year, 1938. By then I had played another season for the Zincs, once again managed by Joe Barbao, whose ankle I broke one day with a hot line foul when he was coaching first base.

Another old friend was the man who brought high school baseball back to Donora after 13 years, Michael (Ki) Duda. President of California (Pa.) State College when he died much too young, in 1968, Dr. Duda inspired more than one poor boy from the Monongahela Valley by serving as his own example. Although proud of his Viennese heritage, he was, like so many of the Slavic "hunkies," as they called us, a member of a large family and extremely poor. Because a partial athletic scholarship helped him work his way through college, he had a soft spot for sports as well as for the youth of our financially pinched area.

Ki—nicknamed because he played the German Kaiser in boyhood games—came home to Donora to teach in 1934 and to begin the administrative work that has taken him so far in the educational field. He taught me seventh-grade English composition and civics or, as it is known now, social studies.

Dr. Duda remembered me as a bashful, backward, quiet boy with a keen interest in sports, especially baseball. He credited my avid reading on baseball with having helped me scholastically. He remembered, too, that because I so often played with older boys and men, the school faculty and townspeople were pulling for me.

Playing with boys my own age, naturally I benefited from my experience with the Zincs. When Ki Duda used his powers of persuasion to return baseball to the high school sports program—he organized and coached the team—I set a Donora school record by striking out 17 in our first game, a seven-inning victory over Monessen.

I honestly don't recall too much of my one-season high school career, but I do remember one game because of a tremendous home run I hit. And every time I go back to Donora, I hear about it all over again. We were playing Monongahela City at Legion Field, the Donora high school park. My brother, Ed, a ninth-grader who was playing the outfield for us, walked to fill the bases in a late inning of the game we were losing. I was up next. The Mon City pitcher, a righthander named Jack McGinty, threw me a fast ball low and inside. Unlike most young players, I was a good low-ball hitter. I hit the ball so far, about 450 feet against the distant right field fence on one bounce, that I had circled the bases before the ball was touched by the retrieving fielder.

In spite of this famous clout, I was signed to a professional contract not as a hitter, but as a pitcher. I was not quite 17 when the business manager of the Cardinals' Monessen farm club, Andrew J. French, approached me after seeing me play sandlot baseball. He invited me to work out with his Class D Penn State League club a couple of miles south of Donora, and, as you can imagine, I was excited.

When I reported, Andrew French turned me over to the manager, Ollie Vanek, a stocky, ruddy-faced man in his mid-20s, a man I was going to meet again. At that time, Ollie, a pretty good hitter sent down with injuries from Class B at Decatur, Ill., was just breaking in as a manager—and I was the first ball player he ever tried out.

Honestly, I'm hazy about the details. I know I had my well-worn glove and a pair of baseball shoes that belonged to the Donora Zincs. My usual summer apparel included a T-shirt, cotton work pants and sneakers, so Monessen fitted me out in a uniform. I recall warming up on the sidelines and cutting loose for Vanek.

The Cardinals' office has the first scouting report on me, filed June 5, 1937 and signed by A. J. French. Using a standard questionnaire for the organization's card-index in St. Louis, French wrote:

"ARM? . . . Good . . . FIELDING? . . . Good . . . SPEED? . . . Fast. Good curve ball. Green kid . . . PROSPECT NOW? . . . No . . . PROSPECT LATER? . . . Yes . . . AGGRESSIVE? . . . Yes . . . HABITS? . . . Good . . . HEALTH? . . . Good . . ."

I worked out three or four times at Monessen that summer and French and Vanek visited my home in Donora a couple of times to try to soften up my father. Finally in late August, just before the Penn State League finished, French came again to persuade my parents to sign a contract with the Cardinals' organization.

Not many people know that I had been contacted by other ball clubs. The Indians had asked me to work out in Cleveland. A Yankee representative, Bill Reinhardt, scouting football players for George Washington University and bird-dogging baseball players for the Yanks, stopped through to see the Donora athletic director, James K. Russell, and talked to me briefly. Later, there was a letter inviting me to New York for a tryout.

What made me sign with the Cardinals? Because they used salesmanship, the personal touch. Where others wrote, they talked. Where others waited, they acted. That early bird that got the worm must have been a Redbird.

To this day, I don't know why my boyhood favorites, the Pirates, didn't show any early interest. The answer, I guess, is that that far back they just weren't scouting as vigorously as St. Louis, which pioneered farm-system baseball, or other clubs that had felt the weight of the Cardinals' "chain gang." Between 1926 and 1937, the year I signed, the Redbirds had won five pennants and three world championships.

Some of my old friends in western Pennsylvania still haven't forgiven the Pirates for letting me get away. I've been extremely happy in St. Louis, where no man could have asked for a more loyal following, better business or happier home. Yet if my boyhood favorites from Pittsburgh had got there first—or any time before I signed—I would have cast my career with the Pirates, not the Cardinals.

4

Moment of Decision

If I had it to do all over, I'd go to college before playing professional baseball. Perhaps that sounds like what I should say, the usual remark one's expected to make, but I mean it. Although baseball treated me wonderfully, I missed something. Call it a feeling of inferiority, call it what you will, but I believe sincerely that it takes a man who doesn't have one to appreciate the value of a college education.

I know now what I've missed, but when I was 17 years old, dreaming a dream that miraculously came true, I couldn't be reasoned out of leaping before I took a good look. Now, I hate to think what would have happened if I had failed in baseball. Although I like to think I would have made my mark in some other way, the fact is I might be working at the steel mill my father so desperately wanted me to avoid. And the way things are today in Donora, I might be struggling to get by on only part-time work, facing middle age and a final layoff, perhaps with lungs affected by silicosis, the disease that attacks many who work in mills, mines and foundries.

My father thought of those odds when Andrew French called at our house on Marelda Street. Pop really didn't know too much about baseball. Oh, he liked it, especially since he'd seen me play, and he did like to talk about Babe Ruth, a name that has cast a spell over many a man, past or present, including me. But even if Pop didn't understand the fine points of the game, he did know that to sacrifice higher education in favor of pro ball was a risk. To an immigrant who had had to struggle with a new language and the handicap of a limited education, the idea of college was dazzling. He glowed happily the first time he heard an athletic scholarship mentioned.

I was quite a high school basketball player. The deflating fact is, both my wife Lil and my brother Ed think I was better in basketball than in baseball as a kid. With Ed, I'm not sure whether that's praise for my basketball ability or a rap at my baseball talent. I imagine he's a typical brother—he even thinks I would have flunked out of college. Certainly I wasn't a good student in high school. I like to think, though, that like many a kid who loafed in high school, I would have found myself in the tougher competition at college. I never claimed to be a brain, but I was a solid "C" student even though my study habits were terrible.

I do remember one course I had a "B" in because I got the grade by swallowing my pride. When I was still wavering between college and pro baseball, I found I'd need algebra for enrollment at the University of Pittsburgh, which was chiefly interested in my basketball ability. To take the subject, I'd walk down to junior high school every morning and for an hour I'd sit among kids three years younger than myself.

As an old Polish Falcon, I probably ought to be ashamed that I got no better than a "B" in gym. The only "A" I ever received was in junior high electrical shop, but what I learned in that course didn't stay with me. As Lil knows all too well, I have trouble doing the most modest electrical repairs around the house.

I'm disappointed that I never had the chance to play football, but my folks were firmly opposed to the game as too rough. They could be stern and neither the coach nor I could change their minds. Coach James K. Russell was particularly eager to have me after the non-uniformed sandlot team I quarterbacked—on the sly—beat some of the high school varsity, soundly. The coach thought I had the speed to be good running back and the arm to make a good passer. My folks had to be stubborn, all right, because Jimmy Russell, an effervescent little man, is cut from the oratorical mold of the man he admired most, Knute Rockne.

Describing me to a mutual friend recently, the old coach said, "A flower of rare cultivation is gratitude, and this boy has cultivated it." See what I mean? Rockne—or Branch Rickey—couldn't have said that more eloquently.

Rockne, for whom he played briefly at Notre Dame, recommended Russell for the Donora job in 1931 just before the Rock was killed in a plane crach. Jim never has stopped talking about Rockne and never has left Donora. The coach takes justifiable pride in two things. He made Donora known widely as "the home of champions" because of the winning football teams he developed in football and because of the athletes he sent forth—Arnold Galiffa to Army, Dan Towler to Washington and Jefferson and the Los Angeles Rams, Bimbo Ceccone to Pitt, Frank Dabiero to Notre Dame, Musial to the Cardinals, and others.

Russell is ever more proud of having seen nearly 160 Donora boys go through college on athletic scholarships, boys who in almost all instances wouldn't have had the opportunity otherwise.

Coach Russell tried his best to interest colleges in me and to interest me in college after I had played basketball for him. By the time I played regularly as a sophomore, my father's eyes danced with the thought of a Musial going to college. So Pop resisted Andrew French's sales talk about professional baseball when the Cardinals' representative called late in the summer of 1937. The Monessen business manager painted a rosy picture of my future. How rosy? Oh, not enough for a bonus, virtually unheard of then, but for a $65-a-month Class D contract the next summer.

I wanted so much to play ball. My mother weakened, but Pop remained firm. French prepared to leave. This, he said, might be my last chance. I wasn't 17 yet but, for me, the world had come to an end. I cried—tears of disappointment, anger and frustration.

That did it. Mom put an arm around me, dried the tears and told me to blow my nose. Then she stood up. She was a big woman, taller than my father. In typical old-world custom, Pop wore the pants in our family, but now Mom spoke up to him quite sharply.

"Lukasz," she asked, "why did you come to America?"

"Why?" my father said, puzzled, in his broken English. "Because it's a free country, that's why."

My mother nodded triumphantly. "That's right, Lukasz," she said. "And in America a boy is free NOT to go to college, too."

Pop grumbled, then paused. "All right, Stashu," he said with a sigh, "if you want baseball enough to pass up college, then I'll sign."

Both of my parents and I signed the baseball contract in late summer, 1937, but in a practice that I understand was common then, the Cardinals did not file the contract with the baseball commissioner's office until the following June.

My father wasn't happy that he had relented, and his displeasure increased during the winter of 1937-38 when I starred for a basketball team that was probably the second best in Donora's history. Only the 1944-45 team went farther, reaching the state finals with two players later famous in football—Arnold Galiffa and Dan Towler.

I look back with pleasure at having played with that team and with pride on the accomplishments of a gang that, as old teammate Flor Garcia says, used to hang around and shoot the gas while I sold it. During the summer of 1937, thanks to the efforts of my brother-in-law, Frank Daniels, who ran a service station in Pittsburgh, I got a job pumping gas in Donora for $25 a week. That was a lot of money in the Depression. I gave Mom $15, kept $10 and really was in the chips. Now and then I'd have to battle brother Ed to run the station for me so I could get away for a ball game.

I have to thank one of my old teammates, Dick Ercius, who was later mayor of St. Petersburgh Beach, Fla., for having introduced me to my wife. Actually Lillian Labash knew me, but I didn't know her. She was a pretty little blonde. Her mother had migrated as a girl to the United States from the Carpathian-Russian section of Czechoslovakia. Lil's father, Sam, a second-generation American of Russian descent, was a grocer who had been a good enough ball player to warrant a professional chance.

The Labashes—there were eight in the family—were good sports fans who often went to local games. Lil saw me first when I was a 14-year-old pitching against older players. A man nudged her father, she recalls, and said, "Keep your eye on that Polish kid."

Lil did. She likes to tease and say that when I was playing high school basketball she fell in love with my legs. Our first date came when Dick Ercius, who was dating one of Lil's sisters, asked me to take the other Miss Labash to a dance after a basketball game.

Lil and I began dating frequently, and more and more often in our little city of hills I began to walk the mile or more from our house up on the north hill down to the Labash grocery at the

Even after Stan made more money in the 1942 World Series than he had all that rookie season, he continued to clerk part-time in his father-in-law's grocery store in Donora.

south end of town. Lil says she's not sure whether I really came to see her or to wolf down the lunch meat and milk that her father generously provided. My real reason, I tell her, was that I always did like older women. Lil was a year ahead of me in high school—but just two months older.

My high school coaches knew I had signed with the Cardinals, but under eligibility rules then in effect I still was able to play high school sports because I had not yet played professionally and had received no money. The coaches were disappointed and not only because they stood to lose me as a senior once I played pro ball. They knew the tremendous odds against making it in baseball, and I'm sure, too, they felt that I might be better off going to college. Coach Russell, who knew I was dating Lil, went so far as to corner her and appeal to her to urge me not to play pro ball in the summer of 1938. Lil politely, but firmly, told him the decision was mine, not hers.

In a further effort to encourage me to try college first, Russell urged Charles H. (Jerry) Wunderlich, gym teacher at Donora junior high school, to take me to his old college coach at Pitt, Dr. H. C. Carlson. Doc Carlson had seen the district tournament. He lent encouragement as well as strong hope that he would be able to offer an athletic scholarship when I graduated a year later. As Doc told it not so long ago:

"I tried to steer Musial off professional baseball. I told him to go to college. I figured he would throw his arm out in the low minors and wind up working in the mill at Donora for the rest of his life.

"Well, they say you're more flattered if someone asks for your advice than if he takes it. Stan was a fine, modest boy who thanked me, departed—and grabbed the contract."

Actually, I wavered. Ki Duda, for whom I played baseball in the spring semester, knew how strongly I felt about the game. In his discerning way he felt that I wouldn't be able to concentrate in college. He suggested that if I really wanted an education, I could continue in school while playing baseball. The clincher, however, was provided by a woman to whom I'm extremely grateful, Miss Helen Kloz, then the librarian at Donora high school.

"Stan," she said softly, when I laid my problem before her, "I've never known a boy who wanted something more than you do. College is a wise course for a man to follow, but you've got to want it enough, almost as much as you want baseball. If you're going to try baseball, the younger you start, the better. You can't afford to lose your head, but you can afford to follow your heart."

I did. Baseball was—and is—my first love. I've often said that the greatest thrill in a career of happy and exciting moments was just putting on a big league uniform, especially opening day of every season. Among my thrills, Miss Kloz figured prominently in one. She moved to eastern Pennsylvania and in 1961 visited me before a game in Philadelphia. "This probably is the last time I'll see you play, Stan," she said. "Won't you hit a home run for me?"

By this time my home runs had become fewer and farther between, and no one hits home runs on order, anyway, except in fiction. And to crown it all that night at Connie Mack Stadium, with Miss Kloz in a box seat behind the Cardinals' dugout, a strong wind blew in from right field.

But, somehow, I was lucky. I caught a pitch down on the fat

part of the bat and rode it through the wind and over the high right field fence. As I trotted around the bases, I thought of my dear old friend, whose kind counsel to follow my heart had meant so much in a boy's moment of indecision. I thought, too, of her request. The Phillies' infielders could have been excused if they thought I was balmy because, circling the bases, I laughed for joy.

Back there in the spring of 1938, when Miss Kloz confirmed her faith in my own judgment, I ran into Johnny Bunardzya, young sports editor of the Donora *Herald*.

"How would you like to ride down to Pittsburgh with me and see the Pirates play the Giants?" he asked.

Even though Donora is only 28 miles from Pittsburgh, I had never seen my favorite team play. The distance was short, but the price was high for a kid who didn't have the money or, when he did, didn't have the time because of a summer job or ball game he was playing in himself. Much as I wanted to see the Pirates—I listened to their games frequently and read the newspaper accounts daily—I'd rather have played than watched any time. The closest I had come to Forbes Field before this had been in 1935. I'd saved up for the inter-urban trolley fare and the ticket to the ball game, but a friend had touched me for a loan and hadn't paid it back in time. So I missed seeing the one and only Babe Ruth make a grand exit with three home runs for the Boston Braves.

When Johnny Bunardzya offered three years later to take me to a big league game on his press pass, I played hooky from school.

Bunardzya remembers that I was bug-eyed when, from the upper tier behind first base, I got my first glimpse of the field and the tree-shrouded backdrop of Schenley Park, just beyond Forbes Field's red brick left field wall.

"What a beautiful park!" I said then—and still do. To someone who has played on assorted hillside and riverfront ball fields in the Monongahela Valley, any big league diamond is a jewel.

I don't remember too many details about that first big league game I saw, though I believe the Giants won, 5-3. A big New York lefthander, Cliff Melton, who was always tough on Pittsburgh, beat Pie Traynor, the Waner brothers and the rest of my favorites.

I do remember, and so does Bunardzya, that after a few innings, I turned to him and said, "John, I think I can hit big league pitching."

That probably sounds pretty brash, and I guess it was, but you'll notice that I didn't say anything to those major league hitters about pitching and getting them out. That 17-year-old Musial must have been a little smarter than his grades indicated!

I didn't realize it at the time, but Johnny Bunardzya was not yet aware that I had signed with the Cardinals late the previous summer, and he was trying to interest me in the Pirates and, particularly, the Pirates in me.

As a matter of fact, my enthusiasm for the Cardinals had cooled somewhat. That spring, Judge Kenesaw Mountain Landis, the baseball commissioner, had declared that Branch Rickey, father of the farm system, had violated baseball law because the Cardinals controlled two or more clubs in minor leagues. Ninety-one St. Louis baseball farmhands were declared free agents, one of them Pete Reiser, who in three years became Brooklyn's batting champion and base-stealing star with a magnetic—and tragic—attraction for the outfield wall at Ebbets Field.

I honestly hoped I had been among the players released. If the Cardinals really were as bad as Judge Landis portrayed them, I didn't want to be a part of their organization. Disillusioned, but also disappointed because I had heard nothing from the Cardinals about where to report, I was quite ready to listen when Irv Weiss, a sports-minded Donora merchant and ardent Pirates' fan, said he'd take me to Pittsburgh for a workout with the Pirates.

"Bring along those letters you had from the Yankees and Cleveland, so we can impress them if we have to," he said.

We had to. But the letters did get me the tryout, three or four tryouts, in fact.

I remember one time I pitched batting practice for the Pirates themselves. Bill Brubaker seemed huge and Paul Waner so little for such a great hitter. Of those 1938 Pirates, I think particularly of three—Gus Suhr, because 19 years later I broke his National League record for consecutive games played; Paul Waner, because he provided incentive to the 3000-hit goal, and Arky Vaughan, because he was a wonderful line-drive hitter, a rival in the thrilling 1942 pennant race and altogether a fine fellow. Poor Arky drowned several years ago.

Although naturally nervous and normally wild, I got the ball over the plate well enough to keep the Pirate regulars from complaining. On the sidelines I must have made some impression because Pie Traynor took me aside finally and talked contract with me. Traynor, a kind, courteous and handsome man, who had been a great player, said the Pirates would be glad to give me a chance in their minor league organization.

"I'd like to, Mr. Traynor," I said, "but I signed this agreement with the Cardinals last summer. I don't know, though, I guess they've forgotten me."

Traynor shook his head. "I doubt that, son," he said. "You'll be hearing from them one of these days. If they do release you, let us know. Good luck, boy."

A few days later I had my orders from St. Louis to report to Williamson, W. Va., in the Class D Mountain States League.

5

$5 Meal Tickets and Marriage

I was so homesick on the long, sleepless bus ride to Williamson on the Kentucky-West Virginia border that I wanted to quit professional baseball even before I started. If E. S. (Lefty) Hamilton, a former player who was general manager of the community-owned ball club, hadn't met me, I think I might have turned around and grabbed the first bus back to Donora. And I had no one to blame except myself.

When Andrew French persuaded my parents to let me sign with the Cardinals, I was just a bashful, inarticulate kid with a desire to play ball. But on one point I expressed myself clearly: I didn't want to play too close to home.

Most teen-agers want to flap their wings and take off, but, added to that, I was extremely self-conscious. I didn't relish the idea of my friends and family watching me play all the time. And if I failed, I wanted to suffer the embarrassment alone.

So French said he'd send along a memorandum that the St. Louis office assign me to a Class D club not too near home. Now every mile the bus traveled, the more I wished I hadn't left. And in the morning when it rolled into Williamson, 240 miles from Donora, my homesickness turned to disillusionment.

Williamson was even smaller than Donora! I hadn't expected a metropolis, but I'd certainly hoped to see a town in which you didn't run out of main street within three blocks. That's when Lefty Hamilton met me. He was a man who understood a 17-year-old boy's loneliness. He and Mrs. Hamilton helped to make my two fractional seasons in Williamson as pleasant as possible.

In those days Williamson was a tough little mining town with a population of about 9000, and hard-drinking mountaineers came to town and tore up the place every Saturday night. The town was almost as tough as my first professional manager, Nat Hickey.

One of the original Celtics, the brilliant professional basketball team of the '20s and early '30s, Hickey was a hawk-nosed man who chewed tobacco constantly and had one of the most sulphuric vocabularies I ever heard. He reminds me of one of the best managers I ever played for, Fred Hutchinson. Hickey, like Hutch, could cuss out a team, really dress it down in blue language, yet keep his remarks so impersonal that you never felt cut.

Looking back, I feel that Hickey was pretty tolerant of a green kid from Donora. The Mountain States League season was in full swing when I reported and a few days later, Hickey, who played center field, started me in a game at Huntington. I soon realized how little I knew and how much I had to learn.

Not only was I wild and knocked out by Huntington within a few innings, but I also was jarred by the umpires. Back home in sandlot ball, I'd had a lefthanded pickoff move to first base that was my pride. The first time I used it in pro baseball, the umpire called "balk." And every time I tried again to pick off one of the many runners I had put on base in that horrible debut, the umpire charged me with a balk. I was striding toward the plate, not toward first base, before I threw to the bag.

That first summer away from home was an experience, all right. First I lived in a rooming house that charged $5-a-week rent. You could get a $5 meal ticket at more than one restaurant and it lasted nearly a week in those days. So I lived comfortably, even managed to save a little, on my $65-a-month salary.

The players spent quite a bit of time traveling in the Mountain States League, riding in their own cars or a bus. Except when we played at Huntington, we'd drive right back to Williamson after a night game so that the ball club could save on expenses. In the minors as well as the majors, the club pays expenses only on the road, not at home.

Because we played at night, there was the whole day to kill. We'd take in the town's one movie—or were there two?—and we shot so much pool I felt like Minnesota Fats.

That first year out, I won six and lost six for a Williamson team that had a so-so season, too. My earned-run average was an unimpressive 4.66. I don't remember playing the outfield at all, but I might have. I pinch-hit a few times and finished with a .258 average. I'm not alibiing, but not until you've seen lights as poor as we had at Williamson can you appreciate how hard it was to hit—or how easy it should have been to pitch.

When I returned to Donora, I felt I'd learned a lot. I'd learned about signs, about backing up bases, about breaking to first base on all ground balls hit to the right side of the infield, and about relay throws and cutoffs.

The one scouting report in the Cardinals' files that was made on me in 1938 was signed by Wid Matthews, then a troubleshooter for Branch Rickey. It read:

"Arm good. Good fast ball, good curve. Poise. Good hitter. A real prospect."

As far as the Cardinals' card-index shows, Matthews is the first to have described me as a "good" hitter. And Wid had to be going on potential.

As a professional athlete, I was now ineligible for high school basketball, so I played semi-pro basketball with a team sponsored by a hustling Monongahela City automobile dealer, Frank Pizzica, who was to become one of my closest friends. I played with the Pizzicas three or four winters, the youngest member of a team that included two or three college graduates. Good thing we had a lot of fun because we certainly didn't make much money. After every game, home or away in the Mon Valley, we'd hurry back to an Italian restaurant or over to Frank's house—I still vote for Molly Pizzica's cooking.

Frank Pizzica has been a thoughtful friend in many ways. "You've got to quit being shy with strangers, Stan," he scolded me once. "Keep your head high, look 'em in the eye and give 'em a warm, firm handshake, not a dead fish."

I believe I was helped, too, by the opportunity to be with friends always a little bit older, more experienced and more knowledgeable. After I came back from Williamson, Lil and I spent much of our time dating with the younger high school

Musial was 17 and a professional, but not very accomplished, pitcher with Williamson, West Virginia, in the old Class D Mountain States League.

faculty members and their wives. For instance, Ki Duda, who had written me encouraging letters that helped during the discouraging months of the previous summer. Duda's wife, Verne, was—and still is—a concert violinist. She's as able with a bow and string as Ki was with his lively larynx.

I finished school in the spring semester—I'm afraid I wanted the diploma more than I did the task of studying for it—and I helped Duda coach the Donora high school team. I pitched for my old friends, the Zincs, until I reported back to Williamson, this time for $75 a month. I waited until I was sure I would graduate, but not long enough to receive my diploma. Lil, who had graduated the previous year, stood in for me at my graduation exercises.

At Williamson in 1939, I felt stronger and more certain of myself. Our new manager, handsome Harrison Wickel, a shortstop, was as soft-spoken as Nat Hickey had been hard-boiled.

I rented an apartment with three other teammates, including Walt Sessi, a big outfielder from Finleyville, Pa., close by Donora. Although Sessi played only briefly with the Cardinals, he hit an important game-winning pinch homer in the 1946 National League pennant race. We needed every ounce of effort because that year St. Louis and Brooklyn finished in the first tie in major league history.

I'm vague about the 1939 season at Williamson, so vague, in fact, that, honestly, I was surprised when I was reminded that I'd been shelved for a time with arm trouble. I do know that although I still could throw hard, I'd had soreness in my left shoulder from time to time—ever since I'd been shoved hard into the wall at the Donora high school gym during a basketball game.

When I returned to action at Williamson after that layoff of "several weeks," I pitched good ball, though I don't think Harrison Wickel would have entirely agreed. On July 15, 1939, his report on Musial to the home office in St. Louis had said:

"This boy is quite a problem. He is by far the wildest pitcher I have ever seen. He hasn't pitched a complete game here in ages and he must average at least 10 walks a game. He has fair stuff and at times he has a good fast ball and pretty good curve. He will strike out just as many as he will walk, but I certainly can't depend on him, and most of the games he has won we have given him a dozen or more runs, or (Wayne) Bruce has been called in to finish his work. I recommend his release because I don't believe he will ever be able to find the plate.

"I don't think he has enough stuff to get by. I've noticed that when he does get the ball over, he is hit rather freely, and I am led to believe that his wildness is his effectiveness. The opposition never gets anything good to hit. The only place he can pitch is Class D, where the player strikes at almost anything a pitcher tosses up there. I am at a loss to say definitely what to do with him. He has the best of habits and is a fine boy."

Wickel was so right—about my pitching, I mean, though I was better later than early for him. I pitched three straight low-hit victories that helped put Williamson into the Mountain States League playoffs before Bluefield beat us for the President's Cup.

I headed home with a 9-2 record, but my earned-run average was 4.30 and, though I had allowed only 71 hits in 92 innings, walked only one less batter than I'd fanned, 85. More important, since Class D clubs carried only 14 players, I'd been pressed into outfield service when one of the Williamson regulars was hurt. And I'd hit, batting .352 in 71 times up. More and more, I liked to hit.

That fall, Lil and I, desperately in love, slipped away on my nineteenth birthday and were married secretly. We've been very happy, blessed with four fine children, and we have been lucky enough financially. But still we'd urge young couples to wait longer than we did, to complete their educations before they marry. We're proud and happy that our son, Dick, graduated from Notre Dame before he married and that the two older of our three girls, Gerry and Janet went to college. Jeannie will, too.

In 1940, for the first time, I was ready to play a full professional season, and for the first time, too, I went to spring training. I was ordered to the Cardinals' minor league camp for Class B and C clubs at Columbus, Ga. The Asheville club was managed by its third baseman, Bob Rice, later the silver-haired, suave traveling secretary of the Pirates.

I wasn't ready for B or even C ball, so I was sent to Daytona Beach, Fla., in the Class D Florida State League. My pay, as an experienced player in the lowest classification of minor league ball, now was $100 a month. I sent for Lil. She was expecting our first child and we wanted to be together. My father-in-law paid Lil's way to Florida.

At Daytona Beach, we met the Kerrs, Dick and Corinne, or "Pep," as everyone called the manager's wife. The Kerrs had no children, but they were always ready to help young players with their problems, including Musial and his. We lost those dear friends, Lil and I, in my last year in the big leagues. Dick died early in the season, and we flew to his funeral. I'd had a chance to visit him in Houston just a couple of weeks earlier when he was dying of cancer, but still cheerful. Pep followed him that same fall.

Dickie Kerr was a pixy who got considerable zest out of the little things in life. He had to have wit and optimism because baseball hadn't been too kind to him. As a big league rookie in 1919, the little 26-year-old lefthander from St. Louis won 13 games for the Chicago White Sox, a gifted team from which eight key players were charged with conspiring to throw the World Series. In the midst of this shame, Dick rode like a knight on a white horse. He pitched and won two games for the team that was trying to lose, and he became a national hero. But his loyalty went unrewarded because after he won 21 games for Chicago in 1920 and 19 in 1921, he was refused a pay increase for 1922.

The reserve clause never seemed more one-sided than when Charles A. Comiskey suspended little hero Kerr for holding out for more money. Dick was out of organized ball for the next three years, playing semi-pro and wildcat baseball until 1925. By then, his skill was blunted. Still he did not become bitter at baseball. By the time I came along to join him at Daytona Beach, he was managing for the Cardinals in the lower reaches of their far-flung organization—and he was happy.

Perhaps because Dick had been a pitcher, too, I learned more from him in a few days than I had in parts of two seasons at Williamson, playing for an outfielder and a shortstop. I learned about concentration, control and helpful pitching techniques, enough to win 18 games and lose only five for a team that came from 13½ games behind Sanford to win the regular-season championship. My ERA was good, too, but I still walked nearly as many as I struck out. Dick Kerr couldn't throw the ball for me.

Between pitching assignments, Kerr played me in the outfield, and I hit .311 in 113 games that 1940 season. Cardinal scouts began to get the idea—as I was getting it—that maybe I was a batter.

As early as April 10 of that year Harrison Wickel, my former Williamson manager who once had recommended my release, filed a report in which he said: "Pitched only one game while I was here. I still think he will never reach the majors as a pitcher, but he might as an outfielder."

Two weeks later Wid Matthews reported to St. Louis: "Good fast ball, curve fair. Nice poise, big boy. He can hit and may be too good a hitter to keep out of the game."

On May 1, Ollie Vanek, who had recommended that the Cardinals sign me three summers earlier on the strength of workouts at Monessen, Pa., took another look and wrote: "Good form and curve, fast ball a bit doubtful. Also a good hitter. May make an outfielder."

All I know is that I liked to play, talk—and listen—baseball. I've still got a scrapbook that shows my radio-side scorecard of the 1940 major league All-Star game at St. Louis. Dreaming as I did of one day reaching the majors, I certainly wasn't optimistic enough to believe that 15 months later I'd be playing in that same major league park against the same man, the Boston Braves' Max West, whose three-run homer in the first inning had led to a 4-0 victory for the National League All-Stars.

Until just before our son was born in August, Lil and I lived in a small hotel in Daytona Beach. Now, with the baby about to arrive, we had a problem and the Kerrs kindly solved it. Among the erroneous stories that have grown up around me is one that Dick Kerr even rented a larger house so that he and Pep could take us in. I'm not saying Dick wouldn't have, because he was a generous man. Just to set the record straight, the Kerrs took us into the house they had. They showed us so much kindness that, in gratitude, we named our son Richard. Inevitably, too, like the former World Series hero, our son became known as "Dickie" until, as a young man, Richard Stanley (Dick) Musial made it plain that he didn't care for the diminutive.

The night after Dick was born in August, 1940, I pitched against Gainesville and celebrated with a 3-2 victory in 12 innings. A Daytona Beach sports editor, Bernard Kahn, ribbed me about the questionable quality of the two-for-a-nickel cigars I passed around.

A few nights later when Dick Kerr was honored in pre-game ceremonies at home plate, gift-minded Daytona Beach fans added an endearing postscript. They gave me a baby carriage. It was a happy night all around because I was pitching and wanted to win for the Islander fans. When I beat Sanford in another 12-inning game, 3-2, Daytona Beach moved into first place in the Florida State League for the first time since the league was reorganized in 1936.

Then "it" happened.

In late August, I played center field at Orlando behind Jack Creel, our best pitcher. A low line drive was hit to center. I charged and dived. Hundreds—no, thousands—of times since then I've somersaulted for a ball and escaped injury because, turnverein-trained, I knew how to fall. But that night my tumbling techniques didn't help. My spikes caught and threw me heavily onto the point of my left shoulder.

The pain was immediate and intense. During the night, a knot rose on the shoulder. In the morning, X-rays indicated merely a bad bruise for which heat treatments were prescribed. Dick Kerr said I probably wouldn't miss more than one pitching turn. A few days later I beat Ocala, 4-3.

Among the romanticized versions of this turning point in my career is that, in discouragement, I talked of quitting and that Kerr talked me out of it. That's as completely false as the story that I wanted to give up and go back home to get a full-time job when my son was born. You'd be surprised how far $100 a month would go in 1940, even for only six months a year, especially if you were frugal. Besides, thanks to my father-in-law, I knew I could count on working in his grocery for our winter keep.

Denying those fables can never detract from Dick Kerr, whose help we tried to repay, secretly, a few years ago. Lil and I told Dick and Pep to pick out a house they wanted in Houston, where since World War II our good friend had worked as a timekeeper for a construction company. Dick, who was about to retire, was so pleased he told a newspaper friend and there was no more secret.

My point is that I hadn't discouraged easily. Maybe I was just a dreamy-eyed kid. Besides, none of us was the slightest bit aware that my throwing arm had been damaged permanently.

When the Florida State League All-Star game was held August 30 at Sanford, Kerr did say he would not pitch me because of the "strain" required in the league race, but there was no hint of anything more serious. I got into the game at Sanford, playing part of it in center field. In early September, Daytona Beach clinched its first pennant, but was knocked out of the playoffs by underdog Orlando, three games to one. I didn't help with my pitching. Making only my second start since I hurt my shoulder, I was knocked out in a 12-5 loss.

The ineffectiveness was blamed on the "overwork" of pitching and playing the outfield. Obviously, though, my arm had begun to lose its throwing strength by the time I played my last game in Class D. As a center fielder I tripled and scored our only run, but Creel lost a tough one to Orlando, 2-1.

There was discord at Daytona Beach at the end of the season. I've never been part of a baseball insurrection, but I mention this unpleasantness to show the plight of the pre-war minor league ball player, especially in the depths of Class D.

Our salaries ended on the final day of the regular season and we received only $2.50 a day during the playoffs for rent, board and other expenses. Homesick, obliged to forego better income in off-season jobs during the playoffs, and hurt because none of the Daytona Beach board of directors had congratulated them for winning the pennant, the players grumbled with reason. Daytona Beach's sports editors, Bernard Kahn and George Rood, wrote critically of the failure of the league to provide incentive purses for the playoffs.

Personally, I look back fondly on Daytona Beach, Dick's birthplace and our first winter home away from Donora. The Florida east coast community was clean and attractive and when a Pennsylvania acquaintance offered me off-season employment in the sporting goods department of the

Montgomery-Ward store, we leaped at the chance to stay south. The job paid $25 a week.

My 1941 contract was assigned first to Asheville, N.C., in the Class B Piedmont League, then to Columbus, O., of the Class Double-A American Association, just one step below the big leagues. Before I reported for spring training at Hollywood, Fla., Bernard Kahn wrote a complimentary column predicting a future for me as a major leaguer.

"Musial," he wrote, "runs like silk hose, throws like a bullet and hits like, well, like hell."

Raising the question of whether my future would best be as a pitcher or outfielder, Kahn pointed out that Dickie Kerr felt, with better control, I could become an outstanding pitcher. Bernie put the question to me.

"I don't know whether I'm a pitcher or an outfielder," I told him. "I'll let the Cardinals decide that. I'm only a player. When I'm getting hit hard or when I'm hitting hard myself, I want to be an outfielder."

Here, though, is the quote about which I am most proud because I still don't believe I could express any better my feeling about baseball than I did as a 19-year-old kid. "Naturally," I told Bernard Kahn back there in 1941, "I want to play with Columbus, but the Cardinals will probably farm me out to Asheville or some other B team. I don't want to play any more D ball, but, if I have to, I want to play it right here in Daytona Beach. I'd play in an E league if they told me to. I like baseball too much to ever give it up."

6

Year of Magic

If I saw a movie about a dead-armed pitcher from Class D who became a major league outfielder within one year, I wouldn't believe it.

But that's what happened to me in 1941, certainly one of the most fantastic seasons ever experienced by any ball player.

As soon as I reported to Hollywood, Fla., I realized something was wrong. My arm didn't really hurt, but it was weak. I couldn't throw hard, and here I was in a Class Double-A camp of experienced players who were headed for the major leagues or who already had played there.

The Columbus manager was a dignified, bespectacled man best known for later managing the Brooklyn Dodgers to two pennants—Burt Shotton—a man who never seems to have received enough credit for the help he gave me.

Batterymen reported ahead of the rest of the squad so that the pitchers would have their arms loose, ready to throw hard, when the hitters arrived. We took a lot of batting practice against each other and we played a few informal squad games. From time to time, as I pitched batting practice or worked out on the sidelines, I'd see Shotton watching me. I knew that I wasn't cutting loose as freely as before and I was even wilder than I had been.

Finally, Shotton took me aside. He was kindly, this former major league outfielder and manager.

"Son," Shotton said, "there's something wrong with your arm. At least, I know you're not throwing hard enough to pitch here. I think you CAN make it as a hitter. I'm going to send you to another camp with the recommendation that you be tried as an outfielder."

I wasn't disappointed at Shotton's decision because, as I had told Bernard Kahn, I frankly had figured I wouldn't make the climb immediately to Class Double-A. If I could make Asheville or another Class B team, I would be satisfied.

I was sent to Albany, Ga., where the Cardinals' Class D clubs trained, then to Columbus, Ga., where the Class A, B and C teams had assembled. I was in a player pool, awaiting reassignment, working out and a bit bewildered, too, when Clay Hopper, who managed the Columbus, Georgia team, told me he wanted me to pitch against the Cardinals. Yes, against the BIG club itself, stopping off to play an exhibition game as it barnstormed back to St. Louis.

"But I'm supposed to be an outfielder now," I protested feebly.

"I know," said Hopper, "but you're lefthanded and you've had a couple of years' experience."

The Cardinals were building another dynasty under Branch Rickey in the office and Billy Southworth in the field. The team I faced had such outstanding ball players as Johnny Mize, Terry Moore, Enos Slaughter and Jimmy Brown. Among the younger ones were Marty Marion and Walker Cooper.

I didn't start against the Cardinals, but it wasn't long before I was needed. Before Hopper could get me warmed up and into the game, the Cardinals had scored six runs in the first inning. I retired the side without further scoring and felt pretty good about it. Maybe Burt Shotton was wrong. Maybe I still could pitch.

In the second inning, I changed my mind. Or, rather, Moore and Mize changed it for me. Moore hit a long home run with a man on base and Mize hit a homer that went even farther.

I got through three more innings, all scoreless, but I had few illusions left. In one horrible inning of relief against the Phillies a few days later, I gave up four hits, six walks, two wild pitches, seven runs—and all ambitions as a pitcher.

By now, Hopper and all the managers of St. Louis farm clubs training at Columbus were as convinced as Burt Shotton that as a pitcher, I might make an outfielder. Yet outfielders had to throw, too, and most of them weren't convinced that my hitting would offset my throwing.

Shortly after reporting at Columbus, I'd seen a familiar face and said, "Mr. Vanek, remember me?"

Ollie Vanek, the man for whom I had tried out four years earlier at Monessen, now managed the Springfield (Mo.) club of the Class C Western Association. He looked at me and shook his head.

"I place the face, kid," he said, "but not the name."

"Stan Musial . . . Stan Musial of Donora, Pennsylvania."

He smiled. "Oh, sure, I remember," he said, "you're the kid whose father needed so much persuasion to let you play."

I was relieved. At least I had one friend in court. I explained my problem. Could I work with his team? "Why, sure," said Ollie, "glad to have you."

Behind the scenes, as I worked out with Vanek's club, my case had created a problem for Branch Rickey, who had seen me hit line drives in batting practice during one of his whirlwind visits. By the time Rickey held a staff meeting at which clubs were to be stocked for the minor league season, I was not just an unknown quantity as an outfielder and hitter, I was damaged goods.

Rickey, the old master of mental gymnastics, oratory and intrigue, liked to see—and hear—his minor league managers maneuver for talent. He enjoyed quick-witted repartee. Far more important, by pitting one manager against another, he learned a great deal about the young players in the system. At that time, by the way, St. Louis had nearly 30 farm clubs, compared with the approximately half-dozen each that big league teams now operate. From players to be reassigned, managers were permitted to pick in order of priority, and Class A managers picked first.

When the name of Stan Musial came up, my pitching background and arm trouble were reviewed. The observation was made that I had shown hitting potential. Mr. Rickey nodded. Who wanted Musial?

No one in Class A.

No one in Class B.

In fact, there's a legend that not until Rickey thrust me on

Ollie Vanek with the promise to replace me when the top clubs started cutting, did I escape a dreaded return to Class D for a FOURTH YEAR. But the way I understand it, it didn't happen that way. When B. R. got to Class C, Vanek spoke up.

"I'll take Musial, Mr. Rickey," Ollie said. "I like the way he hits."

If, as I've said, Burt Shotton hasn't been given sufficient credit for steering me in the right direction, certainly Vanek has been shortsuited even more. He's the man who first tried me out for the Cardinals. He recommended to Andrew French that I be signed. He indicated in an early scouting report that I might have more future as an outfielder. And he volunteered to give me the chance.

Ollie said to me recently, "Look, Stan, I had no idea you'd get as far as you did, but I felt you had a chance. You handled yourself like an athlete. You were quick, coordinated, threw well originally, and you had a good stroke at the plate."

Vanek was the first manager to contemplate using me at first base. In 1941, Ollie knew my arm was weak, though time gradually improved it. However, his first baseman, a big, powerful fellow named Buck Bush, was too slow for the outfield. So Ollie put me in right because it was the short field in Springfield. And to show his confidence in my hitting ability, he batted me clean-up.

The first day in White City Park, I hit three straight pitches onto Boonville Avenue in right field—in batting practice. My debut in Class C was less than sensational. We clobbered Joplin, 13-1, and our left fielder, Roy Broome, belted three triples, but I had only one hit in four times at bat.

I showed at once that I needed education in the outfield, and Vanek saw that I got it. He'd have me out mornings to correct two faults, one of them common to young outfielders. I had trouble gauging line drives hit directly at me. The tendency is to break in too quickly. The ball often rises and sails over a charging outfielder's head. The other trouble was more of anxiety than judgment. Trying to cover up for that weak throwing arm, I rushed too fast trying to handle ground balls. White City Park's bumpy outfield was no help.

I welcomed the chance to learn to field. I had enjoyed being a pitcher because no player is more directly involved in a game or controls the action more. Yet, I had begun to recognize my limitations, specifically my lack of pitching control. Too often I had fallen behind on the ball-and-strike count with my fast ball and couldn't get the curve over the plate—and this was before my arm was hurt.

I never would have made the major leagues as a pitcher. My injury merely hastened a switch that was inevitable. From the time I'd seen my first major league ball game, I'd felt I could reach the big leagues—as a hitter. I'd just never dreamed how much heartbreak there would be early, or how much happiness later, or how quickly I'd move once I got started.

At Springfield, after collecting only two hits in 13 times up the first three games, I began to rip. In one night game against St. Joseph, Mo., with Branch Rickey in the stands, I had a triple, homer and single to account for all Springfield runs. I had had to rely on scrapbooks and the file of *The Sporting News* for many details of my career, but I don't need anyone to jog my memory about coming through in front of the Cardinals' general manager, the man who eventually would have to decide whether I belonged in the big leagues.

Approaching my twenty-first birthday, getting daily batting practice and playing regularly, I had begun to show power. One night at Springfield, hitting .430, I hit three home runs against Topeka. Just outside the clubhouse where Lil had waited after the game, the Musials must have seemed a little crazy. I was grinning broadly, Lil was in tears, and nine-month-old Dickie, the rascal who had driven her to the ladies' room from diaper changes in each of the homer-hitting innings, was asleep on her shoulder—and very, very dry.

I'll never forget one night in a hotel lobby at Topeka. Vanek said, "Stan, the way you're going, I wouldn't be surprised to see you reach the major leagues in a couple of years."

I laughed. The laugh was on both of us, Ollie and me, because the chance came within a couple of months. On a late-July open date, we were out fishing on the White River when a reporter from the Springfield paper reached us. I had been ordered to report to Rochester, N.Y., the International League farm club, just one rung below the big leagues on the baseball ladder.

I was flabbergasted. Sure, I had been hitting—.379 for 87 games with 26 homers and 94 RBIs—but, somehow, I had expected to finish the season in Class C. Instead, I was jumping to Class Double-A. We were leaving good friends behind in Springfield. Fats Dantonio had more reason than the rest to remember us. We left Fats with Dickie's whooping cough!

When I joined Rochester, the team was in fourth place with a 53-47 record. I knew two Red Wings by reputation, former big leaguers Floyd (Pep) Young, the shortstop, and Jimmy Ripple, the left fielder. Others were bound for the big leagues, but I didn't have much chance to get acquainted. I reported to the Wings at Syracuse, N.Y., and the Rochester manager, Tony Kaufmann, immediately put me in right field. The same night, another rookie, a broad-shouldered Chicago kid named Erv Dusak, checked in from Mobile and played left field. Dusak, a righthanded hitter, had the better night in a 7-1 Rochester victory, getting three hits and making a leaping catch. I contributed only an infield single in four tries.

I remember Rochester because I broke in before the home crowd with four hits, including a double and homer, and I remember it even more for offering me the chance to meet Babe Ruth. He came to town to put on a hitting exhibition and to present a trophy in behalf of Rochester fans to their most popular player that 1941 season, first baseman Harry Davis.

The Babe was 47 then, heavy-bellied and out of competition for six years. His timing was way off, but finally he connected with a pitch from Kaufmann, who served as his special batting practice pitcher, and lifted it far out of the ball park. I got a big thrill out of watching that ancient, still-fabulous hitter demonstrate why my father thought there was only one Bambino. Pop was so right.

I confess, though, that I was awed—and maybe a little disillusioned—when Ruth sat on our bench during the game, pulled out a pint of whiskey from his pocket and emptied it. I'd wanted to hit one while the Babe was there—a homer, I mean, not the bottle—but I managed only one single in five trips against Montreal. The Bambino would have thrown that one back as a minnow.

For only the second time, to my knowledge, Branch Rickey saw me in a regular game when the Rochester club was at Newark. I got four hits that night, part of a tremendous series against a powerful Yankee farm team. In three games I got 11 hits.

One game stands out in my mind, as it did in Kaufmann's. Hank Majeski, Newark's third baseman, had a habit of charging fast whenever he anticipated a bunt and, therefore, it was difficult to move a runner along with a sacrifice. When I came up in the eleventh inning with a man on first, Kaufmann, coaching third base, called me aside and said: "I'm giving you the bunt sign, kid, but if Majeski charges, try to push the ball past him."

I squared around to bunt, a lefthanded hitter facing third base. Majeski charged, as expected, and, swinging instead of bunting, I pushed the ball past him into left field for a double. However, we failed to score.

In the thirteenth inning the game still was 4-4 and once more there was a runner on first base when I came up. This time Kaufmann flashed the bunt sign from the coaching box. Figuring we wouldn't try the same trick twice, Majeski charged with the pitch. Again faking a bunt, I swung away and lined the ball past

Hank's ear and into the left field corner for a run-scoring double. We won the game.

I learned later, when I played for the Cardinals and Kaufmann coached for us, that Tony had glowed over those two improvised offensive plays in a written report to the St. Louis office.

Rochester, by winning 16 of its last 20 games, drove toward a playoff berth. In our final Sunday home game—minor league ball drew crowds of 7500 then—the Red Wings virtually clinched a playoff spot with a double victory over Buffalo. I was fortunate enough to be hot at bat, getting six hits in those two games and three more the following night in a 4-2 victory that gave us fourth place.

I hit pretty well in the playoffs, too, but Newark, the regular-season champion, knocked us off in five games. During the playoffs, it was announced that the Cardinals had purchased pitcher Hank Gornicki, third baseman George Kurowski, Dusak and me for delivery after the International League season. None of us actually expected to be called. For one thing, we hoped to last longer in the playoffs than we did.

The last night at Newark, after I had singled and doubled in a 9-6 loss, I phoned Lil, who had gone back to Donora with Dickie. I said I'd grab the train and be right home. To save money, I rode a night coach to Pittsburgh, where Lil and her sister Helen met me.

It was a Sunday, I remember, and I was dead-tired. After Mass, I was taking a nap when Lil awakened me excitedly.

"There's a wire from Rochester for you. I think they want you to report to St. Louis."

"You're kidding."

"I'm not."

I'll tell you, there never was more bedlam than there was in the Labash household that Sunday afternoon. We held a quick pow-wow and decided that, because the big league season had only two weeks to run, Lil wouldn't go with me. Instead, she and her wonderful mother spent that Sabbath washing and ironing my dirty clothes—my wardrobe was skimpy in those days—so I'd be presentable in the big leagues.

Then the Labashes drove us hurriedly into Pittsburgh, where we figured to have a feverish good-bye. Instead, we had more than enough time for farewells.

I had missed my train.

7

"Nobody Can Be That Good!"

The first pitch I saw in the big leagues was the first knuckleball I'd ever faced. And I popped it up, feebly, an easy out.

The day I broke in, St. Louis reporters wondered about the pronunciation of my name. Was it "Meusel," like Bob and Irish, two former major league outfielders? Or like "Musical" without the "c?" Maybe I didn't do a good job of phoneticizing because I was a little overwhelmed, and my name popularly has been mispronounced ever since. Perhaps some of the distortion can be blamed on my good friend and eminent linguist, broadcaster Dizzy Dean, who, letting the vowels and consonants fall where they would, talked enthusiastically about the young "Mews-ee-al."

I've always had a three-syllable surname in the majors, though back home in Donora, with foreign inflection, the name properly is pronounced "MEW-shil." Hearing it for so long the other way, I even have trouble myself. The best I can manage, usually, is "MEWS-yil."

I have only the vaguest recollection of anything in St. Louis in mid-September, 1941, except Sportsman's Park and the Fairgrounds Hotel, located only a few blocks north. Many of the ball players, particularly the unmarried ones, stayed there. But if my recollection is dim of my earliest look at a city in which I was to make my fortune and, finally, my home, my memory of the 1941 Cardinals is bright. I joined one of the gamest, most gallant teams in baseball history.

St. Louis hadn't had a National League winner until 1926 when Rogers Hornsby's team slipped home in front and upset the Yankees in the World Series. Then, and quickly, the city learned about the money crops from Branch Rickey's farm system. Over nine seasons, the Cards won five pennants and three world championships, but since Frank Frisch's Gas House Gang of 1934 the Redbirds hadn't finished first.

In 1941, Billy Southworth was making a pennant bid with a young, incredibly fast team of strong defense and excellent pitching. Only the center fielder, Terry Moore, and the third baseman, Jimmy Brown, really belonged to the post-1934 Gas House Gang. Enos Slaughter, the right fielder, had been a rookie playing regularly in 1938, the year an era ended. When the club finished sixth that season, Frisch was fired.

The cast was different in 1941, but not the spirit. This was the period when the "Cardinal type" was used generally by baseball men to describe any young, eager, fast athlete who played hungrily and a bit recklessly.

The 1941 club certainly showed the old college try, staying in close pennant contention throughout the year with Brooklyn. The Cardinals had lost key players with the kind of injuries that don't shrug off. Walker Cooper suffered a broken shoulder. Slaughter fractured a collarbone. Mort Cooper underwent arm surgery. Brown suffered a broken nose. Moore was sidelined for a month after being hit on the head with a pitched ball. And Johnny Mize wasn't hitting homers because he was in and out of the lineup with a jammed thumb.

Other injuries had been so numerous that only one regular—and of all people, the skinny young shortstop, Marty Marion—hadn't missed a game. Yet when I joined the Cardinals, they still were only two games out of first place after losing the crucial rubber contest of a three-game series in Brooklyn.

I walked into the home clubhouse at Sportsman's Park for the first time early in the morning of September 17, 1941. With me were Erv Dusak and George Kurowski, also up from Rochester, and Walt Sessi, my old Williamson teammate reporting from Houston. The varsity hadn't arrived, but, as I was to learn through more than 20 years of pleasant association, the Cardinals' little equipment manager, Morris (Butch) Yatkeman, virtually lived there. Butch led us back to a cubbyhole where batting-practice pitchers and rookies dressed. It was called the Red-Neck Room because players who crowded into it traditionally were the unhappiest with their conditions, opportunities, salaries and, sometimes, themselves.

Not me. I was nervous but completely happy. I'd started the season as a $100-a-month Class D pitcher and had made the grade as an outfielder at $150 a month in Class C, then at $350 a month in Double-A. The morning I'd reported from Rochester, Branch Rickey had signed me for the last two weeks at a rate of $400 a month—and for 1942 at the same salary, too.

If I sound naive, remember this was 1941. Terry Moore, the best defensive center fielder in the league and an eight-year veteran, was making only $13,000 a year.

Mr. Rickey hadn't anything particularly memorable to say to me that first morning. It was obvious then, as the Cardinals since have confirmed, that the player on his mind was Dusak, not Musial, and I can see why. Erv was a strapping righthanded power hitter who ran well, fielded well and threw considerably better than I did. Unfortunately, Erv had too much trouble with the breaking ball to last long in the big leagues.

When Butch Yatkeman handed out uniforms, he surveyed us with the experienced eye of a tailor and threw us what he thought would fit best. The uniforms, of course, bore numbers then unassigned. I drew number "6." I've never worn any other in the big leagues and, long before I laid it aside, Mr. Busch decided that for the first time the Cardinals would retire a number.

My first big league manager, Billy Southworth, was a sturdy little man, a good outfielder in his day. He was deep-voiced and brisk, but he had a way with young talent. As a player, they'd called him Billy the Kid. At 48, he still looked—and acted—young. He even wore sliding pads to the coaching lines.

Southworth said he would play me at once. The Cardinals were scheduled for a doubleheader that afternoon against the seventh-place Boston Braves, managed by a seamy-faced, jug-eared man who would make his biggest mark at another time in another league—Casey Stengel. With Slaughter hurt, the Cardinals needed lefthanded hitting, so after the Redbirds had won the first game, 6-1, behind a 20-year-old lefthander, Howard Pollet, just up from Houston, I was a second-game starter.

I'll never forget facing my first big league pitcher, Jim Tobin, and the challenge of the first knuckleball I'd ever seen. It fluttered up to the plate, big as a grapefruit but dancing like a dust-devil. Off stride, fooled, I popped up weakly to Sibby Sisti, playing third base for Boston. When I trotted to right field, head down, I had a problem on my mind, a problem—and a challenge.

The knuckleball is a challenge, indeed, and I've looked foolish missing my share of knucklers. But I learned to delay my stride, cut down my swing and just stroke the ball. When I batted next against Tobin, two were on and two were out. This time I hit the ball smack against National League President Ford Frick's signature for a line drive to right-center. The ball bounced off the wall, two runs scored, and I ran joyously to second base with my first big league hit—a double.

I finished that game with two hits in four trips, the other a single, and the Cardinals won, 3-2, on a ninth-inning home run by the veteran Estel Crabtree. I was a happy kid, all right, and pretty lucky. I got a basehit the next day in a 4-1 loss to the Braves, then had my first perfect day in the majors—"3 for 3," including a double—as we beat a big Chicago righthander, Paul Erickson, 3-1.

As a result, the Cardinals were only two percentage points behind Brooklyn with nine games to play, and a crowd of more than 26,000 the most I'd ever played before—came out for the Cardinals' final home games, in a Sunday doubleheader with the Cubs. And at 20, a big leaguer less than a week, I enjoyed one of the finest days I'd ever have in the majors.

In the first game, playing left field, I made two good catches and threw out a runner at the plate. At bat, I doubled off the right field screen in the first inning. Next time up, I singled to center and stole second. On my third trip, I doubled off the screen again. The fourth time, with the score tied in the ninth, 5-5, I hit a one-out single for my fourth straight hit and moved to second on an infield out.

After Cubs' manager Jimmy Wilson ordered Frank Crespi passed intentionally, Coaker Triplett, swinging hard at one of lefty Ken Raffensberger's fork balls, squibbed a little grounder in front of the plate, toward third base. The Cubs' catcher, Clyde McCullough, pounced, fielded the ball and fired to Babe Dahlgren at first base. Umpire Lee Ballanfant spread his palms—"safe!"

Dahlgren whirled to argue with Ballanfant. McCullough stood watching, hands on hips. Rounding third base, I saw my chance and, without breaking stride, raced home and slid across, ahead of Dahlgren's hurried return throw to McCullough, who was scrambling back to cover home plate. I'd scored the winning run from second base on a hit that had traveled about 15 feet.

In the second game, I played right field in a 7-0 victory. I dived to my right for one low line drive and charged for another, turning a double somersault. I bunted safely toward third base and singled to center to make it a memorable six-hit day of all-round delight—for me, anyway.

The Cubs' manager, Jimmy Wilson, was fit to be tied. *"Nobody,"* he exploded, "can be that good!"

I agree. I wasn't. But I'm proud to say that, until age slowed me on the bases and afield, I did a lot more than just swing a bat.

By the time the Cardinals left town that Sunday night for their final trip, they accepted me as one of the boys. They congratulated me, not because they particularly liked my apple cheeks, but because, if I stayed hot, I still might help them take home World Series checks.

In the Pullman, I was talking with Terry Moore, saying how things had happened so fast since spring training in April, when he hit that home run off me in Columbus, Ga., that it seemed unreal to be an outfielder with the Cardinals in September. Terry looked at me, first in disbelief, then in laughter. "It can't be," he said, "you're not that kid lefthander."

I nodded.

Moore called over to Mize, kibitzing a card game. "Hey, John," he said, "you won't believe this! *Musial* is the lefthander who threw us those long home-run balls at Columbus this spring."

Neither Moore nor Mize, I might add, ever let me forget it.

Our first stop that final week was in Pittsburgh. The first game, Ken Heintzelman, a lefthander who would bother the Cardinals for years, shut out the ball club, 4-0, and stopped me, too. Fortunately, I had another chance because this was a doubleheader. As we walloped Rip Sewell in the second game, 9-0, I got three hits, including my first major league home run. It was quite a thrill to trot around the bases at Forbes Field, where three years earlier I had watched the Pirates as a schoolboy, and to know that Lil, my parents and many friends were watching.

That first big league home run carried with it a little dividend that had special meaning for me. A telegram arrived informing me that I would receive a shipment of Wheaties, an advertising gimmick in those pre-war days. Many a time as a kid, listening to baseball play-by-play broadcasts sponsored by General Mills,

I had dreamed that one day an announcer would say: ". . . And for that home run, a case of Wheaties to Stan Musial."

After the doubleheader at Pittsburgh, I waited until my new teammates had cleared out of the clubhouse. Then, almost timidly, I brought my father into the dressing quarters to introduce him to manager Billy Southworth and his coaches, Mike Gonzalez and Buzzy Wares. Pop and I may have been shy, but we were two happy, proud Poles that evening.

I was even prouder, but a bit embarrassed, two days later when my friends and neighbors from Donora put on a Stan Musial Day celebration at Forbes Field. I really hadn't done anything yet, but they thought I had, just by becoming the first home-town boy to reach the big leagues since Bob Coulson went up in 1908. A small town swells up for joy when one of its own makes good—or acts as if he will. A school holiday was granted Donora youngsters so they wouldn't have to play hooky. A good bit of the Monongahela Valley must have been in Pittsburgh that afternoon. Not only was I given a traveling bag and money, but Walt Sessi, from nearby Finleyville, also was remembered with a wrist watch.

So pleased I didn't know whether to laugh or cry, I managed to deliver two hits. They were consolation for Donora, but not St. Louis, because the Pirates beat us, 3-1. And with Brooklyn shutting out Boston, the Cardinals were eliminated from the pennant race. I can't forget the sudden silence in the dugout, as the scoreboard in left field posted the bad news. Faces that had been alive with grim determination now were sad and weary. A team that had tried so hard against heavy odds and handicap all season had run out of time—and hope.

There's nothing deadlier than playing out the string after the race has been run, unless you're a wide-eyed kid just breaking in. The Cardinals finished the season at Chicago with 97 victories, good enough to win many a pennant, but not when another team has won 100. I had good reason to wish we were just getting started. In my first 12 major league games, getting 20 hits, I had batted .426.

I had been on the move so much that year—from Class C in the spring to the majors in the fall—that I didn't win a single hitting title even though I actually hit for higher average than the batting champions of the Western Association, International League and National League. I hadn't played enough games in any league, most certainly the big one, to qualify.

When I returned to Donora that fall, still a bit numb over my good fortune, the Donora Zinc Works Athletic Association honored me with a banquet. The presentations of a wrist watch and trophy were made by the man who had helped build my baseball dreams, Joe Barbao.

Western Pennsylvania's greatest hero, Honus Wagner, was there. The old legendary Flying Dutchman of the Pirates and I became good friends. Even in my most fanciful dreams, I never would have dared imagine that I would play long enough and hit well enough to break many of Old Honus' National League records.

8

"Pass the Biscuits, Mirandy!"

If I hadn't come up to the Cardinals in the fall of 1941 and hit so hard, I'm convinced I would have been sent down in the spring of 1942 because I hit so softly.

Because of my spectacular climb from Class C to the majors the previous year, I was the rookie most talked about in spring training, but, frankly, I was a lemon in the Grapefruit League.

The Cardinals were favored to win the pennant, though the trade of slugging first baseman Johnny Mize to the Giants made our power questionable. But I couldn't count on if-coming World Series money to pay our way now. So, draft-deferred as a pre-war father, I left Lil and Dickie in Donora. And I had more than a few sleepless nights, rooming with Ray Sanders, rookie first baseman, as I struggled trying to live up to my great expectations.

Was I trying too hard? I think not. After two decades of trying to hit in Florida ball parks with high blue skies, waving palm trees in the background and no proper backdrop, I'm convinced that it's too difficult to hit down there. But I didn't know that then. And it didn't help, as I failed to hit, to read that many baseball men had expressed doubt about me as a left fielder because I threw lefthanded.

I appreciated it very much, therefore, when a man considered then as just a craggy-faced comedian voiced a strong vote of confidence in me. Casey Stengel, Boston manager against whom I'd broken in the previous September, told writers in spring training:

"You'll be looking at him a long, long while . . . 10 . . . 15 . . . maybe 20 years. He's up to stay."

In Florida, the pitching that seemed certain to be the Cardinals' strength was even better—and deeper—than expected. In addition to Mort Cooper, Max Lanier, Howard Pollet, Ernie White, Lon Warneke, Howard Krist and Harry Gumbert, there were Murry Dickson, Harry Brecheen, George Munger, Al Jurisich, Henry Nowak and a righthander named Johnny Beazley, up from New Orleans.

A New York writer, Harry Grayson, said Beazley looked like "another Dizzy Dean." Grayson was bold, but absolutely right about Beazley. Handsome, hard-boiled Johnny won 21 games as a rookie and two more games in the World Series. If he hadn't hurt his arm later in military service, he could have been the best righthanded National League pitcher of our time.

Sam Breadon was right, too, when he told Grantland Rice that spring, "Pollet isn't 21 yet, but he's the smartest young pitcher I ever saw. Others may have more all-round stuff, but they don't know how to use it as well."

I doubt if any ball club before or since has had more pitching talent than the Cardinals had at the time World War II came along. We had speed, too, and defense, but our hitting was poor in spring training, and I was the biggest disappointment of all.

En route to St. Louis to open the season, manager Billy Southworth indicated concern over the first base and left field positions (Harry Walker was sharing time with me in left). But by the time we reached St. Louis to play a pre-season series with the Browns, Billy had made up his mind. "Don't worry, Stan," he said. "You're my left fielder. You can do it."

Billy had a way with young players, and his confidence when I was hitting under .200 helped. So, too, did those double-decked big league stands, which provided a better batting background.

Facing the Browns on a Saturday, I tripled and hit two singles, and on Sunday I hit a pinch double as the Cardinals won again. The next day, 24 hours before the season began, Branch Rickey called me into his office. Remember the $400-a-month contract I had signed in September, 1941?

"I'm tearing it up, my boy," Mr. Rickey said. "We're going to pay you $700 a month."

I called Lil at Donora that evening and told her to pack her things. I went apartment-hunting that night and basehit-hunting the next day when I tripled and singled off the Chicago Cubs' Claude Passeau as Mort Cooper lost the opener, 5-4.

I got off strongly in 1942, hitting a home run and two singles the next afternoon, but a couple of days later over at Pittsburgh, with the folks watching, I was lifted for a righthanded-hitting pinch-batter, Coaker Triplett, as lefty Ken Heintzelman shut us out. This wasn't the only time I went out for a pinch-hitter that season.

As much as I wanted to hit, I couldn't fault Southworth, then or now. At the time, like any young lefthanded hitter, I wasn't as sure against southpaws as I became later, and Triplett was a fine hitter against lefthanded pitching.

Platoon baseball is overdone, but in some form it's necessary—and not at all new. Most people don't realize it's done, in part, to discourage the opposition from saving certain pitchers for certain teams. I learned early that if I didn't intend to ride the bench, I'd have to hit lefthanders because opposing teams hoarded their southpaws for us.

Around St. Louis, they still chant the names of three polysyllabic portsiders who bothered us with lefthanded slow stuff—Ken Heintzelman, Ken Raffensberger and Fritz Ostermueller. Later, we helped keep Dave Koslo in the league and enhanced Preacher Roe's reputation.

For a time in 1942, the Cardinals couldn't hit any kind of pitching. We were shut out in five of our first 24 games and were lucky to break even. What we obviously needed—and this proved to be true throughout much of my career—was a series with the Dodgers or, more specifically, against a team managed by Leo Durocher. Front and center always was agitating, aggressive Lippy Leo, the former Gas House shortstop. All Durocher succeeded in doing was to bring out the best—and the beast—in the Cardinals.

The Dodgers, product of Larry MacPhail's madcap front-office genius and Durocher's driving managerial efforts, not only were defending champions, but they were improved after having added veteran Arky Vaughan from Pittsburgh to play third base.

We didn't always beat them, but they did wonders for us. The first time they came into St. Louis in 1942, we took one look at the gray uniforms splashed with blue-script "Dodgers" and came out of our slump. We won a doubleheader and I had five hits.

The club vendetta that had started in 1940 when St. Louis' Bob Bowman beaned ex-Redbird Joe Medwick hadn't cooled from one season to the next, either. Players spilled onto the field in the second game of the doubleheader after Ducky stepped on Ray Sanders' ankle at first base. Darkness finally halted play before the second game was six innings old. How so? Because a half-dozen players, some off each side, had been chased by the umpires after long, heated arguments.

Not all Cardinal-Dodger games were long or loosely played. Mort Cooper and Whit Wyatt, the finest duelists since Dizzy Dean and Carl Hubbell, hooked up for the first time since Wyatt's 1-0 victory the previous September virtually had clinched the 1941 pennant. This time Cooper won by the same score.

After four straight victories, we still were six and a half games behind Brooklyn, and that's the way it went most of the summer. We began to win regularly after playing only .500 ball for our first 30 games, but the Dodgers just were unbeatable, it seemed, except when they played the Cardinals.

I narrowly escaped breaking an ankle Memorial Day at Chicago when my spikes caught the plate as I tried to score from first on a short double. I was sidelined a week and then had trouble adjusting so that I was down to .298 in mid-June.

Later that month when the Dodgers whipped us four out of five at Ebbets Field, extending their league lead to seven and a half games, the St. Louis situation appeared grim. Even our mild-mannered, skinny shortstop, Marty Marion, was mad enough to fight—and did. Medwick slid hard into him. Marty and Joe exchanged words and squared off. Frank Crespi, rushing to Marion's aid from second base, floored Medwick, and a free-for-all followed. Dixie Walker tackled Jimmy Brown and suffered a twisted leg that took him out of the lineup.

In the only game we won in that series, I hit a triple and a homer, boosting my average to .315. Judson Bailey, writing for the Associated Press, listed me most prominently among players "overlooked" for the All-Star game at the Polo Grounds. Five Cardinals already had been selected by the National League managers. Besides I was just a rookie. For more than 20 years the only All-Star game in which I didn't have the honor of playing was that one won by the American League, 3-1.

When I hit a two-run homer off Boston's Dick Errickson to give the Cardinals a 7-5 victory over the Braves in 11 innings, we finished the first half of our schedule with a 47-30 record, a pace that would produce 94 victories and many pennants. But we were eight games behind Brooklyn, and when Lon Warneke was waived to the Cubs in early July there was feeling that the management had given up.

Sam Breadon bristled at suggestions that he had unloaded Warneke to get rid of a $15,000 salary, highest on the club. "We've sold Lon to make room on the starting staff for young blood like Johnny Beazley," Breadon snapped. The next day Beazley shut out the Giants for his ninth victory. As a clubowner, Uncle Sam was good—and lucky.

I remember well a series with Brooklyn at St. Louis in mid-July because for the first—and only—time in my major league career, I charged after a pitcher.

I've been knocked down plenty. Hit, too, even though I stood deep in the batter's box, away from the plate. For instance, in later years when Durocher managed the Giants, I remember his standing on the steps of the dugout at the Polo Grounds and yelling to Windy McCall, a lefthander: "Hit him in the back, Windy, right on the '6.' "

And Windy did, too.

By then, I could cuss to myself, say nothing to McCall and vow quietly to do just what I did—beat hell out of the Giants that day with my bat.

In 1942, though, I was just a kid and I saw red when Les Webber, a Dodger righthander of limited ability, decked me with four straight pitches. I started toward Webber, but our coaches, Gonzalez and Wares, prevented a fight.

We won a doubleheader from the Dodgers that day, but two inuries occurred that promised to affect the pennant race—and one did.

Our wheelhorse righthander, Mort Cooper, a stouthearted guy who chewed aspirin to dull the pain of persistent arm trouble, strained a ligament. Dr. Robert F. Hyland, whom Judge Landis called the surgeon-general of baseball, said that Mort would be sidelined a week to 10 days.

The more serious injury was Pete Reiser's. Brooklyn's terrific young center fielder ran head first into the outfield concrete while catching—then dropping—Enos Slaughter's game-winning inside-the-park home run in the eleventh inning of the second game. A brain concussion kept Pete out of the lineup a few days, but he suffered recurrent dizzy spells. His hitting dropped sharply. The youngest batting champion in National League history the previous year, an exciting baserunner who once stole home seven times in a season, Pete never again was the same player.

By early August, we were 10 games behind Brooklyn. The tide turned on a Saturday, August 8. At Pittsburgh, trailing 5-0, we tied the game in the ninth when I tripled and faked a steal of home so that Luke Hamlin committed a balk. The game went 16 innings and ended in darkness—tied. That day Whit Wyatt lost for the first time in four years to the lowly Braves, 2-0, in a game of unparalleled beanball pitching.

The league, at this point, had been experiencing so much deliberate dusting by the Dodgers that even the National League office became alarmed. I've heard old-timers build up a case for the ruggedness of their day and I've heard players more recently complain about high-and-tight pitching, but I'll match that period in the early 1940s against any era. Brooklyn was riding high and Durocher, roaring defiance, aroused every club in the league.

At Chicago, where his hatchet-men-of-the-mound obliged, Durocher sang out in intimidation, as each Cubs' hitter came up, "Stick it in his ear, stick it in his ear." Leo so infuriated Hi Bithorn that the Puerto Rican righthander tried to stick the ball in Durocher's ear. He fired it from the mound into the Dodgers' dugout.

The first National League manager to speak up was the Cubs' Jimmy Wilson. "The Cardinals," he said, "knock you out of the way on the bases just for fun, yet we don't have any trouble with any team except Brooklyn. Seven teams can't be wrong. When a guy starts hitting you in the clinches, you've got to protect yourself.

"When the Dodgers start something and you don't hit back at them, they go around throwing out their great big chests and calling you yellow. Well, we're not asking for it, but from here on in, it's every man for himself. The funny part about the whole business, when you come right down to it, is they don't have to do things like that to win."

Our old friend, Lon Warneke, the lean Arkansas Hummingbird with the homespun humor, put it another way. Old Lonnie, listening to Wilson sound off to Sid Feder of the AP, drawled:

"You know, it's this way: When you got a sundae in front of you and somebody reaches to take the chocolate off it, you've got to stop him right quick or first thing you know he'll be reaching for the ice cream next. They started it in Chicago, throwing at Bill Nicholson's head. Well, if they start again, we're the boys who can finish it."

Club by club, unnecessarily, Brooklyn alienated the entire

league. The payoff came at Boston the day Wyatt lost to the Braves for the first time. Boston's Manny Salvo, who had been troubled with a sore arm, retaliated in one of the wildest knockdown demonstrations ever. After Solvo won the battle of beanballs, Casey Stengel sat steaming over a cold bottle of beer in the Braves Field press room. "If I had a ball club as good as Durocher's, I wouldn't throw at a ball club as bad as mine," Ol' Case said. "We're going to battle those guys all the harder from now on, and I've talked to Frisch, Wilson and other managers who feel the same. Sure, Brooklyn has got a big lead, but they're not in yet. In case you guys didn't notice, St. Louis is winning steadily."

Boston and New York reporters smiled.

"I mean it," Stengel went on, "those jack-rabbits from St. Louis are coming. Why, I've never seen anything like 'em. Every sonofagun can run like a striped-tailed ape. They don't steal many bases, but they sure put the pressure on your infielders and outfielders, making 'em handle the ball faster than they can, to keep 'em from taking an extra base.

"My guys get jittery and field like this"—and Stengel imitated a nervous fielder trying to throw a ball before he had it under control. Ol' Case was right about one thing. The 1942 Cardinals did exert pressure on the defense. Infielders couldn't afford to juggle a ground ball. We challenged outfield arms boldly, going from first to third on even short, sharp singles, forcing the play with speed and hard sliding.

The club was young and carefree. Capt. Terry Moore, the center fielder, was the only regular of 30. The oldest man on the team, Harry Gumbert, veteran relief pitcher, was just 31. I was the youngest at 21, but most of the players were under 25.

We were young enough not to worry. Pepper Martin's Missouri Mudcats were gone—Warneke and his guitar had been the last—but a zany musical depreciation still hung over the clubhouse. Led by our trainer, Dr. Harrison J. Weaver, who could pick a mean mandolin, we banged out many a wild number before a game or after a victory. I could do pretty well with the slide whistle or beating time with my coat-hanger drumsticks. Doc Weaver kept his clubhouse phonograph well-stacked with records selected to bring out the best in his boys.

When we returned to St. Louis in mid-August for a 22-game home stand, we were still eight and a half behind Brooklyn. Along about that time, Harry Walker, a rookie outfielder, took a shine to "Pass the Biscuits, Mirandy," a clattering Spike Jones novelty that became our victory song, and Mort Cooper, our pitching ace, decided to change uniform numbers. Cooper never had won more than 13 games. When he tripped twice over 13 in

1942, Mort decided that the No. 13 uniform number he wore as a lucky piece had been a hex instead. The night we came off the road, he shucked his shirt and borrowed "14," worn by Gus Mancuso before he was sold to New York earlier in the season.

Cooper pitched a two-hit shutout over Cincinnati's Paul Derringer and thereby began a delightful—and profitable—bit of byplay in a season I'll never forget. Four days later, wearing brother Walker Cooper's "15," big Mort won his fifteenth game, 5-1, over the Cubs.

Coop and the Cards were rolling.

We just had ended an eight-game winning streak when the Dodgers came in for the last time in late August, leading by seven and a half games. We won the first game behind Max Lanier, 7-1, before a record St. Louis night-game crowd of 25,-814.

The next night 33,527 people jammed into the small ball park to watch Mort Cooper, squeezing into Ken O'Dea's "16," try for his sixteenth victory in another of his famous duels with Whit Wyatt. By the time Brooklyn broke a scoreless tie, Mort seemed to be caught in the same old jinx. The Dodgers' run came in the *thirteenth* inning! But in the home half, Enos Slaughter walked with one out and I singled. A base hit by Walker Cooper tied the score and brought an exultant avalanche of seat cushions and straw hats onto the field. And we won the game in the fourteenth.

After Johnny Beazley also won his sixteenth game in another overtime contest, taken in 10 innings by the same 2-1 score, the Dodgers bounced back to take the fourth game, 4-1, and still led by five and a half with only 30 to play. We'd meet them just twice more—*in Brooklyn.*

We didn't gain on them every day. In fact, some days we fell back, but we kept coming. Still four games out as we began our last trip early in September, we sent our wives and children home, hoping they would return to St. Louis for a World Series. We had to be practical. Hotels cost money.

At our first stop, Cincinnati, our speed paid off again. In the sixth inning, I caught the Reds napping and scored all the way from first base on a two-out pop fly single by O'Dea. It tied the game. In the ninth, Johnny Hopp turned an ordinary single into a double, then scored the winning run on a basehit by George Kurowski. We were only three games behind.

I remember what a blow we suffered at Pittsburgh on Labor Day. We led 5-0 behind Lanier in the first game of the holiday double-header when the Pirates scored 11 runs in the sixth. Our victory in the second game seemed hollow.

In the East for the last time, with a record of 26 victories in our last 31 games, we were under par physically. Injuries had sidelined Ernie White, Marty Marion and Coaker Triplett, and the club called up minor leaguers. One, a veteran Rochester righthander, Bill Beckmann, contributed an important victory later. A winning club needs good fortune. Our old former teammate, Lon Warneke, made the Dodgers pay again for their mistreatment of the Cubs. And when we moved into Brooklyn for the make-or-break series, we were only two games out.

I've said what a carefree ball club we were, but by the time we dressed at Ebbets Field we were as tense as mainsprings, and the clubhouse was silent. You could feel it—p-r-e-s-s-u-r-e.

I remember how even a seasoned warrior like Jimmy Brown shook going out for a pop fly. We shrugged off the pennant clanks in the early innings and big Mort Cooper beat Whit Wyatt, 3-0, for his twentieth win of the season. Cooper beat Brooklyn five times that year and allowed them only 10 runs in 53 innings.

The next day we climbed into a tie for first place. In the second inning, George Kurowski, who murdered lefthanders, hit a two-run homer off Max Macon. Our own star southpaw, Max Lanier, always at his best against Brooklyn, was a bit wild, but strong in the pinches. Lanier's 2-1 victory was the Cardinals' twenty-ninth in its last 34 games.

Even up, with 14 games to go, we moved happily that Saturday evening to Philadelphia, where disaster nearly took us out of the race just after we'd got back into it.

As we detrained at old Broad Street station, Johnny Beazley tangled with a redcap he wouldn't permit to carry his bag. Beazley contended that the baggage-hustler cursed him. Hotheaded Johnny threw his bag at the redcap, who pulled a knife. As Beazley flung up his arm in self-defense, he was slashed on the right thumb. Beazley chased the redcap out of the station and returned dripping blood from a wound that was deep, but not serious. How could he pitch Sunday?

He did, though, carrying a 1-0 lead into the ninth when our usually strong defense faltered and we lost, 2-1. We won the second game by the same score when Terry Moore hit a tie-breaking homer off Rube Melton. Bill Beckmann delivered six strong relief innings. An even split could have been damaging, but the Dodgers dropped a doubleheader to Cincinnati.

With two weeks to go, the Cardinals were in first place by a game. If anyone had told me then that Brooklyn would lose just two of its 12 remaining games, I would have doubted—for all my youthful confidence—that we would hold the lead. We scored some incredible victories.

The day after we took the league lead, we went into the ninth trailing Philadelphia, 3-2. With one out, Harry Walker tripled and scored on Slaughter's single. I doubled and Slaughter surged so hard into Mickey Livingston that the Philadelphia catcher dropped the ball. We won, 4-3.

The following day I hit a two-run double early off Si Johnson, but we were forced to go 14 innings before little Murry Dickson, starring in relief of Mort Cooper, doubled to set up the run that won for him, 3-2.

Two days later we were down two runs in the ninth inning at Boston and rallied. I was hitting .314 at the time, tied with Slaughter for the club lead, but when lefthanded Willard Donovan replaced Al Javery on the mound, Southworth lifted me for Triplett. Billy was holding a hot poker hand because Coaker singled in the run that won the game.

Pittsburgh beat Brooklyn that day and we had a two-game lead. Back in St. Louis, old Singing Sam Breadon, humming a happy tune again, announced that the Cardinals would accept World Series reservations.

Only our blinding speed salvaged a doubleheader split the next-to-last Sunday at Chicago, where Hopp and Kurowski pulled a double steal for the run that gave Mort Cooper a 1-0 victory over Warneke, whose friendship was not nearly as strong as his integrity.

Returning home to Sportsman's Park, we trailed Pittsburgh into the fifth inning, 3-0. Two runs were in and the bases were loaded with one out when I faced Rip Sewell. The first pitch was high. The second was a slider, and I timed it for a tremendous drive over the right field pavilion. My first big league grand-slam homer had come off the same pitcher I touched for my first major league home run.

Although we couldn't seem to lose for winning, the few veterans on the ball club studiously saw to it that we avoided using the word "pennant." Terry Moore, who had been on four second-place clubs in seven previous seasons, explained why to reporters:

"We're not saying a thing. That 21-game winning streak the Cubs had in 1935, my first year up, taught me—us—a lesson. We didn't go into any tailspin. They just overhauled us. So the thing is to say nothing, but do plenty, until you're really in."

I've never heard it expressed better.

There was a bit of tartness in an exchange of telegrams in the final week of the 1942 season. Army-bound Larry MacPhail, the volatile redhead who ran the Dodgers, accused deeply religious Bill McKechnie of having favored the Cardinals by not pitching lefthanded Johnny Vander Meer in St. Louis. MacPhail wired the Cincinnati manager: "All the deacons and choir singers of the Methodist organization appreciate your sportsmanship in not pitching Vander Meer against St. Louis."

Good-humoredly, McKechnie wired back: "Congratulations on your appointment as a lieutenant colonel in the Army. Please accept this as my application for the job as your orderly on your private staff. Believe I could be of great assistance in keeping you orderly. The Deacon."

After Beazley and Mort Cooper pitched successive two-hitters at the Reds—I had three hits in the one game and drove in three runs in the other—McKechnie said he believed the 1942 Cardinals were "about as good" as the 1928 Redbirds he'd managed to a pennant. But Rogers Hornsby, then managing Fort Worth in the Texas League, watched us against Cincinnati and said that we "couldn't carry the bats" of his 1926 St. Louis champions.

For a more objective comparison, I prefer the evaluation of J. Roy Stockton, long-time St. Louis *Post-Dispatch* baseball expert who traveled with the Cardinals' nine pennant winners between 1926 and 1946. He considered the 1931 and 1942 clubs the best. That's good enough for me.

To clinch that '42 pennant, we reached the final day needing only a split of a doubleheader with the Cubs at Sportsman's Park. The Dodgers, fighting to the bitter end, defeated the Phillies that day for their eighth straight victory and wound up the season with 104. We wrapped up the flag when White beat Warneke in the opener, 9-2, and we finished with a flourish, a 4-1 World Series tuneup for Beazley.

Down the stretch, the St. Louis Swifties, as New York sports cartoonist Willard Mullin had called us, took 43 of 52 games to finish with 106 victories, the most by a National League pennant winner since the 1909 Pirates.

I'll never forget the thrill, the feeling of great joy, when I ran back into the left field shadows for a long fly ball hit by the Cubs' Clyde McCullough and grabbed it for the official pennant-clinching putout.

9

Double Whammy

If I had hit to the right field roof instead of to the first baseman in the ninth inning of the 1942 World Series opener at St. Louis, the Cardinals might have swept the mighty Yankees in four straight games. And the Yankees had lost only four of their 36 Series games since 1927.

World championships were a habit with the Bombers. They had won eight in eight tries since Hornsby's 1926 Cardinals topped them in a Series that made old Pete Alexander a legend. The nucleus of a team that breezed through the last three World Series was intact. The 1942 Yanks had coasted to a pennant by 10 games with power, pitching and defense, long-time keynotes of Yankee success.

The Yankees were 9-to-20 favorites, but Branch Rickey felt his "imaginative, daring young club" could win. "The Cardinals," he said, "are fast, and a fast-running team throws a defensive club into a chance-taking mood. The defense has no time to hesitate—and haste sometimes leads to errors."

The Series proved Mr. Rickey was right, but not at first.

The 34,769 crowd that squeezed into little Sportsman's Park for the opener saw a game that must have seemed typical to the Yankees. Until the ninth inning, the daring, dashing Cardinals just had rolled over and played dead.

By the time I fouled out, leading off the ninth, we could claim only one hit, Terry Moore's two-out single in the eighth off Red Ruffing. Meanwhile, aided by four errors behind Mort Cooper and Max Lanier, the Yankees had built a 7-0 lead. And they were within one out of a two-hit shutout after Walker Cooper beat out an infield hit and Johnny Hopp was retired.

Ruffing never got that third out. Ray Sanders, pinch-hitting, walked. Marty Marion tripled. Ken O'Dea, also pinch-hitting, singled. Jimmy Brown singled and now Spud Chandler, a 16-5 pitcher in the regular season, replaced Ruffing to throw his sinker. Spud had trouble getting us out, too. Moore singled and when Enos Slaughter's grounder took a bad hop against shortstop Phil Rizzuto's face for an infield hit, the bases were loaded and I was up. The score was 7-4.

I desperately wanted to pump one onto the pavilion roof. Chandler, experienced and capable, kept the ball down. I've always been a good low-ball hitter, but I couldn't get the pitch in the air. I hit it sharply on the ground to first baseman Buddy Hassett, who beat me to the bag, and the ball game was over.

Having made two of the Cardinals' three outs in that last round, I certainly wasn't happy. But, like the rest of the Redbirds, I felt a strange sensation of relief. Why, the Yankees weren't supermen, after all. We'd had 'em on the ropes, hadn't we? The pressure was off now. You can't underestimate it, the tingling excitement of playing in a World Series game. It's different, something special. The tension is enough to rob a man of his reflexes.

The turning point of the Series came in the second game.

Behind Johnny Beazley, our 21-game rookie righthander, we took a 3-0 lead over Ernie Bonham, a brilliant 21-5 righthander with a 2.27 earned-run average. Then, with their explosive power, the Yankees tied us in the eighth with two out. Roy Cullenbine beat out an infield hit, Joe DiMaggio singled and Charley Keller homered onto Grand Avenue. Most observers thought the St. Louis kids would crack. We didn't.

With two out in the home eighth, Slaughter doubled and I

singled him over, giving Beazley a 4-3 lead that held up, thanks to Slaughter's fine defensive play in the ninth. With none out, the Yankees seemed certain to have runners on first and third as pinchrunner Tuck Stainback raced for third on a basehit. But Slaughter, grabbing the ball quickly to his left, wheeled and fired a perfect strike to George Kurowski at third. The clutch play saved the day.

Now came a tough personal decision. Lil had come hurrying back from Donora when we won the pennant. Sam Breadon had provided $100 toward each player's wife's expenses. Still, when Lil and I talked over finances, estimating the St. Louis-New York round trip for the Series, Lil thought it would be too expensive. She could, of course, go to New York on our special train and get off at Pittsburgh on the way back.

"If I've got my choice," Lil said, "I'd rather see the windup of the Series here than the middle part in New York."

In her decision, Lil had plenty of company. But the girls who stayed behind never did see any more of the 1942 Series.

A ball player's introduction to old Yankee Stadium was impressive even if the big ball park in The Bronx was empty. When it was filled with a record World Series crowd of 69,123 and a young player is seeing it for the first time under pressure, as I was, well, I still can't quite describe the sight—or the feeling. The triple-tiered stands with the sea of faces and the swell of noise make the stadium awesome. I sympathize, too, with ball players who have failed at bat or afield there. I sympathize particularly with left fielders in Yankee Stadium. I slipped and fell enough there that, to hear some people tell it, I took more pratfalls than a burlesque comedian. I've heard all kinds of explanations. Stage fright . . . cheap baseball shoes . . . worndown spikes . . . even the suggestion that, trying to adjust for the lefthander's awkward throw from left field, I was having difficulty handling my feet.

I'll admit I was a little numb at first because of the Series pressure, but the only valid cause for my trouble was a situation now well publicized: Near-zero visibility between left field and home plate. October's late-afternoon sun and shadows conspired with the haze of cigarette smoke rising out of Yankee stadium's high stands to hide the ball as it left the bat. I'm fortunate that my foot faults didn't prove costly.

In the third game of the World Series, Ernie White took a 1-0 lead over Chandler because the Yankees complained so loudly that, of all things, an umpire changed a decision. When Marion bunted for a sacrifice, Joe McCarthy squawked that the ball had hit Marty's bat a second time. Marion, required to bat over, then swung away and beat out a slow roller toward third. A sacrifice and slow-hopping infield out produced the run.

In the Yankees' sixth, with Cullenbine on first, DiMaggio lined a drive into the spacious left-center field for an apparent triple. I broke to my left, slipped and went down, just as Moore, charging to his right, flung himself over me and made a backhanded diving catch. We must have looked like the flying Wallendas without tanbark.

In New York's seventh, I ran back to the curving left field corner and grabbed Joe Gordon's drive, which was headed for the lower stands. Immediately afterward, Slaughter pulled one even better. He raced back to the low right field barrier, leaped and deprived Keller of a home run.

The Yankees were having a tough time. After we scored again in the ninth, Frank Crosetti was so incensed that he jostled umpire Bill Summers and later was fined part of his Series share. So, outhit six to five, we won that game, 2-0, with speed, defense and Ernie White's spunk. The blond lefthander, who had pitched the pennant-clinching victory over Chicago after a mediocre 7-5 season of frequent arm trouble, thus became the first pitcher to shut out the Yankees in a World Series game since 1926. Back then, another Cardinal, Jesse Haines, had done it.

That victory at Yankee Stadium, combined with the Yankees' constant crying, completely brought out the old confidence in a team of young contenders.

After having made two outs in one inning under opening-game pressure, I offset that dubious distinction by collecting two hits in one inning in the fourth game. We trailed Hank Borowy in the fourth inning, 1-0, when I led off with a safe bunt toward third. By the time I came up against Atley Donald and drove in the sixth run of the inning with a double, basehits were bouncing like banter from our bench.

The Cardinals' dugout in those days was like Olsen and Johnson's Hellzapoppin'. Chief cheerleader and conspirator was our veteran trainer, Doc Weaver. He'd always concoct some silliness to keep spirits up, tension down. At times, his efforts would be elaborate. Imagine hooking up an electric stop-and-go sign from a toy train so that it flashed green when we were batting, red when the opposition was up.

Other times, Doc led the bench jockeying, reinforced by Redbird reserves and occasionally our little equipment manager, Butch Yatkeman, as harmless as he is inconspicuous.

After we won that wild fourth game, 9-6, batting orders were being exchanged the next day at home plate when Yankee coach Art Fletcher, representing manager McCarthy, demanded that the umpires keep "that little guy" out of the Cardinals' dugout.

Our captain, Terry Moore, who represented Billy Southworth in pregame discussions, couldn't believe that the mighty Yankees could be so upset.

"You don't mean little Butch," Terry said, increduously. "Why, he's in the dugout for all our games."

Fletcher did mean Butch. Sympathetically, Bill Summers, the veteran American League umpire, informed Moore the umpires had no choice under the rules. They had to order that Yatkeman leave the dugout, which meant that Butch would have to return to the clubhouse and listen to the game on radio.

"That's all right, Bill," Moore said to Summers, then addressed himself to Fletcher. "This is just one more reason why there's going to be no tomorrow in this World Series."

There wasn't, either. The fifth game was a 2-2 duel between Beazley and Ruffing until the ninth inning. Three times Ruffing had struck out Kurowski in the opener at St. Louis and Whitey still hadn't had a hit off big Red, but now he rifled a two-run homer into the left field stands.

There was a moment of drama left in the Yankees' ninth. Gordon singled and Bill Dickey was safe on Brown's fumble. The potential tying runs were on base with none out.

On the Cardinal bench, Doc Weaver nudged Frank Crespi to pass the word to other Redbird reserves. "It's time for the old double-whammy," Weaver said.

Ceremoniously, the colorful trainer crossed his wrists, hands back to back, then closed the second and third fingers of each hand so that the first and fourth fingers protruded like horns. He pointed the twin horns at Gordon, straying off second base. Grimly, the benchwarmers followed his witchcraft.

Beazley pitched to Jerry Priddy, who missed a bunt attempt. Marion had slipped in behind Gordon at second base, and Walter Cooper's quick, accurate peg to Marty picked off the runner. The good old double-whammy had worked. Priddy popped to Brown and the World Series ended—the first time the Yankees had lost four straight since 1922 against the Giants—when pinch-hitter George Selkirk grounded to Jimmy.

The young Cardinals, the St. Louis Swifties, were world champions. It seemed so fitting that the Series-clinching homer had been hit by a young fellow who had battled physical handicap and discouragement to reach the majors.

Kids under handicap would do well to remember George (Whitey) Kurowski, who played baseball—and played it well—without part of the ulna bone of his right forearm, a result of boyhood osteomyelitis. To compensate for the diseased bone that was removed, George developed powerful muscle. Because the arm was short, he crowded the plate in a defiant stance that made him an inviting target for high-and-tight pitches.

In 1937, just before Kurowski left Reading, Pa., for his first professional baseball job, his brother Frank was killed in a mine cave-in. Then in the spring of 1942, as Whitey was trying to win a place on the Cardinals' roster, his father fell dead of a heart attack.

But now, Whitey was the center of a shrieking clubhouse mob. We grabbed old Judge Landis and hoisted him to the ceiling, ripped National League president Ford Frick's hat to pieces, lifted Branch Rickey to the roof, then picked up Kurowski. And we roared our good-luck number down the National League stretch, "Pass the Biscuits, Mirandy."

When Kurowski's cleated shoes hit the clubhouse concrete again, we grabbed him by the seat of the pants and ripped off the back. We tore pieces into shreds for souvenirs. The only thing Whitey wouldn't give up was the bat with which he'd hit the home run. You know, it was the only bat he had taken to New York.

When I could stop to think, I wired Lil at the Fairgrounds Hotel in St. Louis. I would be in the following afternoon on the Cardinals' championship special. Then I thought again. My wife had passed up the trip to New York in the interest of economy. Now, it was my turn to be more careful. I sent Lil another telegram. I'd decided to go directly to Donora with my parents, who had come to New York for the three games at Yankee Stadium. I asked Lil to meet me half way—at home.

She did.

That rookie season ended for me standing at Pennsylvania Station, watching the Cardinals' world championship train pull out for St. Louis just before mine left for Pittsburgh. Marty Marion says he still remembers me crying as the guys were piling aboard.

Those were tears of sheer joy. After having played a full season for $4250, I'd just earned $6192.50 in one week. Now Lil and I could buy the clothes we needed. I could do things for Mom and Pop and also put some money in war bonds.

And just 21, I could walk down the streets of Donora as a member of baseball's world champions. I still felt a little like I'd gone to a banquet with a sandwich in my pocket, but I'd won my gamble that the game I played for fun could also be a profitable profession.

There was another reason for the tears. I knew that some of my teammates were bound for military service at once. Would this great gang ever be together again?

10

Business, Batting, and Bellbottoms

For the first time I held out in the spring of 1943. I didn't get the money I wanted, but I got something else—a lesson in the art of negotiating salary—and it paid off the only other time I balked at contract terms.

With Branch Rickey having gone to Brooklyn, Sam Breadon, who for years had kept an eye on the size of contracts, just as he'd reserved for himself the right to change managers, was serving now as his own general manager. Although Mr. Breadon was considerably more generous than he has been portrayed, he did have an over-abiding fear of once again being poor. He had been a grease monkey who rose to wealth as an automobile dealer and then to prosperity as a baseball clubowner.

Times of uncertainty, which a war represented to baseball, alarmed him and made him cautious. I found that out when my first contract arrived at Donora, where I was working at the zinc works after the 1942 season. The boss was offering me a raise of only $1000 even though I had finished third in the National League batting race. Boston's big Ernie Lombardi had hit .330, teammate Enos Slaughter .318, and I had batted .315.

With the help of my old friend, Frank Pizzica, a good businessman for whom I was playing war-charities' basketball, I drafted a reply asking for $10,000. The amount was Frank's idea. We—I—pointed out that with both Moore and Slaughter in service, I would have to play "even harder."

That was a foolish mistake. There are no degrees in playing your best. Mr. Breadon had me. He wrote stiffly:

"Your letter of March fifth was a disappointment to me. In fairness to players who have been on the club as regulars for years, it is impossible to consider the sum you ask for 1943. You will have no more to do this year than you had last year. I thought you were the kind of ball player that gave all you had in every ball game. Of course, we expect the same in 1943, if you sign a contract with us . . ."

Uncomfortably, I countered with a request for $7500, but Breadon wouldn't budge.

"No one in our organization has been advanced faster than you have been," he wrote. "We have had great outfielders on our ball club, including Hafey, Medwick, Moore and Slaughter, and none of them in their second year received a contract for as much as $5500 . . . In your first year you were on a ball club that allowed you to make $6200 in the World Series. I don't question but what you are a good player and have a chance to be a great player, but in fairness to the other men on the club, your contract must be in line with what they received in their second year . . ."

I wrote back that higher taxes and increased costs made his comparisons with depression-era salaries unfair, and Mr. Breadon replied:

"We could write letters until the end of the season and get no place. Therefore, I suggest that you come to St. Louis and if you do not sign a contract and want to stay out of baseball in 1943, we will pay your round-trip expenses."

I wouldn't be trapped into making that trip. I knew that once I sat across from the square-jawed, white-haired Irishman whose blue eyes could warm you or chill you, I'd succumb. I declined to make the trip, so the boss sent Eddie Dyer to see me. That did it.

Dyer, who later managed the Cardinals, had become farm

director after a brilliant minor league managerial career. The polished, articulate Texan knew how to appeal to a young fellow whose feet were itching for baseball. Besides, he brought a compromise offer—$6250—and my adviser, Frank Pizzica, was out of town.

I signed, flew to St. Louis, then drove to Cairo, Ill., before Pizzica could give me what-for.

Cairo, Ill.—that's where the Cardinals trained. Baseball had been restricted to spring training north of a geographical line drawn by baseball commissioner Landis and the Office of Defense Transportation. Doc Weaver had urged the players in a letter to wear hats and topcoats to camp. Further, he prescribed long underwear for outdoor workouts and gym shoes for indoor practice. We needed both. Already in shape, I reached condition quickly even though I had reported a week late.

We had lost four men to service—Moore, Slaughter, Beazley and Crespi, and Pollet was to be called up in July at a time he had pitched 29 consecutive scoreless innings. But we won the pennant easily even though the Dodgers had been co-favored with us at 9 to 5 in the pre-season odds. Every club had lost heavily to the military, and we'd had more talent to spare.

Brooklyn dogged us into July, when the old rivalry flared up. The trouble began when Les Webber—remember him?—dusted me off with four straight pitches. Walker Cooper, next up, blasted the pitcher as he stepped into the batter's box. Grounding out, big Coop stepped on Augie Galan's foot at first base, spiking him. Mickey Owen, who had followed down the line to back up the play, thought the spiking was deliberate. He leaped on Cooper's back, and players from both sides piled on.

Angrily, we swept a four-game series, ripped off 11 straight victories—and the race was over.

I made my first All-Star appearance that summer. It was at Philadelphia, the first night game in All-Star history. The American League knocked out Mort Cooper early and won disdainfully, 5-3. They rubbed it in by declining to use a single member of the American League champion Yankees.

My first time up as an All-Star, I hit a long run-scoring fly off Washington's Dutch Leonard in the first inning. I had one hit in four times up, a double off lefthander Hal Newhouser.

I played regularly against lefthanders in 1943. Billy Southworth, late in the 1942 season, had said he thought he'd made a mistake in platooning me. In '43, I won my first batting championship and first Most Valuable Player award. I batted .357 on 220 hits, including 48 doubles, 20 triples and 13 home runs, but I'm afraid those figures would have been smaller if we'd kept using the balata ball.

Because rubber was a war-priority item, the Spalding Company, which manufactures the major leagues' baseballs, decided to use re-processed rubber or, as it's more accurately known, balata. Opening day at Cincinnati, the world champion Cardinals lost to Cincinnati in 11 innings, 1-0—and only 11 runs were scored in four big league games that day.

The next day when I tripled off Ray Starr, the ball sounded like a nickel rocket. But we still didn't score and lost again in 10 innings, 1-0. A frowning Southworth told us, "You'll have to choke your bats, fellas, as they used to do in the old days, and bunt more often."

One thing I did like was the extra emphasis on speed—with a little bit of luck. We trailed again in the sixth inning of the third game, 1-0, when I tried to steal home with our first run of the season and was safe when catcher Ray Mueller dropped the ball. And when I singled again in the eighth inning, raced to third on a wide infield throw and scored on a passed ball, we'd finally won one, 2-1.

In fact, with only three runs to show for our first four games, we managed a split at Cincinnati. Eleven games were played in the majors in '43 before the Yankees' Joe Gordon hit the first home run. Baseball brass was alarmed that the ersatz ball would kill interest. As a stop-gap, clubs with 1942 baseballs on hand were given permission to use them. Spalding, meanwhile, promised to replace the balata ball, which the company agreed was at least 25 per cent less resilient.

To show what difference the ball can make, the American League, then the so-called power league, hit only nine homers in 72 games before a new 1943 baseball came into use. The day it replaced the balata, Sunday, May 9, the American League hit six homers in just eight games.

I know those figures would make no great impression now, but the livelier ball gave us hitters reason to cheer then. I say that even though I was hitting .323 at the time and had managed five doubles and three triples among 21 hits. To this day, I'm proud of having done that well because I learned in just a couple of horrible weeks how Willie Keeler must have felt 45 years earlier, trying to "hit 'em where they ain't."

Although we'd beaten the Yankees in the 1942 World Series and then breezed to the 1943 pennant by 18 games, the Yanks were slight favorites to regain the championship. We thought the oddsmakers were odd, but they weren't.

Because of war travel restrictions, the Series for the first and only time was limited to one round trip. It began in New York before 68,676 who saw the Yankees win the opener, 4-2, largely through a wild pitch and error by Max Lanier. I had one single of the seven hits off Spud Chandler, who had been a 20-4 pitcher in the American League that year.

I'll never forget the second game and not merely because it was our sole victory in that Series. Early that morning, Robert Cooper, father of our brother battery, died unexpectedly of a heart attack at his home in Independence, Mo. Mr. Cooper, 58, a rural mail-carrier, had planned to go to St. Louis for one of the weekend games.

There had been other occasions when World Series participants lost loved ones. In Mort Cooper's case, though, there had been more than one suggestion that our great righthander couldn't win the big ones under less emotional circumstances. People had forgotten Mort's big clutch victories over Brooklyn and could remember only that he had been knocked out twice in the 1942 Series and had failed in the All-Star game.

Southworth put it up to Mort and Walker Cooper whether to play or head for Independence. They decided to play, then go home. With an open date between the third and fourth games, they could attend the funeral and rejoin the ball club for the Saturday game, the one their father had intended to see.

Mort Cooper is gone now, prematurely in his grave, too. He was one of the best three or four pitchers in the National League in my years with the Cardinals, and I remember best the ball game he pitched—and won—when his heart was as heavy as his fork ball. The score, when brother Walk squeezed a game-ending pop foul off Joe Gordon's bat, was 4-3.

I ran so fast in determination that day, trying to help my teammate win the big one, that I literally ran out from under my cap as I scored from second base on a short single.

We didn't win again. Errors and a three-run clutch triple beat Al Brazle the next day, 6-2. Back in St. Louis, facing lefty Marius Russo, I got two hits, but so did Russo, and his were important doubles that beat Lanier, 2-1. So the Yankees wrapped us up in the fifth game when Bill Dickey hit a two-run homer off Cooper. Chandler, though touched for 10 hits, shut us out, 2-0.

A losing share of the Series, $4321.99, still looked awfully large to a Polish kid who was lucky not to be laboring in the mill or, at this time, toting a gun. I wanted to do something in the war effort and welcomed the chance to entertain American troops stationed in Alaska and the Aleutians.

That winter, after putting in a stretch working in the mill, I made a six-week tour for the government with Frank Frisch, Danny Litwhiler, Hank Borowy and Dixie Walker. Four times a day, we'd talk to servicemen, answer questions, run off World

Series movies and autograph baseballs. Some nights we'd go back to our huts so hoarse we didn't bother to tell each other good night, but the experience was rewarding.

Every doughfoot up there in the frozen north seemed to have lost money betting on the Cardinals in the 1943 Series. Wherever we went, the first question I'd get was: "How did the Cardinals happen to lose to the Yankees?"

Borowy, a member of the Yankees' pitching staff, would beam when I'd say, invariably, "The Yankees deserved to win because they played better ball and had the better pitching."

I didn't have any contract worries for 1944 because I'd signed a three-year contract without much difficulty. I can remember players telling me, "Man, if you ever get $10,000 out of Breadon, you're doing darned good."

On the basis of my league-leading .357 average and 347 total bases, I asked for a three-year contract totaling $40,000 and effected a compromise. The boss offered $36,000 and I agreed. The salary was scaled at $10,000, $12,500 and then $13,500 for the third year, 1946.

Even though the Cardinals, like other clubs, continued to lose players to the armed forces, we still had more material. We won the 1944 pennant even more easily than in 1943. We led every Monday of the season and even after losing 15 of 20 in September, we still won 105 games, our 1943 total.

That summer's All-Star game was played in my "home" territory, Pittsburgh. For the first time in four years, the National League won, 7-1. I played both center and right fields, had one hit and drove in a run, but Vince DiMaggio did the heavy hitting for the National League, and we bombed out my winter-touring buddy, Hank Borowy.

When the Cardinals slumped just after Labor Day, I was hurt in a wicked collision with another Redbird outfielder, Debs Garms. I was out 10 days with a bad knee and then, because we were losing, tried to come back too soon. However, Dixie Walker, the peepul's cherce of Brooklyn, deserved the batting title with his .357 average, 10 points higher than mine. My collision with Garms kept me out of eight games, so I missed the 200-hit goal by three.

The 1944 World Series was a baseball oddity, the first all-St. Louis Series and, in fact, the only time the late, lamented Browns won a pennant in this century.

Lil remembers the Series atmosphere as her "rude awakening." She'd lived two full summers at the Fairgrounds Hotel, within earshot of the ball park. Time was, when the Browns and Cardinals swapped hotel rooms and home stands, that the Grand-and-Dodier area fell relatively quiet for

American League games. But 1944 was busy every day and close to bedlam as the Browns finished at home. After the Series opener, Lil said, dazedly, "This is a *Brownie* town."

The Browns, sentimental favorities, had won the pennant the last day of the season before nearly 38,000, largest crowd ever to see an American League game in St. Louis. They were a team of 4-Fs, veterans and castoffs, cleverly put together by Bill DeWitt and ably managed by Luke Sewell. We were solid 1-2 favorites to beat the Browns in St. Louis' Streetcar Series, but we had to battle like hell to win.

They took the first game, 2-1, even though Mort Cooper allowed only two hits, one a decisive homer by George McQuinn. And the Browns really might have won the Series if my old Springfield (Mo.) teammate, Blix Donnelly, hadn't made a great fielding play in the second game. With the score tied in the eleventh, McQuinn on second base and none out, Donnelly leaped off the mound to make a great play and throw on a bunt, retiring McQuinn at third base. In the home half, Ken O'Dea's pinch single gave us the ball game, 3-2.

Without Donnelly's pinch pitching and fielding, we would have been down three games because the Browns won the third contest, 6-2, as Jack Kramer beat Ted Wilks. We got back into the Series largely on the clutch pitching of Harry (The Cat) Brecheen, a well-seasoned rookie for whom my admiration was to increase through the years. Having been on a hit-a-day ration, I helped in the 5-1 game with three hits, including a two-run first-inning homer off righthander Sig Jakucki.

On a Sunday before nearly 37,000, the Cardinals finally went ahead, but only after a great duel between Mort Cooper and his first-game conqueror, Denny Galehouse. Homers by Ray Sanders and Danny Litwhiler gave us a 2-0 victory in a game in which the pitchers set a World Series record of 22 strikeouts, 12 by Cooper.

The background at Sportsman's Park made batting difficult whenever a white-shirted crowd jammed into the center field bleachers. And I say that without trying to detract from Cooper or Galehouse. A couple of years later I helped persuade Sam Breadon to rope off the center field section of the bleachers. Subsequently, Gussie Busch turned that vacated area into an arboretum that improved the appearance of the ball park and helped the hitters even more.

The Cardinals won the 1944 world championship with a 3-1 victory in the sixth game, in which Lanier and Wilks, who took over in the sixth inning, allowed only three hits. Fact is, the Browns wound up with a .182 team average for the Series. Yet I salute them as an inferior team that just wouldn't quit.

I hit .304 in that Series, but, like many a batting champion, including greater ones like Ty Cobb, Rogers Hornsby and Ted Williams, I never was a World Series standout. I'm just thankful I never was a Series bust, either.

The top men that Series were the Browns' McQuinn, who batted .438, and our feisty second baseman, slender Emil Verban, who hit .412. The instant the Series ended, Verban, annoyed at the seats his wife had been given for the Browns' home games in the World Series, rushed over to a box and told Dan Barnes, the Browns' startled owner:

"Now YOU'RE sitting behind a post!"

To me, a highlight of the Series was the superiority our shortstop, Marty Marion, displayed over Vern Stephens, the Browns' shortstop. There had been some static during the regular season in St. Louis about which was the better. Marty didn't have Stephens' power, of course, but his edge afield, as he proved in the Series, was decisive. Marion was brilliant defensively; Stephens committed three errors.

I had another reason to respect Marion. Even though he had batted only .267, Marty won the Most Valuable Player award in the National League. I think this was the greatest tribute to defensive play in the history of the MVP award. This one and the MVP won six years later by a relief pitcher, Jim Konstanty of the Phillies.

The World Series share in 1944 was skimpier—$4626.01 for winning—because the St. Louis ball park was small, but I was grateful. Grateful for playing, for winning and for the birth that December of our second child, daughter Geraldine.

I had been able to play ball for two war years—in baseball I don't believe you'll find many who consider 1942 a war year—and I was really relieved to go into service when my Donora draft board finally called in January, 1945.

I chose the Navy and was sent to Bainbridge, Md., for basic training. A merciless barber at boot camp skinned my head like a grape. A photographer took my picture and the barber said, apologetically, "Why didn't you tell me who you were? I wouldn't have cut it so short."

I ran my hand over the fine head of fuzz he'd left me and said, lamely, "Thanks, but now I know how a guy feels when he's going to the electric chair."

During boot training or just after—I can't remember exactly—I played four or five ball games at Bainbridge. Then I was assigned to Special Services and shipped to Hawaii by way of Treasure Island, the Navy's shipping-out point at San Francisco. I found at both places how eager the sailors were to see a ball game.

At Bainbridge in just a few games, two things happened that were to affect my career. Although by then I had a reputation as a good defensive outfielder in the big leagues, the Bainbridge athletic officer, a lieutenant named Jerry O'Brien, put me at first base. I was amused. O'Brien was not.

"Get out of there, Musial," he fumed two days later, "you're terrible. You'll never make anybody's team at first base."

At Bainbridge, too, service personnel wanted to see the home run. So to pull more often, to hit the long ball, I altered my batting stance a bit. I moved up closer to the plate. This proved to be an important step in my evolution as a hitter.

From San Francisco, I was shipped out with about 10 other ball players, including Bob Scheffing and Cookie Lavagetto, and wound up assigned to the ship repair unit at Pearl Harbor. Every base or unit had a ball club, and we had an eight-team league composed mostly of big-league ball players.

For the first few weeks I was assigned mornings to a liberty launch that transferred men and officers from the big men-o'-war, many of the flat-tops and battle-wagons limping in damaged. Every afternoon I played ball to entertain soldiers, sailors, Marines and other service-attached personnel who crowded into the games, eager for the entertainment. I was extremely fortunate, therefore, to be able to keep reasonably sharp.

I never did learn how to repair ships. I was still stationed at Pearl when, a few months after V-J Day, my father fell ill with pneumonia. He wasn't expected to live, and Mom appealed through the Red Cross for an emergency leave. Even with priority, transportation to the States in January, 1946, was so agonizingly slow that I lost hope of reaching my father's bedside in time. By some wonder, my homecoming was a day of thanksgiving. Pop was not only still alive, he was recovering.

To this, Dickie added his own surprise. He'd saved the Christmas tree for me, Nativity scene and all. Gerry toddled around during the excitement, happy but standoffish. I was a stranger to her.

When my leave was up, I was assigned to the Philadelphia Navy Yard. There, I was listed among ship repairmen assigned to dismantle a British destroyer. The day before I was scheduled to work, I walked over to watch men already at work, wearing goggles and heavy gloves and carrying blow torches. I realized that, a greenpea like me could wind up maiming himself or someone else. I went to the athletic officer and said:

"Sir, I'm a ship repairman who never has repaired a ship. For my sake and the Navy's, can't you please have my orders changed?"

Thank heavens, he did.

Stan was called home to Donora from Pearl Harbor on emergency furlough in January 1946, because his father was seriously ill. Mr. Musial never did recover fully and died just before Christmas in 1948.

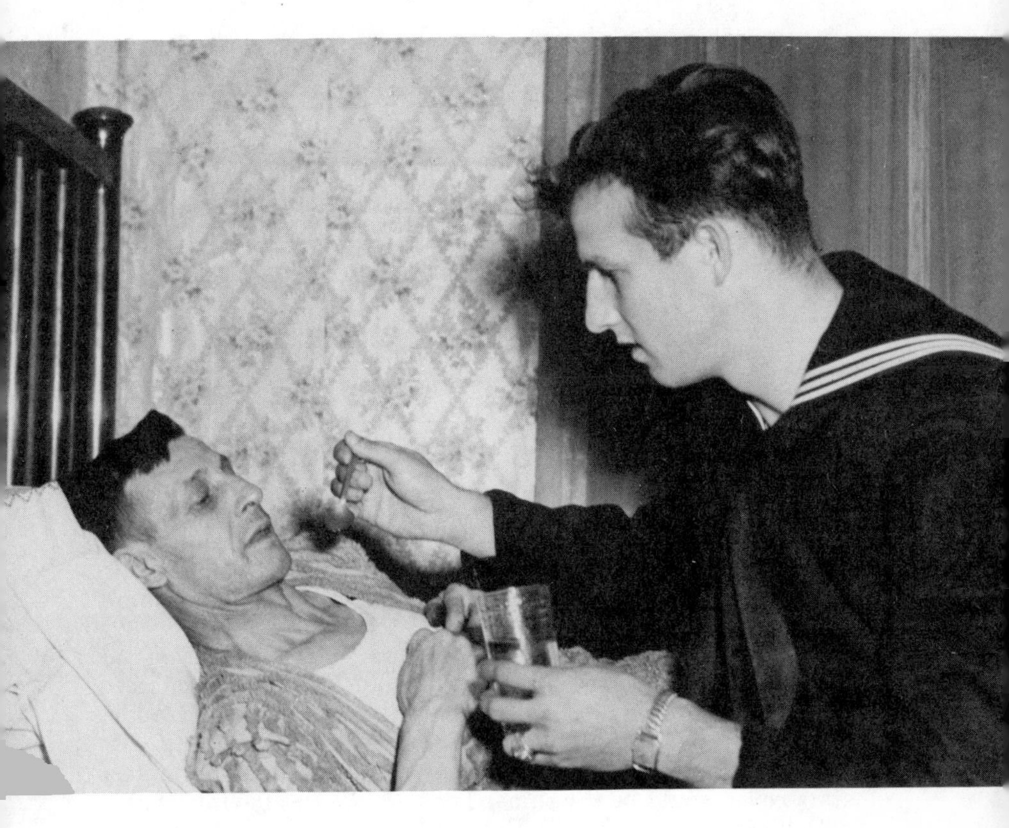

11

Playoff and Payoff

I really gassed the gang at our spring training reunion in 1946. Every time I'd shake hands with a guy, I'd leave my right thumb in his grasp!

I've been interested in parlor magic ever since I became a good friend of a St. Louis insurance man, Claude Keefe, who practiced the black art. Magic has given me—and others—many a laugh. But there was sadness, too, at St. Petersburg that spring.

It was apparent early that a few of the Cardinals' brightest stars never would be the same. Terry Moore was having trouble with his legs in center field. Ernie White and the most promising pitcher of the era, Johnny Beazley, had sore arms.

Our new manager, Eddie Dyer, was on the spot, taking over a heavily favored club which had won three pennants and two world championships in four years. Eddie had played briefly in the big leagues and had managed and supervised for years throughout the Cardinal organization. He had built a reputation among baseball people, but to the man on the street in St. Louis he was an unknown trying to replace Billy Southworth.

Southworth, right after the Redbirds narrowly missed a fourth straight pennant in 1945, asked Sam Breadon to release him from a two-year contract so he could take a more attractive offer from Lou Perini, the new owner at Boston. Breadon, too proud to ask Southworth to reconsider and too hurt to hold the manager to his contract, appointed Dyer—and immediately handicapped him by selling Walker Cooper to the Giants for $175,000.

Breadon said Coop didn't want to play for Dyer, but the boss gave the persuasive manager no chance to talk to the catcher. The truth is, Mr. Breadon was annoyed at the Cooper boys for squabbling over salaries in 1944. In '45, Singing Sam had dealt Mort Cooper to the Braves for Red Barrett and cash.

The sale of Walker Cooper, then the best catcher in baseball, proved to be disastrous in the years that followed. Ken O'Dea, scheduled to inherit the first-string job, had been troubled with sciatica, which worsened and quickly ended his career. The Cardinals were left with inexperienced catchers who couldn't hit.

Dyer's problem was to separate the men from the boys, to decide which players had been only war-time wonders. To add to the manager's woes, coach Mike Gonzalez came over from Cuba and predicted that a winter-league wonder, rookie first baseman Dick Sisler, would hit 30 home runs—"ceench."

Without really waiting to see whether Sisler could make it at first base, Breadon sold Johnny Hopp and then Ray Sanders to the Braves. Pittsburgh bought Jimmy Brown and New York purchased Danny Litwhiler, belatedly discharged from service. The Cardinals did have a surplus, but we questioned the recklessness with which some players were sold.

We had general leg miseries from the sandy condition of old Waterfront Park, where we trained in St. Pete. The old ball park always had too much sand in its soil, but never so much as after soldiers had used it for a drill field for nearly four years. Reporting late from service, I slipped during pepper practice and strained ligaments in my left knee, which has bothered me at times ever since. But I was just 25 and didn't need much work to get ready.

However, our holdout third baseman, heavy-legged George Kurowski, wasn't ready. Whitey failed to hit or move well and he committed a damaging error as we lost our 1946 opener to Pittsburgh, 6-4, on a raw, cold day in St. Louis.

Sentimentally, Dyer started Beazley, but Johnny's arm wasn't sound. Facing Fritz Ostermueller, a cunning long-sleeved old lefthander with one of the few good sliders I've ever seen a southpaw throw, I singled my first time up, and our rookie first baseman, Dick Sisler, gave us a momentary two-run lead with a double in his first big-league appearance.

When Kurowski proved he wasn't ready in the opening game loss, Dyer corrected a mistake he had made in spring training. There, he had tabbed freckle-faced Red Schoendienst as his No. 1 utility man. Although Schoendienst, a shortstop by trade, had played left field by necessity as a rookie in 1945, leading the league in stolen bases, Dyer said:

"I can't play anyone regularly who batted only .278 against wartime pitching."

Eddie didn't know Red. I didn't, either, but we all soon did. With him at third base, hitting hard and fielding like Pie Traynor, we won seven in a row. Then Marty Marion was hurt, and Red moved to shortstop because by now Kurowski was ready

Musial was extremely proud to be a member of an outfield considered by many to have been one of the best ever. Here they are shown in spring training in 1946, having just returned from the service. Enos Slaughter, the right fielder, 30, was the greatest hustler Stan ever saw. And Terry Moore, 34, was a defensive master in center field and an aggressive, inspirational team captain.

to play. Schoendienst proved to be the next thing to Mr. Shortstop himself.

What comes after short? Second base, of course, and it soon became evident that Dyer's No. 1 utility man wouldn't stay irregular long. To thin out second basemen—Lou Klein was playing the position—Emil Verban was traded for a catcher, Clyde Kluttz.

Our first eastern trip reflected the immediate post-war turmoil. Baseball was in a state of unrest, bordering on revolution, as we reached Brooklyn in mid-May, a game and a half behind.

After Max Lanier went 11 tough innings to win the series opener, we proved behind Howard Pollet in the second game that our great outfield truly had returned from service. I'm very proud to have played with Terry Moore and Enos Slaughter in an outfield considered to have been one of the best ever, all-round.

Although Moore and I made good clutch catches that prevented runs, our return to Ebbets Field really belonged to Slaughter, a hypochondriac who hypoed the ball club. The more Enos complained, the better he played. He was, as anyone who ever saw him will remember, a stocky, large-rumped athlete who ran hard and hustled even when the ball wasn't in play. Bosco had a picture-book batting stance, a flat level swing. Together, I believe, we battled more lefthanded pitchers than any two lefthanded hitters who ever lived.

That day in Brooklyn, pitching irritant Les Webber threw too close to suit old Enos. So he tapped one along the first base line and, when Webber fielded the ball, nearly bowled the pitcher over. They squared off and players of both sides poured onto the field. Dyer and the umpires prevented the rhubarb from sprouting.

When Slaughter trotted to right field and 25,000 Brooklyn fans booed, Bosco silenced them with as fine a retort as I've ever seen. After Carl Furillo led off with a single, Augie Galan hit a low line drive. Slaughter rushed in, slid on his seat and plucked it just off the grass. Then on a hit-and-run play, with Furillo rounding second, Slaughter raced to the scoreboard, made a backhanded catch at Ferrell Anderson's expense and, wheeling, pegged the ball to first to double off Furillo.

You could have heard a pin drop in Greenpernt after Slaughter's 1-0 game which put us in first place—temporarily.

The Cardinals moved into Boston, where Robert Murphy, a labor relations man trying to unionize ball players, visited our club. He was persuasive—came close actually to inciting a sit-down strike among Pittsburgh players—but despite dissatisfaction with salaries and other conditions, we held fast. For the moment, that is.

I'll never forget one day late in May, 1946. While we were in New York to play the Giants, our pennant chances seemed to fly south of the border with Lanier, Klein and Fred Martin, a well-seasoned "rookie" pitcher. They had been lured to Mexico by Jorge Pasquel's money. Martin had been relegated to the bullpen and Klein had lost his second-base job to irrepressible young Schoendienst.

Lanier's loss was the big blow. He had won his first six starts, all complete games. The week before, when we were in Brooklyn, the Pasquels, who already had signed other big league players, contacted Max and reportedly offered more ($150,000) than Lanier felt he could make "in a lifetime here."

The bottom seemed to fall out all at once. The same day our players jumped, a national railroad strike caught us with our chins down. Traveling secretary Leo Ward finally wangled a chartered DC-3 that would take just part of the ball club to Cincinnati for the game the next night. The flight was rough. Finally a wall of black weather forced us down at Dayton, about 50 miles short of our goal, close to game-time. Ward rounded up taxicabs and a police escort for a race to Crosley Field, where a large crowd was gathering.

I loved it. Especially when the hood of our ancient cab kept popping open. The cabbie, desperate, finally suggested that one of us players ride on the hood to keep it in place.

"Oh, no, you don't," I told him. "You ride the hood, cabbie, and I'll drive."

Man, that was something. With my head out the side window so I could see around the cabbie, I drove at high speed and we managed to keep up with the caravan. When we wheeled into the Crosley Field parking lot, I was laughing, but some of the guys with me were a little white.

I wasn't laughing, though, when Alfonso Pasquel, one of the wealthy Mexican brothers, and Mickey Owen, the former Brooklyn catcher who was serving as an emissary, began to talk to me about joining the others who had followed the heavy sugar south. I don't think I ever seriously considered going, but Pasquel was determined. His offer kept going up.

By the first week in June, I was hitting hard, leading the league, but the Cardinals were faltering. Lil and the two children were moving from the Fairgrounds Hotel to a bungalow I had rented furnished in newer southwest St. Louis. This would be the first time we hadn't lived in a hotel room or cramped apartment since I reached the big leagues, and we were pretty excited.

Excitement increased when Pasquel and Owen came to the hotel. As I recall, Alfonso plunked five cashier's checks for $10,-

000 each onto a bed and said I could consider them a bonus. The brothers Pasquel, he said, were prepared to offer me a contract for $125,000 additional to sign for five years.

My eyes bugged out at the sight of so much money. I was getting only $13,500. How long would I have to play to be assured of $175,000?

The Pasquels even had old teammate Max Lanier phone me from Mexico City, but I had made up my mind. I told Lil I frankly didn't want to see or hear any more temptation. Eddie Dyer, an eloquent man, had talked to the ball club—the Pasquels wanted Moore and Slaughter, too—about what it meant to be a big league ball player in the United States.

Soft soap? Maybe, but I remembered how I had dreamed and worked to get to the big leagues, and Eddie offered the clincher when he said to me, privately:

"Stan, you've got two children. Do you want them to hear someone say, 'There are the kids of a guy who broke his contract?' "

So I turned down the Pasquels' generous offer. Not everyone believed me at first because there had been amusing confusion. With the town buzzing as to whether I might jump, reporters and lounge lizards at the Fairgrounds had been thrown a red herring by Dickie, my six-year-old son. When they asked him what I was doing, he answered innocently:

"Packing."

I was, too, but to move to Mardel Avenue, not to Mexico City.

That hectic night, after I'd played and collected a couple of hits, we moved to Mardel with reporters at our heels. Again I was forced to reassure them that I wasn't going anywhere except home to bed. Only then could I sit down to a cold beer with Lil in the quiet kitchen of our new home.

"What date is this?" I asked. "June 6?"

"Yes," Lil said, "and Gerry is 18 months old today."

I sighed heavily. "Yeah, I know. I just wanted to be sure because I want to remember this date. I don't think I'll ever forget it."

I wasn't offered a salary increase or promised a raise not to jump to Mexico. Later, Dyer did go to bat with Sam Breadon for a few of us who had turned our backs on Mexican offers and had made key contributions during a prosperous season. In August, Mr. Breadon called me into his office and said he was giving me a $5,000 raise at once. I was nearly floored.

By then, we had fought back from an eight-game deficit and I had become a first baseman.

Except for those few games in the Navy at Bainbridge, I hadn't even fooled around the bag. But by mid-June, with our

In mid-season, 1946, Musial moved to first base, little dreaming he would play there—or anywhere—long enough to become the only guy ever to put in 1000 major league games each in the infield and outfield.

attack weak and young Dick Sisler having trouble hitting, Dyer decided on a bold move. A pretty good psychologist, Eddie began thinking aloud about his first-base problem. One night when I reported in the clubhouse, I found a new first baseman's glove in my locker. I took the hint and began to work out at the infield position.

The June night Dyer called me aside in the clubhouse and asked me to go to first base—"for the good of the club"—was one of the whacky ones in an era when the attitude of the old Gas House Gang and Pepper Martin's Mudcats lingered. That night, as the slumping Cardinals dressed, Doc Weaver's old phonograph blared Spike Jones' hill-billy dilly, "Pass the Biscuits, Mirandy," the number that had been so lucky for us down the stretch in 1942. The guys grinned about the old gal's return.

As the club stumbled far behind Brooklyn, Harry Walker remembered that in '42 we had begun to move when the club shifted from "Jingle, Jangle, Jingle" to "Pass the Biscuits, Mirandy" as its favorite tune. Trouble was, when mother-hen Weaver went to his record collection, the disc was gone. The conscientious, lovable old trainer, who would trim your toe nails, lecture on foot hygiene and help croon you out of a slump with his mandolin, searched the second-hand music stores without success.

Mirandy had baked her last biscuit.

Desperately, Doc appealed to the Cardinals' physician, Dr. Robert F. Hyland, a dignified man, but a baseball fan, too. He arranged with a St. Louis radio station to cut a record of the dilly disc. So on the night I went to first base, Mirandy passed the biscuits again, and Charley (Red) Barrett, who had failed to finish in five previous starts, held the Phillies to one harmless single!

Still seven behind on the Fourth of July, we had inched up on the Dodgers by the time of the 1946 All-Star game, one of the blackest days for those of us who carried the National League banner. Playing at Boston's Fenway Park, we were completely crushed by the American League, 12-0. Ted Williams put on a tremendous show with four hits, two of them homers. Playing half the game in left field, I went hitless in two trips.

We kept creeping up on the Dodgers and finally caught them with a four-game sweep in St. Louis in mid-July. That series, I think, had much to do with my baseball nickname, which was originated by Brooklyn fans.

We took a Sunday doubleheader before a packed house. In the first game, I singled in the eighth inning and Slaughter homered to give us a 5-3 victory. In the second game, little lefty Vic Lombardi shut us out until the eighth. I tripled, scored the tying run on Kurowski's fly ball and then gave us a 2-1 triumph with a home run in the twelfth.

Next night I had four hits, including a triple and another homer, in a 10-4 rout. And we were only a half-game out when, as we trailed into the ninth, pinch-hitter Erv Dusak hit a three-run homer for a 5-4 victory, a dramatic development that started the guys calling him "Four Sack" Dusak.

I'd always hit hard against the Dodgers, and the next time we were in Brooklyn, Bob Broeg, up in the pressbox, detected a chant when I came to bat. At dinner Broeg asked traveling secretary Leo Ward if he'd heard. Ward had.

"Every time Stan came up," Ward explained, "they chanted,

'Here comes the man!' "

"THAT man, you mean," Broeg attempted to correct Ward.

"No, THE man," Ward emphasized.

So Broeg wrote for the St. Louis *Post-Dispatch* about the Brooklyn fans' peculiar tribute to Stan (The Man) Musial. And a nickname was born. I'd be less than honest if I didn't admit liking it. And liking Brooklyn, Ebbets Field, Flatbush fans and, especially, Dodger pitching.

For much of my early career, a St. Louis-Brooklyn game was a spirited battle royal for first place, and the Dodgers somehow brought out of me a little something extra. That little something extra was necessary in the 1946 race, which resulted in the first pennant playoff in major league history.

The Cardinals and Dodgers went down the stretch neck and neck and ended in a dead heat on the final day, when we missed a chance to win in Cardinal tradition. A season's high of more than 34,000 fans at St. Louis watched the scoreboard as much as the field. At Brooklyn, our old former teammate, Mort Cooper, was pitching Billy Southworth's Braves to a shutout over the Dodgers. We got off in front against Chicago when I hit a third-inning homer off Johnny Schmitz, a troublesome lefthander. But just about the time the 4-0 final score at Brooklyn was posted, the Cubs knocked out George Munger in a five-run sixth inning.

Chicago's 8-3 victory not only set up the historic first playoff, but it enabled the Cubs to tie the Braves for third place. So for having helped us, our old buddies with Boston were $100 apiece poorer than if we had defeated Chicago and the Braves hadn't had to share third-place money.

Although we had backed into the playoff, we were keyed up by the pressure of playing a best-of-three series for the big money. A World Series has the glamour, but it doesn't pack the pressure of a playoff. After all, once you're in a Series, win or lose, you're in the chips. The difference between first place and second in the regular season is considerably greater—financially and in personal satisfaction.

We never felt we'd lose to Brooklyn. The Dodgers had indeed won three of the last four they'd played with us, but we had taken 14 of 22 during the regular season, and that margin had been necessary to reach a tie—96 victories and 58 defeats.

Immediately after the unprecedented tie on the season-ending Sunday, National League president Ford Frick held a three-way phone conversation with Sam Breadon, representing the Cardinals, and Leo Durocher, of the Dodgers. Durocher, always a master gambler, called the flip of a coin. He immediately elected

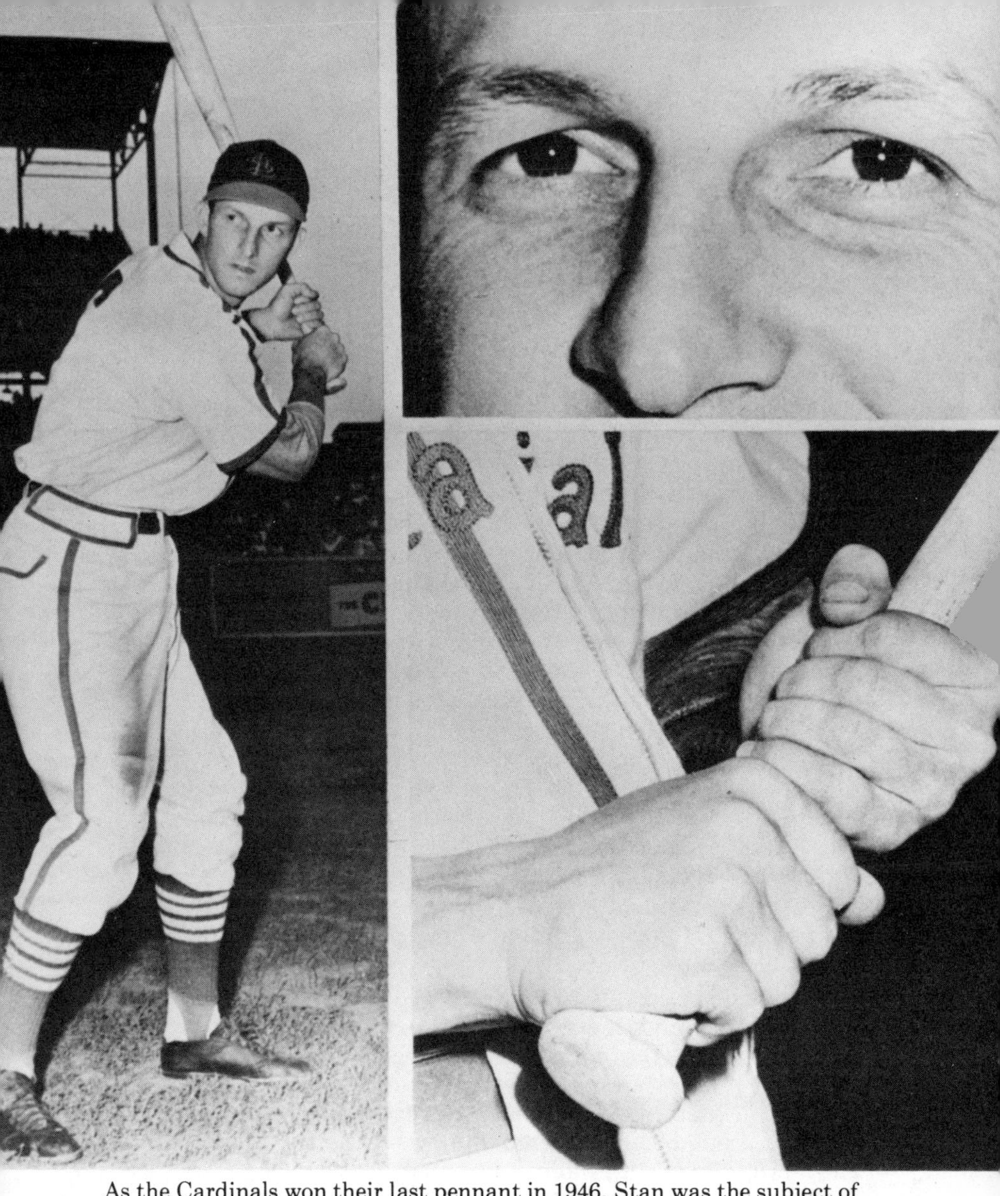

As the Cardinals won their last pennant in 1946, Stan was the subject of a picture study—stance, eyes, and grip.

to take the second game and, if necessary, the third one for Ebbets Field.

En route to St. Louis for the first game, Leo told New York writers, "I wish this was going to be on a winner-take-all basis. I'm that sure we can win two straight."

Despite a bad back, Pollet scored his twenty-first victory and his fifth over Brooklyn in the playoff opener at Sportsman's

Park. I tripled in that game as we beat Ralph Branca, 4-2, but the hitting hero was our 20-year-old catcher, Joe Garagiola, who had three hits and two RBIs. Terry Moore also collected three hits. The Irishman wasn't about to let anyone beat him out of the money.

Two days later at Brooklyn, we won the pennant. We supported Murry Dickson with a 13-hit attack, which included doubles by Moore and me, triples by Slaughter, Dusak and Dickson himself. With the Dodgers trailing 8-2 in the ninth, the crowd came to life when the Bums rallied. But with two runs in and the bases loaded, Harry Brecheen came in and struck out both Eddie Stanky and Howie Schultz.

For the fourth time in my four full seasons in the majors, the Cardinals were pennant-winners. It was a great feeling.

The Boston Red Sox, who had breezed to the American League pennant, were 9-to-20 favorites. Not only did the Red Sox have five .300 hitters to our three—Kurowski, Slaughter and me—but they had greater power in the heart of their batting order. Dom DiMaggio and Johnny Pesky were adept at getting on base, and Ted Williams, Rudy York and Bobby Doerr had the muscle to drive them in.

The big individual duel was expected to be between Williams and me. Ted had hit .342. He had 38 homers and drove in 123 runs. I'd batted .365 to lead the National League a second time and contributed 50 doubles and 20 triples, but only 16 homers. I'd had 103 RBIs.

Boston's pitching was established, and one other thing was going for the Red Sox—tradition. They hadn't lost a World Series in five tries.

We had Series tradition, too, and we lived up to part of it right away. For the eighth time in nine World Series, the Cardinals lost an opener. This one had to be the most disheartening of all. For eight innings, despite his troublesome back, Pollet had the Red Sox beaten at St. Louis, 2-1. In the ninth, though, a bad-hopping ground ball slithered through to tie the score. And in the tenth inning York walloped a home run to give the American Leaguers the ball game, 3-2.

Off Red Sox righthanders Tex Hughson and Earl Johnson, I had only one hit, a run-scoring double. Williams, who had hurt his right elbow before the Series, singled once.

To encourage Williams to hit to left field rather than aim at our close right field fence, we had adopted a version of the shift used by Lou Boudreau, Cleveland manager. We left only Marion, the shortstop, on the left side of the infield, moving Kurowski, the third baseman, to the right side of second base.

Schoendienst, the second baseman, moved deep into the hole toward first, and our outfield swung around toward right field, too. Me, I'd have hit a ton against that kind of defense, but Ted chose to challenge it.

In the five years I played for Eddie Dyer, I never saw him lower than he was after that first game in the 1946 Series. For one thing, he had a deep feeling for Pollet. He'd scouted and signed Howard as a junior American Legion pitcher in New Orleans. He'd found that the good-looking kid was the most apt pitching pupil he'd ever seen. Managing Houston, Eddie had polished Pollet's pitching and then sent him to the Cardinals at 20. In 1946, they were reunited in St. Louis, and Pollet pitched tremendously for his old mentor. He not only won 21 games and saved several others, but, as Dyer knew, he pitched with a troublesome back muscle in the pennant playoff.

And now he had been beaten just when victory seemed certain. With one out in the ninth, Mike Higgins' grounder had skidded freakishly through Marion's legs. After Rip Russell singled the tying run to third, Pollet struck out pinch-hitter Roy Partee. Because Garagiola, just a kid, was behind the plate, Dyer was calling the pitches from the bench. With two strikes on righthanded-hitting Tommy McBride, Dyer gave Garagiola the fastball sign.

Joe relayed the sign to Pollet, who shook it off. Garagiola glanced at the bench. Dyer persisted. Again, Pollet shook off the sign. This time, grudgingly, Dyer yielded. Pollet wanted to throw a curve, his slow curve, and did. He fooled McBride, but not enough. Off balance, Tommy grounded slowly between third and short, just through the hole, for a game-tying single. And in the tenth, York guessed correctly on a "2-0" change-up and—bang!

One thing about baseball—the sun always rises the next day. Brecheen asked that Del Rice, rather than Clyde Kluttz, be his righthanded-hitting catcher against Boston lefthander Mickey Harris. Rice contributed two hits, and The Cat shut out the Sox on four hits, 4-0.

Harris held me hitless, and Williams was stopped so completely by Brecheen that he had a terrible time. Once he missed a third-strike screwball with such a violent swing that his bat flew like a javelin into the visitors' dugout.

I didn't feel so good myself in the third game, the first one at Fenway Park, where we had been humiliated in the All-Star game that summer. I walked and stole second in the first inning, but then was picked off second. In the Red Sox's first try, York hit a three-run homer off Dickson, and Boston righthander Dave

(Boo) Ferriss breezed to a 4-0 victory. I had a ninth-inning triple that didn't help.

We were amused after Williams, in desperation, bunted against our unorthodox defense and pushed the ball on the ground into left field. We were not amused at his hit, but at the Boston headline in big bold type:

"TED BUNTS!"

The experts felt certain that, down two games to one, Dyer would have to come back with either of our top lefthanders. But Pollet and Brecheen didn't have enough rest, so Eddie preferred to gamble with George Munger. We made it easy for Big Red in a 12-3 rout, clobbering Hughson and others for 20 hits that tied a Series record. Three Cardinals—Slaughter, Kurowski and young Garagiola—and old Wally Moses of the Red Sox also tied a Series record by getting four hits apiece. I felt lost with just one hit.

The Red Sox moved within one game of the championship when Joe Dobson beat a pain-racked Pollet, 6-3. As if that loss weren't damaging enough, Slaughter was struck on the right elbow by a pitch and was forced to leave the lineup, considered out of the rest of the Series.

On the train to St. Louis, Doc Weaver worked with hot and cold packs all night, but Dr. Hyland reluctantly recommended that Enos be kept out of the game because a blood clot at the elbow might move. The Old War Horse would have none of that nonsense. Barely able to grip the bat, he delivered the last of five hits by which we knocked out Harris. And Brecheen evened the Series, 4-1.

The seventh game was one of the most exciting in World Series history. Dickson led Ferriss into the eighth inning, 3-1. Then Boston made its bench strength count. Pinch-hitters Rip Russell and George Metkovich singled and doubled to put the tying runs on second and third with none out.

Brecheen, who'd had only a one-day layoff, replaced Dickson and retired two men, but Dom DiMaggio then doubled off the right-center field wall to tie the score. Dom twisted an ankle rounding first base. Leon Culberson ran for him and went to center field in the home eighth, in which the veteran Bob Klinger was the Boston relief pitcher.

Slaughter, still swinging with difficulty, singled to center, but seemed destined to stay on first. Then with two out and Walker batting, Slaughter broke for second so that when Harry lined the ball safely over shortstop Pesky's head into left center, Enos was nearing second. Rounding the bag, he said later, he made up his mind he would go all the way. Frankly, our fine old third-base coach, Mike Gonzalez, had had one of those years when too often he had sent in men who didn't have a chance. At other times, he held up runners who might have scored, including Slaughter, early in the World Series. Enos had groused to Dyer.

"Okay," the manager had told him, "if it happens again and you think you can make it, go ahead. I'll take the responsibility."

So as Slaughter neared third, Gonzalez prepared to stop him. No one could have blamed Mike, because this was really only a single. Pesky knew this as he stepped into short left field, his back to the plate, to take Culberson's throw. The play eventually was ruled a double, but that was an injustice to Slaughter's daring. Walker himself said that he actually *slowed* halfway to second, hoping to draw the throw there.

Slaughter thundered past Gonzalez and sped for the plate. Pesky already had caught the ball just back on the grass, and Higgins yelled a warning from third. The crowd gasped and then roared. Pesky whirled, cocked his arm and threw off-balance so that the ball sagged and, as catcher Roy Partee went out to meet it, savage-sliding Slaughter actually scored easily.

The drama didn't end with that first-to-home dash on a king-sized single, however. In the Boston ninth, singles by York and Doerr put two men on with none out. We huddled around Brecheen on the mound, talking over the bunt defense. So when Higgins pushed the ball hard enough to third to compel the third baseman to handle the ball, eliminating the chance for a play at third, Kurowski reacted quickly. Instead of throwing to me at first base, Whitey pegged to Marion at second for a force-out on Doerr.

That unorthodox play not only kept the potential winning run out of scoring position, but it proved extremely important after Partee fouled to me. McBride, pinch-hitting, grounded to Schoendienst, who juggled the ball. Our hearts stood still as it rolled up the redhead's right arm. Red looked like a magician pulling a rabbit out of his sleeve when he finally flipped the ball to Marion, just in time for a Series-ending force play. If the runner had been on second, not first, Schoendienst wouldn't have been able to get the ball to me in time to retire McBride.

The thrilling 4-3 victory represented St. Louis' sixth championship. In this one, three-game winner Brecheen and shake-a-leg Slaughter had been the Series heroes. I hadn't contributed much, batting just .222, but in my head-to-head test against Williams, I'd had the edge. My six hits had included four doubles and a triple. I'd driven in four runs. Ted had batted .200 with five singles and one RBI in seven games.

The World Series melon was small in 1946. Each winning

player's share was only $3742.34, partly because both Sportsman's Park and Fenway Park had small seating capacities. There was another reason, though, a reason for which we on the Cardinals were extremely proud.

We had voted to waive the $175,000 Series broadcasting money—there was no television swag then—so that the player pension fund could be started. The Red Sox, by contrast, balked at first over giving up the present plum for future promises. Four players, we heard, were unwilling to voice agreement that had to be unanimous. Then, as I understand it, Tom Yawkey, the splendid sportsman who owned the Sox, let it be known that he would make up the difference for any Boston player who declined to approve the deduction of the radio money. The few reportedly dissident Red Sox relented—and the pension fund, now one of the most attractive features of the game, was on its way.

We of the 1946 Cardinals have particular pride in the pension plan because it was the creation of our shortstop and our trainer.

During the season of unrest, when players were jumping to Mexico, troubled clubowners asked dissatisfied athletes to present their requests. The biggest gain came through the pension plan, which Marty Marion and Doc Weaver devised one rainy day at the Hotel New Yorker. Their plan was crude, but, considering that neither had ever seen an actuarial table, it was basically sound. They proposed that players and clubs make matching contributions, that receipts from the All-Star game and radio money of both the All-Star game and World Series be earmarked for the pension fund and that, if necessary, inter-league mid-season exhibitions between natural rivals be played to help sweeten the kitty.

Marion and Weaver didn't know that right around the corner a wondrous cyclops, television, would answer so many monetary questions for both baseball management and labor. The pension proposal was No. 1 among the Cardinal players' requests for improved labor relations; then it became the main plank in the major league players' platform for reform.

Doc Weaver lived long enough to be one of the first to benefit. Marty Marion, like me, has been fortunate enough not to have to depend on the benefits. Already, though, we've seen several examples that show just how much the pension fund can mean. I have had the option, as a 20-year man, of collecting about $800 a month for life when I reached 50, but, happily, didn't need it then. So, automatically, I'll get about $25,000 a year at 65.

12

Money and Misery

I made my biggest financial score in 1947, but I had to work "extra innings" to get it.

I was determined to get a sizable increase. The top stars in the American League—Joe DiMaggio, Ted Williams and Bob Feller—were getting $40,000 to $50,000 or more. So I was disappointed when Sam Breadon's offer of $21,000 reached me through the mails. I'd hit .365. I'd won the batting championship and the Most Valuable Player award, moving from the outfield to first base. And the Cardinals—for the first time—had drawn more than 1,000,000 cash customers.

I wanted $35,000, I told Breadon, then accepted his invitation to negotiate in St. Louis. I was wiser now, not so fearful of giving in too easily. When the boss insisted he already was giving me a pay boost of $7500, I maintained he had offered only $2500 more than I had received. Oh, no, he contended. My salary had been $13,500, not $18,500. That $5000 had been only a bonus, not an increase.

"Mr. Breadon," I told him politely, "I don't care what you call it, but I know two things—I had to sign a new contract and I had to pay income tax on the money."

We agreed to meet again in February at the New York baseball writers' dinner, where I was to receive the Sid Mercer award as the No. 1 major league player of 1946. The morning of that dinner, Mr. Breadon offered $24,000, but I wasn't buying. That afternoon he told me what I had suspected. He wanted to be able to announce my signing at the dinner. He boosted the figure to $27,000.

I still said no.

So we broke off negotiations and I officially became a holdout when spring training began without me. For the first time, I took Lil and the children to Florida with me. We stayed at the Bainbridge and it seemed strange to be around the hotel while the other players worked out. An unsigned player is not permitted to suit up and practice.

Eddie Dyer became a little anxious and talked to me. I told him exactly what I wanted—$35,000—and he talked at length about a compromise.

"Come up to the room," he said, "and we'll call Breadon and see if we can't work this out. I don't want you to miss any more work—for our sake and yours. If the old man will split the difference, how about it?"

"All right," I said. "I'll compromise if he will."

He did and I signed for $31,000. That was a considerable increase over $13,500 or $18,500, and a healthy hike even over the $21,000 I first had been offered for 1947. I consider this the most significant salary boost I ever received.

Mr. Breadon, when he came to Florida, was pleasant despite the hard negotiations. One night Lil, the kids and I were eating in the small crowded hotel dining room when he appeared in the doorway. We asked him to join us. At the end of the dinner when I asked for our check and his, he wouldn't permit it. He didn't offer to pick up mine, but he wouldn't let me pay for his, either. I think that summed up Mr. Breadon—a straight-shooting man who paid his own way.

For all his years in baseball, he never ceased to be a fan. The enthusiasm was good, but there was a gullibility about it that wasn't. Not only would Mr. Breadon change managers almost impetuously—he once fired pennant-winning manager Bill McKechnie because the Cardinals lost a World Series in four straight—but he also could be influenced by irresponsible gossip.

Take 1947 when his world champions started poorly, losing nine straight in the first fortnight, a result of both the pitching and hitting, especially the hitting. As we headed east for the first time, Eddie Dyer held a clubhouse meeting. He informed us that we had been criticized for drinking. The manager said that, reluctantly, he had been forced to bar all public drinking.

No one could make a case for excessive drinking, especially by an athlete, but Dyer, like many other managers, felt that a beer or two would relax a thirsty player and help replenish the body liquid lost on a hot day or night. I know that in later years I found that by slowly cooling out in the clubhouse, sipping a beer, I was calmer and better able to eat when I left the park.

In 1947, though, the players not only weren't allowed to have a beer in the clubhouse, but they weren't supposed to take a drink on a train or in a bar or restaurant. Someone had told Breadon he had seen a player having one too many. Mr. Breadon had been around long enough to know that in many eyes, an athlete is crocked the minute he takes rum ice cream for dessert. But by his unreasonable sternness, the boss was encouraging furtiveness and deceit.

While his slumping champions were playing in New York, Breadon flew to Manhattan. Before talking to Dyer, he privately consulted captain Terry Moore and shortstop Marty Marion. If either Tee or Slats had put the rap on Eddie or just given him halting support, Breadon might have made a change. Instead, Moore and Marion absolved the manager of blame for our poor start.

Mr. Breadon wanted to see Dyer, too, about a delicate problem. He had heard rumors about discontent among southern-bred players because of the presence of the major leagues' first Negro, Jackie Robinson, on the Brooklyn ball club. The boss's question, answered to his satisfaction before he returned to St. Louis, was justified. Frankly, there was unrest over Robinson's presence—on all clubs, not only the Cardinals—but it was mostly hot air. At least, that's the way I regarded it. I'd gone to high school and played with a fine Negro athlete, now a college professor.

At the time, I had my own problem. One of the main things wrong with the world champion Cardinals had been Musial. Opening day, I'd failed in four trips at Cincinnati as Ewell Blackwell whip-cracked his way to a 3-1 victory over Pollet. The next day I'd hit an eighth-inning homer off Eddie Erautt to tie the score, 1-1, in a game we'd won. But that had been only a flash. I didn't have any power or zip and began to over-stride.

I soon found out why. I became deathly ill and was bedded down at the Hotel New Yorker. The same morning that the house physician diagnosed the trouble as acute appendicitis, a story broke in the *Herald-Tribune* that the Cardinals had threatened a protest strike against Brooklyn's use of Robinson. Only Breadon's intercession and league president Ford Frick's counter-threat of indefinite suspension had averted the strike, the newspaper charged.

I, for one, was just too sick to be indignant. There never had been a strike voted by Cardinal players because no vote ever had been taken. I ought to know—I was there.

Newspapers, like ball players, do make mistakes. A little later a story was published that a physical beating at the hands of Enos Slaughter, not appendicitis, had forced me out of the lineup. Naturally, old Bosco was as distressed as I was. Fortunately, St. Louis writer Bob Broeg had been in my hotel room as I lay naked and entirely unmarked, waiting while the hotel physician pondered whether I could go to Pittsburgh with the ball club, return to St. Louis or undergo emergency surgery in New York.

The doctor recommended surgery, but I preferred, if at all possible, to go on to Pittsburgh with the ball club. Dyer, after conferring long-distance with Breadon and Dr. Hyland, decided to have me fly to St. Louis. A reserve catcher, Del Wilber, would accompany me. I was too done-in to argue.

I was doped up for the flight to St. Louis, where Dr. Hyland examined me at 1:30 A.M. He was back at my bed at St. John's Hospital again at 7 A.M. At noon he offered the most encouraging news I'd heard during a horrible period of second-guessing myself. You see, I could remember abdominal distress during the winter back home at Donora, where my family doctor had recommended removal of my appendix. I had put him off.

Dr. Hyland said that I had infected tonsils as well but, aware that surgery would sideline me for nearly a month, he suggested it might be possible to freeze the diseased parts, to put off operating. The famed surgeon knew when not to operate, too. I was all for that.

Five days later, with the Cardinals in last place, seven games out, I returned to the lineup. After morning batting practice, my hands were blistered. I came back prematurely. I went 22 times to the plate without a hit—and then had to beat out a bunt.

My low-water mark was May 19 when I was batting only .140. I was still struggling around .200 when the ball club came home from a trip on June 13 in last place, eight games out. As we opened a four-game series with Brooklyn, Breadon paid a rare clubhouse visit, at Dyer's invitation, to deny reports that he planned to sell the ball club. He also expressed confidence that we would rebound and said that Dyer would remain the manager "at least" the rest of the season.

That night we began to win and I began to hit. We swept the four-game series from the Dodgers, and I had seven hits, including a triple and home run. We went on to win nine in a row.

"I'm getting my weight back gradually and it's because I'm eating well," I told a St. Louis writer. "It's great to be getting home cooking again. Lil is a very good cook."

The way I had been going, I was extremely flattered that the fans voted me even a reserve's spot in the National League All-Star team for the game at Chicago's Wrigley Field. I grounded out as a pinch-hitter against Walt Masterson as the American League again won, 2-1.

The only National League run came on a homer by Johnny Mize, who figured later that summer in an amusing incident at St. Louis. Harry Brecheen nicked him on the head with a curve ball one smothering, sweltering night, and Big John went down. As he was carried out, though, he winked to his roommate, Buddy Blattner.

"Call Jean," he said, referring to his wife, "and tell her I'm not hurt."

Over in the visitors' dugout, however, Mel Ott wasn't taking the incident so lightly. The Giants' manager ranted that Brecheen had tried it once too often.

"Kennedy," he yelled.

Monte Kennedy, wild young Giant lefthander who was pitching that night, was startled. "Yeah, skipper."

"If you don't hit that little so-and-so," Ott said, "it'll cost you fifty bucks."

Kennedy, who had trouble finding a stationary target much less a moving object, protested.

"I'll throw at him, skipper, sure, but, gosh, I can't guarantee to hit him."

"You heard me," Ottie insisted. "Hit him or it'll cost you fifty."

A quavering Kennedy went out to the mound and players on the Giants' bench had difficulty trying not to laugh at his nervousness. However, his first pitch caught Brecheen squarely on the right knee. The Cat, hurt, refused to rub, took two steps toward first base, rubber-legging like Leon Errol, and then collapsed.

Monte Kennedy had saved fifty dollars—and Mel Ott's honor.

They used to say, flatteringly, "As Musial goes, so go the Cardinals." No man can carry a ball club by himself, but the responsibility of the big hitter was reflected in the 1947 figures. In April, I had batted only .146 and the Cardinals won only two games out of 11. In May, during which I missed those five games and batted a feeble .227, the Redbirds were 13-13. In June, I batted .330 and the club won 18 and lost 10. In July, I hit .320 and again we were 18-10. And in August, the point when I reached .300 average for the season, the Cardinals won eight straight.

When I singled off Pittsburgh's Jim Bagby to reach .300 for the first time in 1947, my teammates made me feel awfully good. They broke into a hand-pumping, back-slapping clubhouse celebration.

"If it hadn't been for that terrible start, I'd be hitting about .340 now," I said.

I would have, too, and the Cardinals, I'm sure, would have been out in front, even though our pitching leader, Howard Pollet, had experienced a losing season, and our three young catchers—Joe Garagiola, Del Rice and Del Wilber—had been having troubles that were magnified. Intending no malice, I'm sure, commentator Gabby Street, himself a good catcher in his playing days, analyzed the catchers' deficiencies so thoroughly on the radio that every fan became a self-appointed authority on catching, and extremely vocal. The pressure told, in particular, on home-town boy Garagiola, just 21, but Joe had the wit that, curiously, was to make him highly successful on the same radio job eventually.

"Dyer," Joe said wryly, "has one catcher who can't hit (Rice), one who can't catch (Wilber) and one who can't throw (Garagiola)."

The wear and tear of the hot season on an illness-sapped body began to take effect on me again. I fell back to .284 by the end of August.

"I'm awfully tired now," I said. "Once in a while I can belt a long one—the ball is unquestionably livelier this year—but day in and day out, I can't get that spring into my swing. I especially can't get any power on the outside pitch I hit to left field.

"But we're not through now," I insisted. "I hope the extra rest and care I get at home will help me get as hot this September as I was the last month last year."

September and I made a happy combination over the years. Most players and pitchers lose something the final month because of weariness and boredom. The figures proved, until age overtook me, that I was at my best the last month of a season.

I finished strong in 1947. So did the Cardinals, closing the gap of 10 games in August one to four and a half in mid-September. We missed injured Red Schoendienst's glove at second base, and his bat, too. Whitey Kurowski, a hard .300 hitter that year, also was hurt late. But the Dodgers deserved the pennant. To divide the season's series, they won seven out of the last 10 games they played with us. Two out of three in St. Louis late in September proved decisive. At the finish our 89 victories left us five games behind.

I wound up with a .312 average for 149 games. I'd collected 183 hits, 30 of them doubles, 13 triples, 19 homers, and I'd batted in 95 runs. Pretty good, yes, but not good enough. Harry Walker, whom the Cardinals had traded to the Phillies for Ron Northey in mid-May, adopted brother Dixie's hit-'em-where-they-ain't methods and led the league with a .363 average.

In a losing year we'd lost the world championship and I'd lost the batting championship. The only losing that I liked was my tonsils and appendix right after the season. Without them, I felt I could hit .350 again.

13

The Big Year

From the moment I picked up a bat in 1948, healthy and strong after off-season surgery, I knew this would be it, my big year.

By the time I arrived in St. Petersburg, there had been some changes made. For one, the Cardinals were under new ownership. An era had ended in November, 1947, when Sam Breadon sold out to Robert E. Hannegan and Fred Saigh. To give up the ball club that had become his life, Mr. Breadon had blended sentiment and practicality. Over 70, he decided to choose his successors rather than allow fate that privilege in the event of his death. He feared, on the one hand, that his Redbirds might have to be sold to meet inheritance taxes. On the other, he was reluctant to thrust so large a responsibility upon his widow.

He was certain a woman couldn't run a ball club.

Mr. Breadon chose to sell out after a highly profitable season. We had drawn about 1,250,000, by far the largest gate in the club's history. When Hannegan and Saigh bought the Cardinals, they "purchased" more than $2,000,000 in cash. (Breadon had hoped to build his own ball park.) We all envisioned good-natured Bob Hannegan as a soft touch, but he wasn't.

I came to St. Louis at Hannegan's invitation, hoping to get a pay increase, but I didn't get it then or at St. Petersburg, where the entire family vacationed before spring training. I was grateful, though, for pleasant hours with Hannegan and, particularly, for his kindness to my father. I signed, finally, when Bob assured me that if I had a good year, he and Saigh would adjust my contract during the season.

The other change that spring of 1948 was in me. I was 27 now, at my athletic peak and healthier than I had been for as long as those low-grade infections had been gnawing at my system. Stronger, too, when I picked up a bat and swung it. The bat felt so light that instead of gripping it about an inch up the handle, as I had in the past, I went down to the knob. Gripping the bat at the end, I could still control my swing.

I was returned to the outfield for the first time since midseason, 1946, and put in right field, my favorite position. The reason, Eddie Dyer said, was to get hard-hitting Nippy Jones in the lineup at first base and to add defense and speed to the outfield. If I'd known that before the season was over I'd be playing center field, I wouldn't have been so delighted.

Opening day, I contributed only a double in five trips as Murry Dickson pitched a 10-hit shutout over the Reds at St. Louis. And my position-switching began quickly. Enos Slaughter, not hitting, asked to switch back to right field, which he preferred, too, so I went to left field. I didn't pout. I got five hits that night, including two doubles and a home run.

Of all the years I was credited with having "carried" the Cardinals, 1948 would have to be the season in which that exaggeration came closest to being true. Injuries kept Kurowski out of 61 games, Red Schoendienst out of 50 and Marty Marion out of 10. Worse, our infielders had to play at times when they weren't fit. Near mid-season all three of our catchers were hitting under .200, and our pitching fell off, too, except for Ted Wilks in the bullpen and Harry Brecheen starting.

The Cat, one of my favorites as a competitor, won 20 games and led the National League in earned-run efficiency. One night late in the season when he shut out the Phillies before a collection of former stars at Shibe Park, 81-year-old Cy Young said to another Hall of Fame pitching great, Lefty Grove, "There's a boy who could have won in any baseball generation. He's got that extra fine control."

Grove agreed.

I'll never forget a game Brecheen pitched against the Phillies early that season at St. Louis. The bandy-legged, stoop-shouldered, hollow-cheeked little guy was so good that night he missed the only perfect game of this century in the National League by an umpire's decision. In the seventh inning Johnny Blatnik hit a two-strike, two-out slow hopper along the third base line. Kurowski, hurrying, fielded the ball, but couldn't get too much on the throw with his tormented arm. Still, when umpire Babe Pinelli ruled the batter safe on a hairline play, the crowd hooted.

Pinelli said he had been aware that no Philadelphia batter had reached base. Ben Chapman, the Phillies' manager, said he wouldn't have kicked if the call had gone the other way. Brecheen said, "I thought he was out, but, of course, I'm prejudiced."

I reached a milestone that at first meant little to me. On May 24, 1948, I tripled off a Chicago lefthander, Cliff Chambers, at Wrigley Field. The hit was No. 1000.

Afterward Bob Broeg came into the clubhouse. Instead of congratulating me, he ribbed me as he's inclined to do. (His nickname for me is "Banj," short for "Banjo," a disparaging term used to describe a weak hitter.) Now he teased:

"Look, Banj, if you're going to talk about hits, what about trying for 3000?"

"Three thousand," I said in disbelief.

Broeg told me he'd seen it happen. He'd covered the June, 1942, game in Boston when Paul Waner reached the plateau. But Waner was only the seventh hitter to do it.

"Know how exclusive that 3000-hit club is, Banj?" he said, asking me to name the six others.

I got Ty Cobb right, but when I mentioned Babe Ruth and Lou Gehrig and Rogers Hornsby—and Broeg kept shaking his head—I was astonished.

"You mean to tell me those men—all those *great* ball players—didn't make it?"

"You can," he goaded.

I sat there letting the thought sink in, doing silent arithmetic. Let me see—I had 1000 hits in a little more than five full years in the majors, so I'd averaged close to 200 hits a season. To get 3000, I'd have to average 200 a year for 10 more seasons. To maintain that incredible pace, I'd have to be good and lucky—lucky to escape serious injury, lucky to last that long. I'd be 37 or 38 years old!

I laughed. "That's a long way off," I said. "Too many things could happen."

But I couldn't shrug off the challenge. "Keep reminding me," I said. "This is a team game and I play to win, but a fella has to have little extra incentives. They keep him going when he's tired. They keep him from getting careless when the club is way ahead or far ahead. It'll help my concentration."

So Broeg appointed himself vice-president in charge of Musial's basehits—and we both laughed.

I was hitting .350 at the time and felt I was improving by laying off more bad pitches, hitting the better and faster strikes. Two years before, as a pitch started for the plate, I could tell whether it would be a fast ball or something not so quick, a curve or a change-of-pace. And that gifted sight, or whatever it was, seemed to be coming back.

Broeg wondered about home runs because the year before, though missing a few games, I'd hit 19, my personal high. In 1946, I told him, pitchers generally had thrown high and tight to me, but now they were throwing low and away, a tough pitch to pull. Still, with four in the first 21 games, I figured to hit from 15 to 20. With four doubles and four triples to my credit, I said I thought I'd be good for 35 to 40 doubles, 15 to 20 triples and that I'd drive in 100 runs or bust.

I wish I'd always been so prophetic. In 1948 I finished with 46 doubles, 18 triples, 131 RBIs, and—to my pleasant surprise—39 home runs.

If I could have hit all season at Ebbets Field or the Polo Grounds or, for that matter, if I could have played the 1948 season on the road, I might have hit .400 and ripped the record book apart.

The first time we went into Brooklyn to play the defending champions, we swept three games. I had 11 hits in 15 trips, including four doubles, a triple and a homer. In the middle game of the series I went 5 for 5, a result of two singles, a double, a triple and a home run.

The next five-hit performance came in mid-June at Boston. The Braves, thanks in part to players they had bought from the Cardinals, were making their first pennant bid under Billy Southworth. One of my hits that night was a bunt. By then, though I could lay the ball down well, I seldom bunted because the club had begun to count on my newly found power.

When I started up to the plate in the ninth with the score tied, bases loaded and lefthanded Clyde (Hard Rock) Shoun on the mound, Eddie Dyer called to me:

"Hey, boy, I'm afraid I'm going to have to send up a hitter for you."

I did a double-take, and Dyer and the bench laughed. I hit Shoun's first pitch through the middle for my fifth hit, a two-run single that won the game.

When we went into Brooklyn in late June, I homered and doubled in a four-hit performance that helped beat another lefthander, Joe Hatten. The next night Dyer was holding a squad meeting when a knock on the door brought a hush to the visitors' clubhouse at Ebbets Field.

The sharp-featured head of Preacher Roe popped in. The popular old lefthander of the Dodgers grinned and said gleefully, "I know how to get Musial out."

"How?" our guys chorused.

"Walk 'im on foah pitches an' pick 'im off first," Roe drawled and ducked out, leaving us laughing.

I was hitting .410 at the All-Star interlude, after a July double-header in which I played right field and first base in the first game and center field in the second game. Even so, we were down in third place, six games behind the Braves.

The All-Star game was played in St. Louis' Sportsman's Park. The American League won once more, 5-2, but with most of a crowd of 34,009 pulling for me, I hit my first All-Star home run, lining a pitch off Walt Masterson into the right-center pavillion in the first inning with one on.

Things really popped in the National League at the All-Star interlude. Item: Johnny Sain, the Braves' tobacco-chawing perennial 20-game winner, threatened a sitdown strike if Lou Perini, who had just put out a $65,000 bonus to Johnny Antonelli, didn't come up with some scratch. Item: Bob Hannegan called me into his office to make good that promised salary adjustment, a $5000 increase that boosted my salary to $36,000. Item: Leo Durocher, darling of the Dodger diehards, crossed the Brooklyn Bridge to New York's Polo Grounds, where, despised by Giant lovers, he succeeded old idol Mel Ott as manager. Item: Burt Shotton, who led Brooklyn to the 1947 pennant while Durocher was under a year's suspension imposed by commissioner A. B. (Happy) Chandler, returned to Ebbets Field from his Bartow (Fla.) front porch.

I hit with remarkably good luck in Brooklyn, where I batted .522 that year. In 11 games at Ebbets Field I had 25 hits—10 singles, 10 doubles, a triple and four home runs. But I believe I'm proudest of a fielding performance.

Like the pitcher who likes to talk about his hitting, I like to talk about my fielding, especially because as age finally took the spring out of my legs, my defensive skill waned before my offensive ability did. It was in 1948, you see, that my throwing arm came back much of the way. When they tried to run on me, I threw them out.

In the first game of our final trip to Brooklyn, the Dodgers stopped me cold. Over the years, I'm proud to say, I had some of my best days defensively when I wasn't hitting. I never said much, but I thought my share about players who would let their chins drag when not hitting so that their fielding was affected, too. If I couldn't beat 'em with my bat, I certainly hoped to try with my glove.

Playing center field the September afternoon I *didn't* hit at Ebbets Field in 1948, I took a double away from Jackie Robinson with a somersaulting catch in the third inning. In the sixth I charged over to the exit gate in deep left-center and flung up my glove for a one-handed catch that robbed Pee Wee Reese of a leadoff triple.

With two on and two out in the ninth, Tommy Brown lifted a short fly to center for an apparent two-run game-tying hit, but I sprinted in, dived and snatched if off the grass to preserve a 4-2 St. Louis victory.

I jammed my left hand tumbling in the outfield, but forgot about it in the showers, where Terry Moore, whose center field shoes I was trying to fill, quipped:

"Stash, if you only could hit . . ."

"Yeah," I kidded back, "then I probably could make the varsity."

The following afternoon that left wrist bothered me a bit, but I hit a home run off Carl Erskine, who earlier had hit me on the right hand with a pitch. Still, when Reese doubled to lead off the ninth with the score tied, 2-2, I didn't think I could throw properly if I had to make a play to the plate. I ran in from center field to tell Eddie Dyer I thought Erv Dusak would have a better chance. Dyer agreed, but Pete Reiser, the next hitter, didn't. He delivered a hit too long for anyone to head off Reese with the winning run. And, for the record, I never took myself out of the lineup again.

The next day the jammed left wrist and badly bruised right hand hurt, but not enough to keep me from playing against Leo Durocher's Giants across the river in Harlem. I broke up the second game of a doubleheader at the Polo Grounds with a homer off Ray Poat. We took both games and, as a result, had won 10 straight from New York, including the final five at the Polo Grounds, where I'd had 17 hits that included two doubles and eight homers.

Under Mel Ott, the Giants in 1946 and '47 had been the league's toughest team for us. And in '48 before Ottie was replaced by Durocher, they had taken six out of 10 from the Cardinals. Leo liked to play the game rough, liked to make it a game of intimidation. His tactics turned us from tabbies into tigers.

The facts speak for themselves. After Durocher took over at New York, we won 11 out of 12 from the Giants. By contrast, we won eight out of 11 from Brooklyn before Leo was let out, but just two of 11 after Burt Shotton reassumed command. The year before, Shotton's Bums had split the season's series with us. In 1946 we had won the pennant only because we beat Durocher's team 16 out of 24.

Leaving New York for Boston, we had only a slight chance of overtaking the Braves, who had pulled ahead of Brooklyn, now "too hot not to cool down." That year, 1948, in salute to the Braves' two great pitchers, someone had coined the expression, "Spahn and Sain . . . and pray for rain."

They forgot a guy named Potter . . . Nelson Potter . . . who had been released by Connie Mack at Philadelphia in one of the grand old man's rare fits of temper. Nellie had signed with the Braves in mid-season as a relief pitcher. His screwball gave a lot of hitters trouble, most certainly me.

On our last 1948 visit, the Braves immediately moved within a game of clinching a tie for their first pennant in 34 years. They swept a doubleheader. With my wrists hurt and taped, I wasn't much help.

Generally, the wind blew briskly in off the Charles River, making Boston a cool, invigorating place to play, but discouraging for hitters. When at times the wind did blow out, it favored lefthanded hitters, and the flag at the right field foul-pole would gesture toward the "jury box," as Boston writers quaintly called the small bleachers. On such a day the second-place Cardinals sought to avoid elimination from the race—against Warren Spahn.

At the batting cage beforehand, Bob Broeg pointed to the flag and said, "A great day for the hitters, Banj."

"Yeah," I said, a little bitterly, "but I can't hit like this."

I held up the wrists with the flesh-colored tape. Angrily, I ripped it off.

When the game began I looped a single to left off Spahn in the first inning, punching the ball to the opposite field to minimize wrist strain. In the third, I again hit one to left field—this one harder—and the ball cleared Mike McCormick's head for a double. That inning we knocked out Spahn.

In the fourth inning, garrulous righthander Charley (Red) Barrett took the mound for Boston. Our former teammate had jockeyed us hard the day before about the favor the Cardinals had done him in trading him to a pennant winner. He tried to fool me with a "2-0" change-up, but I saw it coming and said to myself, "To hell with the wrists."

They hurt, but the ball I pulled went into the jury box for a home run.

In the sixth inning, facing a second southpaw, Shoun, I grounded a single into left field between third and short. I was entirely aware—and so was the gang on our bench—that with four hits, I would have one more chance at matching Ty Cobb's 1922 record of five hits four times in a season.

Once before I had come to bat a fifth time with a chance for a fourth five-hit performance and had slashed the ball right back at Bob Chesnes, Pittsburgh righthander. When I came up in the eighth inning, righthander Al Lyons was on the mound for the Braves—and I wanted that fifth hit.

Lyons missed with the first two pitches. Our bench began to ride him. I was anxious, too, for fear he'd walk me. I made up my mind, with the Cardinals far ahead, that I'd swing at anything close to the plate—wrists be hanged.

The next pitch was a bit outside, but I jerked it around. I didn't really hit the ball too hard, but, in baseball vernacular, it "had eyes." It bounced in the hole between first and second and got through for a record-tying single.

Saving the sore wrists as much as possible, I had hit safely five times by taking the absolute minimum number of swings—just five. By contrast, on another of my five-hit days that year I hit safely every time with a two-strike count.

It was a once-in-a-career season.

Although we finished second with 85 victories, I became the first National League player to win a third Most Valuable Player award. My .376 average had been the highest to win a National League batting championship since Arky Vaughan's .385 in 1938. Twice I had been hitless three consecutive games, but the most crippling slump had come the first week in September when I'd had just three hits in 24 trips over a seven-game period. During that stretch, we had lost five out of seven and the Braves had taken five of seven.

The batting average was really not the most outstanding feature of my greatest season. I'd had the first .700 slugging percentage in the National League since Hack Wilson in 1930. My 103 extra-base hits were just four shy of Chuck Klein's league record, set in 1930, and my 429 total bases were only 21 behind the league high established by Rogers Hornsby in 1922. I'd actually had a piece of several great hitters' best seasons.

I led both leagues in basehits (230), runs (135), doubles (46) and triples (18). I was first in the National League in RBIs (131) and just missed the first clean sweep of departmental honors since James (Tip) O'Neill of the 1887 St. Louis Browns. My 39 home runs were one short of the league-leading total which Ralph Kiner and Johnny Mize tied for. And I'd hit one homer that had been washed out by rain.

Most surprising, after playing pro ball since 1938 and as a big leaguer since late in 1941, I'd suddenly become a home-run hitter.

The power surge felt good, mighty good, but it was to hurt as well as help me—and in 1949 it hurt before it helped.

14

Close, But No Cigar

Dizzy Dean surveyed the situation in the Cardinals' clubhouse at Sportsman's Park one night early in August, 1949. We sat with our heads literally in our lockers. Ol' Diz thumbed back his 10-gallon hat, pushed out his expanding belly and roared:

"I alluz knew I started in baseball too soon. Boy, it must be great to be a pitcher now. You can even call back a home-run ball!"

Diz had just seen one of the two extraordinary defeats that brand 1949 into the memory. The Cardinals lost the pennant by one game. In a race that close, every quirk of fate seems to sneer and jeer.

Take that night Dean was there, for instance. In the first inning, Nippy Jones, our first baseman, walloped a two-run homer off the Giants' Adrian Zabala, Cuban lefthander only recently reinstated after having jumped to Mexico. The home run was disallowed because Jocko Conlan, umpiring at third base, had declared a balk. Zabala hadn't come to a stop in his delivery.

In football, a team captain could have said, "No, thanks, Mr. Referee, we don't want the measly offsides penalty on that play. We'll take the big touchdown we scored." Come to think of it, the referee wouldn't even have insulted the captain's intelligence by asking.

In baseball, like football, there now is an option by which the offended team may take the greater gain, but under 1949 rules the penalty went against the Cardinals, not the Giants. Zabala went on to a 3-1 victory.

That season we lost another game as innocent bystanders. This was in July at Pittsburgh, where a kid named Dino Restelli had just come up from San Francisco with a home-run flurry that made him an overnight hero—briefly—and pretty chesty, too. In the course of a scoreless duel between Gerry Staley and Ernie Bonham, Restelli complained frequently on the pitches called by an outstanding umpire, Larry Goetz.

With two on and two out in the sixth inning, Restelli stepped out of the batter's box twice to beef on called strikes. Rednecked now, Goetz gestured for Staley to pitch with the batter OUT of the box. Head down, apparently day-dreaming, the pitcher lobbed the ball to the plate, thinking the umpire wanted to see it. Not until catcher Joe Garagiola fired it back to him, angrily, did Gerry realize he had a golden chance for an uncontested third strike.

Although Staley was hurrying, he checked the runners through force of habit before throwing a pitch that had nothing on it. And Restelli, suddenly recognizing Goetz wasn't kidding, jumped back into the batter's box to belt the "cripple" to the left field fence for a two-run double that gave Pittsburgh the victory.

Goetz, asked for an explanation by the press, was characteristically frank. "I was trying to put the fresh busher in his place," he said, "but St. Louis wouldn't let me."

Almost as if it were a foretaste, 1949 had begun sadly for me when my father died. After the poisonous Donora smog the previous fall, he and my mother had joined us in St. Louis, where Lil and I had decided to make our home.

Frankly, I would just as soon have returned to Donora or, at least, the Pittsburgh area close by our people, but son Dick was eight and we didn't like him to have to miss or change schools. We had met many fine people in St. Louis. When Dick told Lil he wished we could live there year-round, that clinched it.

Just before my folks came to St. Louis, we bought a house in the new southwest section of the city. Close by was the restaurant of Julius (Biggie) Garagnani, a good friend of Sam Breadon and Joe Garagiola.

For some time, I had been thinking of getting into business. Now and then, eating at Garagnani's Club 66, I'd talk about my hopes. I was completely sold on the wisdom of getting started on a second career before the first one was over. I had a moderate amount of capital to invest. My principal asset was my baseball name.

One day Biggie and I were out playing golf and the subject came up again. "Stan," he said, "if you really want to go into business so much, why not become partners with me?"

I liked the idea and so did Lil. The only catch was that we'd just paid cash for the new house and didn't have $25,000 ready to buy in. A check of the books showed that Biggie was being extremely fair. He revealed he could be generous, too.

"Pay me out of your share of the profits," he offered.

So without putting out a penny, I became half-owner in a venture that proved most profitable for me. Sure, business was helped because of my baseball popularity, and Biggie profited, too. But he already had proved himself a sound businessman and, more important, a good restaurateur.

Our partnership, formed in January, 1949, was so successful that in 1960 we built a new restaurant, a real showcase, and sold the original Stan Musial and Biggie's. The partnership with the Garagnanis has since extended long beyond Biggie's premature death in 1967.

In those early days, particularly, I'd hear snide remarks that the restaurant interfered with my baseball. How could it? During the season, I'd drop in around noon partly to take advantage of our secretary's efficiency. Shirley Auen, who once baby-sat for Dick and Gerry, became indispensable in helping me answer my mail and her sister, Pat, proved an efficient successor. Except after a weekend day game, I'd stay away from the restaurant, though occasionally after I'd played a night game, Lil and I would go there for a snack.

Biggie was not only sensitive to any suggestion that business might interfere with my baseball, but was shrewd enough not to over-expose me around the place. "Bing Crosby don't sing every day in public," he'd say.

Actually, in the off-season, I began to spend more and more evenings at the restaurant. It became my school teacher. The more I realized with the passing years how warm people felt toward me, the more I enjoyed meeting strangers. At that, I wouldn't drop in until about 7:30 and I'd be home well before 10:00 so I could say good-night to the kids.

I went into business to make money, but, above all, I wanted something to fall back on if I suffered a career-shortening injury. I'll never forget rounding first base early in the 1950 season at Pittsburgh. Loose dirt went out from under me. I slipped, fell and twisted my left knee. When I tried to get up, I couldn't make it. I thought I was through and said to myself:

"Thank God for the restaurant."

I just wish other ball players had been as fortunate. Even that first summer in the business, when I was slumping at bat, I was able to say:

"If I was doing just half as well as the restaurant, I'd be hitting .400."

At the time in 1949, I wasn't hitting much more than half of .400. Why? Because I'd become a greedy hitter. I outsmarted myself in salary negotiations and at the plate, too.

After my 1948 performance, Bob Hannegan had called me in the last day of the season and offered a $45,000 contract plus $5,000 for each 100,000 attendance over 900,000. In 1948 the ball club had drawn 1,111,454.

Instead, I made a counter proposal. "How about a two-year contract with $50,000 base pay, Mr. Hannegan, and $5,000 each year if we pass 900,000 paid admissions?"

Hannegan agreed, and I glowed, certain that I was increasing my pay from $36,000 to $55,000. If I had gambled and accepted his original terms, I would have drawn $70,000 because the all-time St. Louis attendance record, before the new downtown Busch stadium was built, was set in 1949—1,430,676.

The man who benefited most that year was Fred Saigh. Before the season, the fatal illness that had overtaken Hannegan in political life forced him to sell out to the little lawyer who had proved himself a financial wizard in skyscraper real estate. Saigh and Hannegan, a friend of Breadon, reportedly needed only about $60,000 cash to swing a $4,000,000 deal. Together with the ball club went Breadon's fabulous cash reserve and mortgageable ball parks at Rochester, N.Y., Columbus, O., and Houston, Tex.

Saigh insists a baseball deal arranged by Hannegan with his political friend, Pirate owner Frank McKinney, did not help produce the capital by which Saigh and Hannegan dissolved their partnership. He does contend, however, that the sale of Murry Dickson to Pittsburgh for $125,000, announced a few days after Saigh moved up to the club president's chair, had been arranged by Hannegan.

Dickson, a wiry, rubber-armed guy, not only pitched effectively 10 more seasons, but he beat us five critical times in 1949.

After years as pennant favorites, we had been picked for

fourth place. Surprisingly, we stayed in the thick of the race. Howard Pollet came back after two bad seasons. Joe Garagiola returned from the minors much improved. Red Schoendienst and Marty Marion, physically sound, gave us infield strength we had missed sorely in 1948. Until Eddie Kazak suffered a broken ankle in mid-season, the rookie gave us the kind of sock we'd had from George Kurowski in the past at third base. Even though a bad back sidelined Nippy Jones too often, our first baseman also lent punch.

Enos Slaughter, after a terrible start, came so strong that, despite a weary final-week slump, he finished with the highest average of his career, .336. And I overcame my greediness to have a tremendous second half.

Before spring training, I'd said I was going out for home runs. As Ralph Kiner had cracked, "singles hitters drive Fords, but homerun hitters drive Cadillacs."

But in going for the home run, I played into the pitchers' hands. Trying to pull the ball too often, I lost my timing. I overstrode at the plate. The pitchers suddenly realized they had a different—and easier—hitter to pitch to. In the past, working me in and out because I hit to all fields, they'd tended to pitch me inside, trying to jam me as I strode into the ball, daring me to go for the long one. When I finished with those 39 homers in 1948, however, they were looking for something else.

They found it. After beginning the '49 season by walking me often, pitching too carefully, they began to nibble at the outside corner with slow-breaking stuff, pitches I previously lined into left field. Now, trying to jerk too many pitches to right field, I began to press. All of a sudden, I found myself chasing bad balls.

Home runs have to come naturally or not at all. It took me nearly to the All-Star game in July at my favorite target—Ebbets Field—to get back into the groove. In fact, if it hadn't been for my success against Brooklyn, I wouldn't have reached mid-season hitting .290. In a June series at Flatbush, I came out of the slump. The first night I hit two homers and a single off Preacher Roe. Next night, facing Don Newcombe, I singled twice, tying the score with the second one, then won the game in the fourteenth with a two-run triple off Jack Banta.

I had 8 for 13 in a series in which we began to crowd the Dodgers. We had regained Max Lanier, Lou Klein and Fred Martin, three of the 18 contract-jumping players who had been reinstated by commissioner Happy Chandler. The Mexican bubble had burst, and the fellows were happy to be back. Lanier, not in shape after having scrounged around playing semi-pro ball in Canada, needed precious weeks—and costly starts—to reach his stride.

Just before the All-Star game at Brooklyn, we closed in, a half-game from the lead, with a 2-1 victory in 10 innings at Chicago. I drove in both runs and threw out the potential tying run, trying to score from second on a single to right field.

My bat stayed big for the All-Star exhibition in Ebbets Field, my favorite game preserve, where I hit a two-run homer off Boston Red Sox southpaw Mel Parnell and drove in another run with one of two singles. But Joe DeMaggio also drove in three runs. And, when our side committed five errors, the American League won its twelfth game in 16 tries, 11-7.

In mid-July, I got over .300 on the strength of another fat series at Ebbets Field as the Cardinals took over first place by winning three games and tying one.

In the opener I singled and homered off Preacher Roe. I remember the home run. Roe pitched a slow, sweeping sidearmed curve that forced me to give ground, but, stepping away, I took a full swish at the bad, hanging curve. And as my left hand slipped off the bat, I one-handed a high fly over that tall, close right field fence. Red Munger won, 3-1.

We came from behind in the ninth to win the next night, 5-4, a game in which I walked twice. The following afternoon was one of my biggest. I hit for the cycle—single, double, triple and home run—as Pollet breezed to victory and we took first place.

The fourth game was a 4-4 tie, called after nine innings to permit both teams to catch a train west. I'd had a single, double and triple that day, so it was a really happy ride west over the rails for a guy who was batting .546 for nine games in Brooklyn. Over a two-year period in Flatbush, I then owned a .531 average on 43 hits, of which 11 were doubles, five triples and eight home runs.

And the figures went up during our final trip to Ebbets Field, though I would gladly have traded some of the personal gain for another victory.

Actually, both contending clubs were slumping, and so was I, when we arrived there. The Dodgers had just lost an extra-inning game, their third straight. If they needed outside stimulus, Dick Young gave it. The highly capable—at times caustic—baseball writer of the New York *News* stung them with an implication that they had choked up under pressure.

"A tree grows in Brooklyn," Young wrote. "It's an apple tree and the apple is lodged in the throats of the Dodgers."

Professionals don't choke up, and the Dodgers were champions.

They proved it after we momentarily extended our league lead to three games. In the afternoon half of one of those abortive two-games-for-the-price-of-two programs, I came out of a slump with a single and double off lefty Joe Hatten. And Enos Slaughter, hitting .434 at Ebbets Field, had a single, double and triple. Our 5-3 victory was a replay of that earlier tie game.

For just an instant that night, we seemed to have the Dodgers on the run. In the first inning I hit my sixth Brooklyn homer of the '49 season onto Bedford Avenue, giving Pollet a 2-0 lead over Preacher Roe. But the Ol' Bag o' Bones, working with only two days' rest, proved himself once again to be quite a money pitcher. He beat us, 4-3.

The next night Don Newcombe held Slaughter and me to one hit each, shutting us out in our final game at Brooklyn. We'd won seven of 11 there, but, backed against the wall, the Bums had taken the last two and had cut our league lead to one game. That was championship baseball.

After our last series at Brooklyn, we moved over to the Polo Grounds, where Leo Durocher, despite no love lost for the Dodgers, boasted that the Giants would take three out of four from the Cardinals. Wrong again. We won three, and I hit three home runs.

My hitting was hard and timely the second half of the 1949 season after having had trouble while trying for the long ball. Curiously, when I began to go for base hits instead of home runs, I hit for more power as well as average. I batted .290 for the first 86 games. Only 34 of my first 98 hits were good for extra bases, including 16 home runs. The next 71 games I hit an even .400; 56 of the last 109 hits were good for two or more bases. Twenty were home runs.

As a result of that prolonged surge, I felt I had an outside chance at the batting title when I had a hot weekend at Cincinnati, September 10-11. For the second time that season I beat Howie Fox with a ninth-inning homer. My average moved to .331. At the time, Jackie Robinson led with .345 and my teammate, Enos Slaughter, also paying the penalty for a slow start, was second with .339.

Old Bosco made his grandest bid when Brooklyn came to St. Louis for the last time, with 10 games to go. We held a game and a half lead, but the wear and tear of the long season began to tell on a club that had fought to catch up.

I was a little gimpy myself, having pulled a groin muscle, so Eddie Dyer moved me to first base for the afternoon game of a day-night doubleheader. He put young Bill Howerton, just called up from Columbus, in center field against righthander Don Newcombe.

St. Louis still remembers Max Lanier's duel with Don Newcombe before an excited crowd. In the first inning Marion was out at the plate on Furillo's great throw as he tried to score from second on my double. And the game remained scoreless until the ninth.

Slaughter, getting his third straight hit to take the batting lead, dropped a double just inside the left field line. Ron Northey, next up, was passed intentionally. When Howerton's bunt danced along the third base line for a hit, the bases were loaded with none out.

Jackie Robinson, angry at plate umpire Bill Stewart's calls, used a throat-gripping gesture to indicate that Stewart had choked up. The umpire threw him out of the game. And with Eddie Miksis playing second base, Garagiola's grounder glanced off the substitute's glove for a single that gave us the game, 1-0.

Once more, however, Roe won the critical middle contest for the Dodgers. The Preacher beat us a fourth time in five tries on only two hits, 5-0, before another packed house that night. Because young Chuck Diering twisted his ankle stepping on a ball during practice, Howerton, a lefthanded hitter, had to start in center field against the crafty old southpaw, Roe. When Bill later left for a pinch-hitter, Red Schoendienst—the best second baseman in the league—wound up playing center field.

The Dodgers positively overwhelmed our walking wounded in the final game between the two clubs, 19-6. I had a single, double and homer off Hatten, but those hits weren't nearly enough. We had won the season's series from Brooklyn, 12 games to 10, but the Dodgers had taken four of the last six.

Two days later, we left for the final five games of the season, leading by a game and a half, two on the defeat side. Nippy Jones' bad back had become so troublesome—his replacement, Rocky Nelson, hadn't hit at all—that the Cardinals had called up a big, powerful rookie from Rochester, Steve Bilko. If the Cardinals did win the pennant, Eddie Dyer told writers aboard our train, he would ask that Bilko be made eligible for the World Series in Jones' place.

During a tight pennant race, a ball club's special railroad cars used to be crowded down the stretch with reporters from all over. It was tense and exciting. I remembered how in 1942 we had begun our apparently hopeless final trip with only one writer along and had returned with more than 25.

Talking to writers in the club car, Pittsburgh bound in '49, traveling secretary Leo Ward figured as a joke that if all five of our remaining games were rained out, we would win the pennant by two percentage points even if the Dodgers played and won their last four. The rains came, but not Ward's wishful washouts.

Pittsburgh was our jinx park—and now the Pirates were mad.

Back on Labor Day in St. Louis, as we were breezing to victory over the dozing Pirates, Slaughter slid hard and extremely high into Danny Murtaugh, the Bucco second baseman, slashing Murtaugh on the ribs. They exchanged words and Murtaugh followed Slaughter to the dugout. A fight was prevented, but sleeping dogs had been aroused. In the second game that holiday, Bill Meyer threw his starting pitchers into action as if this were the seventh game of the World Series. And the Pirates won on the tenth-inning double by Murtaugh.

We still heard about Slaughter's slide when we reached Pittsburgh. "My guys and I frankly would rather have seen St. Louis win than Brooklyn, but not now," Meyer told Bob Broeg.

"Your guys are awfully tired," Meyer shrewdly observed.

He was so right. Slaughter had tailed off after his terrific season. Schoendienst's once-high average had shrunk and Red was so weary that, despite the importance of the series, Dyer planned to rest him two games in Pittsburgh so that he might perk up for the final three games in Chicago. Then in infield practice before the first game at Forbes Field, rookie Solly Hemus, who had been scheduled to play second base, was hit in the face with a bad-hopping ground ball which broke his nose. Though exhausted, Schoendienst had to play.

I was tired, too, but I had no excuse. At that stage of my career, Forbes Field was a hex park for me. I'd hit only .255 there during my .376 season in 1948. I was struggling to hit .200 before the home folks in '49, too. And even though I hit 46 of my 75 homers on the road during that two-year span, I didn't hit one at Pittsburgh.

To this day, because I didn't hit there in '48 and '49, many fans think Forbes Field was my least productive park. The truth is that over a career I batted .337 at Pittsburgh, better than my lifetime average, and actually delivered more base hits there than at any park except the Cardinals' own.

In 1960 I almost lost some long-time friendships by beating the Pirates three times with home runs, when Pittsburgh was going for its long-awaited pennant. But in those two games in late September, 1949, I was held to just two singles in nine trips.

We lost the first night, 6-4. Schoendienst had a bad night afield, Munger walked two weak hitters to force in a run and then Tom Saffell, a rookie who didn't last long with the Pirates, hit the foulpole screen in right field—a foot fair—for a grand-slam homer. Our league lead was cut to one game with four to play.

Rain the next night provided some rest, but it increased the anxiety. Murry Dickson, whose sale to Pittsburgh had been so controversial, had dinner with his old roommate, Harry Brecheen.

"I still hope you win, Cat. We can delay our hunting trip until after the Series," Murry said, "but you're not going to beat *me*."

For the fifth time that year, we didn't. Dickson scattered six hits to beat Gerry Staley, 7-2. Our defense was as shaky as our offense. So we lost the season's series to the sixth-place Pirates, 12 games to 10. And when the Dodgers took a rain-shortened doubleheader at Boston that afternoon, we were out of first place—for the first time in 43 days.

Over at Chicago, I singled and doubled in the opener of the final three-game series with Frank Frisch's last-place club. But I lost a fly ball in the sun, too, and the ball glanced out of my glove for a damaging two-run double. Lanier, who had won five straight games after failing his first nine times back from exile, was knocked out. Munger failed in relief. By contrast, Walt Dubiel, replacing Bob Rush for the Cubs, held us to one hit the last four innings to preserve a 6-5 Chicago victory.

Now we were one down with two to go—and miserable.

The next-to-last game in 1949 was one of the most frustrating I played in the big leagues. Brooklyn lost to Philadelphia that day, so we could have regained a tie for first place.

The Cubs scored three quick runs off Brecheen, their old nemesis. The Chicago pitcher, throwing lefthanded lollipops, was Bob Chipman. He was one of those nuthin'-ball guys who had a herky-jerky pitching motion, an effective change-up and good control. He walked four that day, though, and gave up nine hits, including two doubles to me. But we passed up chance after chance, left 12 men on base—and lost, 3-1.

For the first time in major league history, both pennant races went down to the last day. Over in the American League, beating the Red Sox a second straight game, New York nosed out Boston for the pennant. Our league's race went "extra innings" Brooklyn staggered to a 9-7 victory over the Phillies in the tenth.

One day too late, we came out of our slump. I ripped two homers and we pounded out 14 hits as Pollet won his twentieth game, 13-5. A ball club that had been picked to finish fourth and had straggled along in seventh place in late May, five games below .500 just hadn't been able to hold on quite long enough. We lost six of the last nine after Lanier pitched that dramatic 1-0 victory over Newcombe. In the final week, for the first—and only—time all season, we lost four straight.

If we had staggered through, we probably would have made a sorry World Series ball club. Still, I doubt if we would have done worse than the Dodgers, who disappointed us by losing to the

Yankees in five games. We would have gone into the Series without our regular first baseman, Nippy Jones, scheduled for surgery on his back, and without our star second baseman, Red Schoendienst. The tired redhead had suffered a cracked thumb taking a routine throw from the outfield the day before the season ended. Awaiting surgery with Jones were Eddie Kazak, the third baseman, for bone chips in the right ankle broken in mid-season, and our best relief pitcher, Ted Wilks, for a bone spur on his left heel.

While back home that Sunday evening the Cardinals' front-office staff grimly went about returning $1,500,000 in World Series applications from some 120,000 persons, we dressed slowly in the pall of the visitors' clubhouse at Wrigley Field. Instead of preparing to take a special train to New York for the World Series, we faced a late-afternoon trip back to St. Louis.

I was too sick at heart to take much comfort from what I know now was a great season, poor start or not. I'd blown the batting title to Robinson by four points, .338 to .342, and my 123 RBIs had fallen behind Ralph Kiner's league-leading total, but I had finished first again in runs (128), hits (207), doubles (41), triples (13) and once more was second to Kiner in homers, with 36.

The ride back to St. Louis was deadly quiet. Most of the fellows sat in the private parlor car, eyes closed. If they were like me, they were replaying the close ones in the only pennant race the proud Cardinals ever blew, a championship lost by one game.

Up ahead behind the closed door of a compartment, manager Dyer sat, stunned, talking softly to his wife, Gerry. Bob Broeg knocked, entered and offered his sympathy.

"I guess, Colonel, after so many years breaking other clubs' hearts down the stretch, the Cardinals had this one coming," the writer said, seeking mutual consolation. Dyer nodded.

"The only thing is," Broeg added, "I wonder when we'll get this close again?"

Dyer glanced up, then looked knowingly at his wife.

"That," he said, "is what I've just been saying to Gerry."

15

End of an Era

If I ever had a chance to hit .400, I lost it in 1950. That year began with the birth of our second daughter, Janet, which was a good excuse to cut down on speaking engagements. I always used to lose weight worrying about what to say. A public speaker I'm not.

Determined just to meet the ball, I wanted a good start. I got it in the first night opener ever played. We beat Pittsburgh in St. Louis, 4-2, and I homered off Bob Chesnes.

Late in April, when I was batting .448, I suffered the first injury, slipping in soft dirt at Pittsburgh. My left knee gave way. The great team surgeon, Dr. Robert F. Hyland, thought I ought to stay out a week, but the club needed me. I was back in a couple of days, moving from right field to first base.

I got a couple of hits as Joe Garagiola and his roommate, Tommy Glaviano, led us to a 14-inning victory over the Dodgers. I mention this only because Glaviano, who was quite a kid with wild curly hair that looked like Harpo Marx's wig, figured in a most unforgettable loss. Somebody must have shot the albatross.

At Brooklyn, where we ALWAYS fattened up, we led 8-0 in the eighth inning. The Dodgers scored four runs in the eighth and then five in the ninth because poor Tommy committed THREE errors—in one inning. Never again did we hold sway at Ebbets Field.

Disaster followed at St. Louis, where Garagiola, hitting .347, tried to avoid spiking Jackie Robinson on a bunt play at first base, tripped, fell heavily and fractured his shoulder. That was the day that the world lost a promising catcher and gained a great comedian.

Injuries continued to stalk us. After hitting .442 in June, I was hurt freakishly. A-1 Pitcher Brazle fielded a ball near me at first base, and threw too hard. Unable to get my glove across my body, I tried to spear the ball barehanded. It ripped a gash between the second and third fingers.

Forced to cushion the bat handle with an air-foam pad to stay in the lineup, I slumped again when required to wear an elastic, steel-ribbed bandage on that gimpy left knee.

My roommate Red Schoendienst brought the Cardinals distinction by winning the All-Star game at Chicago's Comiskey Park, with a fourteenth-inning homer off Detroit's Ted Gray, 4-3. Red called his shot, too—to our delight on the bench—but we didn't have much to smile about.

I finally wound up at .346, then my career average, and played first base and all three outfield positions for Eddie Dyer. But all that didn't prevent a drop to fifth place, one that really cost the 50-year-old Texan.

This is the kind of year 1950 was:

At Brooklyn, just after getting 17 hits in 29 trips, a 30-game hitting streak was in jeopardy when I was horsecollared until the ninth inning. Then my teammates batted around so that as I came again, the Dodgers brought in 19-year-old bonus righthander Billy Loes.

As the kid warmed up, I overheard Pee Wee Reese and Jackie Robinson, huddled with him on the mound, laughing. Next day I found out what Reese had asked the rookie. Pee Wee wondered if the kid knew I had a long hitting streak at stake?

"Yeah," said the cocky Loes, "and I'm going to throw one right down the middle to him, too."

He did, too, and I hit the fat pitch on the ground, right to

Robinson, for a double play that broke the longest hitting streak of my career!

Most of us thought coach Terry Moore would be chosen the manager for the 1951 season. But Fred Saigh picked Marty Marion, then 32 years old, with his career near an end because of back and knee injuries.

I wanted to become the first National Leaguer to repeat as batting champion since Rogers Hornsby in 1925. But, first, after a wonderful week at Hot Springs, Arkansas, I went to Europe to instruct and entertain American troops. I even learned from an old Bavarian how to pick out a few chords on a zither.

Belgians didn't know much about baseball, but money is a universal language. They applauded when a Baron Munchausen interpreter said my boss valued me at $2,000,000. I don't know what Saigh really thought I was worth, but, insisting vehemently that no one got $100,000, he offered $75,000 and a $5,000 attendance clause.

Saigh and Marion were trading like Bill Veeck, the sports-shirted Barnum who bought the neighboring St. Louis Browns that year, when we opened at Pittsburgh. The batting order was: Peanuts Lowrey, cf; Red Schoendienst, 2b; Enos Slaughter, rf; Musial, lf; Don Richmond, 3b; Steve Bilko, lb; Joe Garagiola, c; Solly Hemus, ss, and Tom Poholsky, p. There were quite a few new names, and these were mentioned only because many more were on the way.

In a Christmas-card, snow-flurry setting at Pittsburgh, with rookie Poholsky pitching, we lost to old teammate Murry Dickson, 5-4. I singled and walked in four trips.

The weather there might have caused the flu epidemic that swept our club in the East, since several of us were out with the flu by the time we got to Cincinnati. To take advantage of our feeble condition, the Reds promptly rescheduled a rained-out game for a Saturday doubleheader. Customarily early-season postponements are played later. I guess we kicked Luke Sewell's strategy in the rear end.

The sun was out that Saturday. Although still weak, I felt the air might be better for me than a stuffy hotel room. So I sat in the bullpen, cap off, and soaked up the warmth until, losing again in the second game, we threatened in the eighth inning and trailed by a run.

Sewell switched from lefthander Harry Perkowski to righthander Frank Smith, confident I was no factor. I walked up to the bench to Marion and offered to pinch-hit.

Although still washed out, I hit one of Smith's sidearmed sinkers for a three-run homer and a 6-4 victory that ended a five-game losing streak. Marion said he never forgot that look of disbelief on Sewell's face!

Marion's turn to register disbelief came the day before the trading deadline at home against the Dodgers. We lost, 2-1, on a ninth-inning two-run homer by Gil Hodges off little Joe Presko. But, wait, here's the rub: We had 15 hits, two walks, the benefit of an error and scored just one run.

The next day Saigh and Marion traded old friends Garagiola, Howard Pollet and Ted Wilks to Pittsburgh for outfielder Wally Westlake and pitcher Cliff Chambers. Westlake disappointed them, but Chambers, until he broke his wrist the following year, pitched well.

Marion had, at Saigh's request, asked my opinion, an unusual thing for him to do. The Cardinals could have Chambers or another lefthander, Bill Werle. Whirlin' Willie, as they call him, had stopped me. And I soon solved Willie's Whirl. I had hit Chambers hard, but I thought he was the better pitcher. He was, too.

I'll never forget about one time at Pittsburgh with Chambers. It was at a game the year before, we trailed by three and, as we rallied, I yelled:

"Load 'em up and I'll hit one."

When we filled the bases, Bill Meyer, the Pittsburgh manager, went out to talk to Chambers, who is a good-natured, gabby guy. Cliff gave Uncle Bill a sales talk. Meyer went back to the bench and, just as he sat down, I teed off for a grandslam homer. Uncle Bill leaped up and hit his head on the dugout.

Another funny one happened at the All-Star game in Detroit. The night before the game the Yankees' Eddie Lopat told the Dodgers' Preacher Roe that he knew how to pitch to me. The next day as the National League won a battle of home runs, 8-3, I hit one into the upper right field stands off Lopat.

Roe, jumping up in the NL dugout, chortled, "I see, I see. Hell, I know how to pitch him that way."

Before the season, I figured a .350 average would win. I figured, too, that leg-hitting Richie Ashburn of the Phillies would be the man to beat. In July we had a Sunday showdown at Connie Mack Stadium. I was four points up going in .366 to .362, and got five hits that afternoon to Richie's two. Two of mine were homers, including one off lefty Jocko Thompson that was said to be among the longest at old Shibe Park. It cleared the right field fence, 335 feet at the foul line, 38 feet high, and the ball sailed far over 20th Street. It landed on the rooftop of a second-story flat and bounced onto another building beyond.

That year I tripled off the right field screen at St. Louis, against New York's young righthander, Al Corwin. It was just inches fair. The next time I homered into the left field bleachers, again less than a foot fair. I don't believe I ever hit a ball harder, deeper or tighter to the line in the opposite field.

By the way, to acommodate the rallying Giants' stretch drive against Brooklyn, we became the first club since 1883 to play two teams in the same day. We met New York in an afternoon contest before a regularly scheduled night game against Boston. We lost to Spahn and the Braves, but apparently hurt the Giants by beating Sal Maglie.

You know what happened, though. New York DID win the pennant on Bobby Thomson's dramatic playoff home run against the Dodgers.

The Cardinals finished a strong third, and I'd hit .355 with 208 hits and 108 RBIs. But we had lost 18 out of 22 to the Dodgers

In January 1953, Sidney Salomon, St. Louis sportsman, presented Stan with an oil painting for his old restaurant. With them are, from the left, the late Biggie Garagnani, Horace McMahon, and Joe Garagiola (with hair!). At this luncheon, Garagiola made his debut as a master of ceremonies—and was great.

and Saigh felt Marion hadn't spent enough time in the front office. So Marty was canned, reminding me of that first flu-ridden eastern trip when Slats had abandoned four traditional red-striped stockings in favor of solid blue baseball socks.

"I don't know, Marty," I mused then. "Know what they look like to me? Mourning socks."

Remember that $80,000 contract I had signed? Well, I had not gotten the $25,000 raise because of a Korean War freeze on pay hikes.

Seated next to handsome Maurice Tobin, Secretary of Labor, at a dinner in Washington, I mentioned my pay-increase problem. Tobin had been the mayor of Boston when I played there. He invited me to bring my lawyer, Mark Eagleton with me to Washington. Tobin took us before the Wage Stabilization Board. And I got the raise, which Saigh waggishly pointed out would be much smaller when applied to my gross income.

I didn't care. $80,000 was $80,000 and, besides, if I had to take a pay cut in the future, there would be more left. A few days later with the press present, Saigh called me in, and extending a blank contract, said:

"I know this puts you on the spot, Stan. But I think you have given some thought to what you want. Anything short of your owning the ball club tomorrow morning is all right with me."

Taken aback, not expecting to conduct negotiations publicly, I stammered that I wanted to be the last to sign because I didn't want my contract to be a hardship on the other players because of the salary-freeze on club, not individual, ceilings.

So I said, "Well, Mr. Saigh, I've been very well satisfied with my contract in the past. I think that if Miss Murphy will come in, I'll sign my 1952 contract under the same terms as 1951."

Miss Mary Murphy, private secretary to Cardinal club presidents from 1941 until her retirement in 1962, brought in a blank contract.

Saigh thanked me for a "tremendous thing." Afterward, a reporter quipped that Saigh must have been a helluva fine crap shooter. Saigh said, smiling, that he had gambled on a man's character—The Man's.

After signing, I wanted to get away to Florida because I felt tired and nervous. I'd had to chase back and forth to Donora because my mother had been seriously ill. And after having played for only two managers my first eight years in the majors, I was facing a new straw boss a second straight season.

Saigh had wanted an aggressive manager and he got one. He gave up two players for Eddie Stanky, who had played on pennant winners at Brooklyn and Boston, and with the 1941 world champion New York Giants. He was a little battler whose blue eyes could flash angrily or freeze a hot tamale. We had known him as both a respected and bitter enemy. He was an ask-no-quarter-and-give-none opponent who had twice been hospitalized by rough-sliding Enos Slaughter.

Most of us felt that Marion had merited another chance. We also felt that Stanky would be under handicap as the first non-organization man to run the club in 20 years. Although he was 36 and had slowed, Eddie came over with the notion that he could play second base and move Schoendienst to shortstop. But in spring training, Solly Hemus, called the Mighty Mouse by Marion, impressed Stanky with his base-reaching ability. And, of course, Stanky wasn't Schoendienst at second base.

So, basically, Eddie sat on the bench except to needle the umpires. One night at Cincinnati, just after the bad news came that Saigh had been indicted for income-tax evasion, Stanky got in a gesturing, jawing match with umpire Scotty Robb. Suddenly, making man-bites-dog news, the umpire pushed the manager. When National League president Warren Giles, a spectator, refused to clear him, Robb quit and briefly went to the American League.

In mid-June, we won a game I'll never forget. In the opener of a hot Sunday doubleheader at New York, we trailed Sal Maglie and the Giants after three innings, 11-0. Leo Durocher began to rest his regulars. Stanky thought of pulling Slaughter, Schoendienst and me, too, but something stopped him.

"Call it a silly hunch, call it anything," he said, grinning, after the greatest rally I ever saw. We won the game, 14-12.

When I went into a slump, the late Ellis Veech, sports editor of the *East St. Louis Journal,* went through a familiar ritual. He hunted up a four-leaf clover, crushed it, sprinkled it in my hair and I went on a 24-game hitting tear, a streak that ended in a rain-abbreviated game at Pittsburgh.

Even the All-Star game at Philly was short-order that season. Thanks to homers by Jackie Robinson and Hank Sauer, the National League won in five innings, 3-2. As the rain fell steadily, home-town hero Bobby Shantz of the A's struck out Whitey Lockman and Robinson in the home fifth. Plate umpire Bill Summers must have decided the Philadelphia fans had had their money's worth. To give Shantz three straight strikeouts, Summers called me out on a very bad pitch, low and away, and hustled for cover.

The Cardinals' club record for consecutive victories—14—was set by the Gas House Gang in 1935. In '52 we saw a 10-game streak snapped by the Phillies at St. Louis, 4-3. Three times Redbird runners sent in by Stanky, a good third-base coach, were thrown out.

Afterward, a surprising clubhouse visitor, Ty Cobb, came in to tell Stanky he had been absolutely right. "Only exceptional relay throws and some wide, poor running kept your men from scoring," Cobb told a grateful Stanky.

Warren Giles, president of the National League, gives Musial his sixth silver bat, the symbol of the 1953 batting championship.

I was thankful, myself, for the outspoken, authoritative Cobb. He had recently written for a national magazine during his playing era of 1905-28, when only Phil Rizzuto, Yankee shortstop, and I would have been stars. Even though I disagreed with the fiery old super-star's conclusions, Ty and I did strike up a pleasant correspondence.

Our pitching was dependent all season on veteran lefthander Al Brazle and rookie righthander Eddie Yuhas, who was the best 1-2 bullpen we ever had. We got a double lift in August by the arrival of two talented young starters, Stu Miller and Harvey Haddix. We won eight in a row, challenged, but then finished, third with 88 victories, the most from 1946 until my last season in 1963.

Although leading the league a third straight year, batting .336, finishing first in hits, run and doubles, I was disappointed for the first time in 10 years to finish with fewer than 100 RBIs. After all, Hemus and Schoendienst had been on base often.

As a cheap gag the last day of the season when I had put Frankie Baumholtz safely away, they asked me to pitch to my batting rival. Baumholtz turned around and batted righthanded. I lobbed the plate to him and he reached base on a questionable error. I'm not proud of that boxoffice circus.

I was proud, however, of the way friends and strangers rallied around me in 1953 with prayers, suggestions and good-luck charms when I couldn't get started. I received enough four-leaf clovers to feed a horse, enough rabbits' feet to make every Easter bunny a basket case, enough hairpins to start my own beauty shop. If a ball player finds a hairpin, you know, it's supposed to bring him a basehit.

I had another good reason to want to break out. In March, Anheuser-Busch had bought the Cardinals after Fred Saigh, convicted of income-tax evasion, agreed to sell for less money to St. Louis interests than to Milwaukee. I was sorry for Saigh. His misfortune set off a chain reaction of franchise shifts when the Boston Braves then beat Bill Veeck and the old St. Louis Browns to Milwaukee.

For August Anheuser Busch Jr., 52-year-old beer baron-sportsman, baseball opened new doors. It opened his eyes, too, just as it had for Saigh, a real estate wizard relatively obscure until thrown into the baseball limelight. Busch traveled by private railroad car to watch us play the Milwaukee Braves' historic opener, which represented big league baseball's first franchise shift in a half-century.

Although I hit Warren Spahn pretty well, I went 0 for 5 that day. The Braves beat Gerry Staley in the tenth, 3-2, on the first—and only—home run hit that year by rookie Bill Bruton.

Busch's home opener was a near-disaster, too. The rooftop elevator broke down. The pre-game aerial bombs failed to burst in air. Governor Phil M. Donnelly had a sore arm and couldn't throw out the first ball, and Irish tenor Phil Regan developed a sore throat and couldn't sing the national anthem. It's a wonder Harvey Haddix managed to shut out the Cubs.

Here and there in the early weeks of the season, I'd have a good game, but then I'd slump again. So, one morning under Eddie Stanky's watchful eye I took a long private practice. Eddie suggested I was striding too far.

He wondered why all clubs didn't take action movies of their hitters at their best. An advertising friend in New York offered films of me hitting from a few years before. The movies confirmed what Lew Fonseca, a former good hitter in charge of instructional and World Series movies then for the majors, had written. At my peak, my stride at the plate was just 12 inches. Now, I was striding nearly twice that far.

Stanky offered to rest me when, still struggling, I pulled a groin muscle at Brooklyn. I told him, "If you don't mind, Eddie, I'd like to fight my way out."

I was worried, naturally, but not enough to burden anyone else with my problem, as roommate Red Schoendienst, off to his greatest season, explained when he told a reporter I hadn't changed. "One thing I know," said Schoendienst, "he's pulling for me as I always pulled for him. He tells me, 'Keep the room full of hits, Red.' "

In mid-June, down to .251, I took an open-date batting workout and hit hard. That day I felt I could predict a .300 season and even held out hopes for another batting championship. "If I can get close to .300 before the All-Star game, I still might make it," I said.

The All-Star game at Cincinnati, where I had two hits, belonged to my 37-year-old teammate, Enos Slaughter. He walked once, singled twice, stole a base, scored two runs and executed a sliding catch of a low line drive.

I was tickled for Bosco. "You should have seen him grinning when he left," I told reporters who were too late to catch the fastest man ever to clear out of a clubhouse.

Despite our new club high for home runs, 140, we finished in a tie for third with the Phillies. The young Polish Falcons, Jablonski and Repulski, had contributed power. However, except for a 20-game season by Haddix, we had been saddled with inferior pitching. The staff's ailing-armed Eddie Yuhas had been missed. And the slow left side of our infield proved to be handicap to sinkerball pitchers like Gerry Staley and Al Brazle.

But remember what I'd said in mid-June? In 12 games before the All-Star game, I went from .251 to .303 with 24 hits in 43 trips, including 10 doubles and four homers. In one calendar week against Pittsburgh, New York and Philadelphia, I had 19 for 27 and drove in 12 runs.

Finishing strong in September, I narrowly missed a fourth straight batting title. Actually, I felt worse that Schoendienst missed with a .342 average, two points behind Carl Furillo. I hit in the 15 last straight games at a .437 clip.

I'm proud of that .337 season, proud to have batted .385 the last 101 games after my stumbling start. In my best power showing since 1949, I finished with 53 doubles, nine triples, 30 homers and 113 RBIs.

Going into the last three games, I needed six hits to reach my sixth 200-hit season in 11 years. With two the last day at Chicago, I wound up with 200—right on the nose.

I had kept faith, I felt, with the thousands of well-wishers who, back there in the lean months, had kept faith with me.

Members of a Mutual Admiration Society meet at the 1951 World Series. Casey Stengel (left), then managing the Yankees, predicted back in '42 that The Man would be a champion batter.

16

Rain or Shine

When I walked into our living room, late for dinner, hungry and happy, I scooped up my five-year-old second daughter, Janet, and mussed the blond hair of 13-year-old son Dick.

"Gee, Dad," he said gravely. "They sure must have been throwing you fat pitches today."

A prophet is indeed without honor in his own country, a father in his own household. This was the May Sunday in 1954 when I had hit five home runs in a doubleheader against the Giants. Rain had almost washed that out, but that's the kind of year 1954 was for the Cardinals. There was very little sunshine.

The new owners, wanting to build a winner quickly, not only had bought and renovated Sportsman's Park, renamed Busch Stadium, but had peeled off the bankroll for talent, too, spending more than $300,000 in money and players for three minor leaguers. During spring training, the club gave $75,000 and two minor leaguers to the Yankees for Vic Raschi, the 35-year-old powerhouse righthander who had been a holdout. Unfortunately, a bad back kept Raschi from showing his old fire, and of the expensive minor leaguers only shortstop Alex Grammas panned out at all.

The club was nominally under the direction of Dick Meyer, the brewery's brightest young executive a former college ball player. But Meyer continued as an increasingly important brewery executive, so that he didn't stay long as our general manager. He impressed most of us, including veteran baseball men in the organization, as a man of unusual aptitude.

After I had talked contract with Dick and agreed on the same $80,000 terms as the previous three seasons, I signed for the first time with Mr. Busch. Amiably, he came that time to his rarely used ball club office, but in subsequent years I signed at the brewery. These became pleasant productions with the press, radio and television men—and Miss Mary Murphy. Until she retired in 1962, her "baseball age" a well-guarded secret, our beloved front-office secretary would come down from the ball park to fill in the figures on my contract.

For the first time, at that 1954 contract session, I expressed the thought publicly that I might reach the 3000-hit goal. Told that, going on 34, I was 777 hits away, I said:

"Those are good figures. I actually think I can make it. I think I can play three or four years at top speed."

I had done some reading about heredity. I knew that, though my father had been worn out from overwork in his 50s, Pop hadn't looked his age, hadn't had a gray hair in his head. The presence of Enos Slaughter who had played ably past 37, also had influenced my thinking. So I was shocked almost as much as Old Bosco when he was traded to the Yankees two days before his thirty-eighth birthday.

Other National League clubs had waived on Enos, probably because of his age and $28,000 salary. When he was notified in the eighth inning of our final exhibition game that Meyer wanted to see him in the Cardinals' offices, Slaughter cried. Neither Meyer nor Stanky had expected that reaction from the hard-playing, hoarse-voiced holler guy. But 16 years in a ball club's uniform can do things to a man—even a strong man.

In the clubhouse, when the rest of us got the word, we were stunned. Dressing even more slowly than usual, I was the last one out. At the lot where I parked my car, across from Busch Stadium, I found Slaughter, still wiping his eyes. We looked at each other—and both burst into tears.

I was now the senior member of a ball club that had undergone a complete change. Of the 30 players on the roster in 1954, only nine were on the squad which Stanky opened with as manager in '52. Of those, only Schoendienst at second base, Rice catching, Staley pitching and I—wherever they decided to play me—could be considered regulars.

Opening day exposed the weakness of that 1954 team—pitching. Wally Moon, a rawhide kid from Texas A. & M., on the spot as the popular Slaughter's replacement, hit a home run his first time at bat in the major leagues, and I also homered, but the Cubs cuffed us, 13-4.

I was hitting the ball hard early in 1954, but I never dreamed I'd have a day like the amazing first Sunday in May. Oddly enough, that noon, just before the doubleheader with the Giants, a New York writer, Arch Murray, told Stanky he was doing a magazine piece on baseball men's views of which player was No. 1. Who was Eddie's choice?

"Number Six," Stanky said, pointing to me. Out of earshot, the manager was most flattering. That day, at least, I made him sound like a sage.

My first time up, I walked. In the third inning I timed one of lefthander Johnny Antonelli's slow curves and hit it to the right field roof. In the fifth, Antonelli fired a fast ball down and in, probably too far inside and, theoretically, a bad pitch. But I was holding my arms closer to my body and was able to get out in front of the ball. I hit it to the right field roof for a two-run homer.

In the sixth I singled to right off righthander Jim Hearn's good overhanded curve. When I came up in the eighth, the crowd was roaring. The score was tied, 6-6, and we had two men on. I was well aware I'd never hit three homers in a big league game, but I was trying only to get a hit when I belted Hearn's slider so solidly that it, too, landed on the right field roof.

Lil called me during the doubleheader intermission, almost as unhappy that she hadn't been there as she was glad for me. Sure, I was excited. I know some so-so hitters have had three-homer games and Johnny Mize, a good hitter, did it five times. But I had never done it before.

Because of the overcast, the lights had been turned on in the ninth inning of the first game, and the second game began under lights. First time up, I walked and the crowd booed angrily. The fans wanted to see me hit.

Second time up, I hit a ball as hard as any that day, but I didn't quite pull this one enough. Willie Mays ran back about 410 feet from the plate and made the catch just in front of the extreme right-center field bleachers. The wind that day blew toward left field. If it had blown toward right, I believe I would have had two three-homer games the same afternoon.

In the fifth inning, I hit my fourth homer of the day. It came with one on. I drilled a slow curve, thrown by Hoyt Wilhelm, clear over the stands onto Grand Avenue. A ball had to have hoist to reach the roof because the right field pavilion at Busch Stadium was nearly 40 feet high, and a screen fronted the stands from the foul-line to the 354-foot mark in right-center. Atop and at the back of the roof was another screen, several feet high, to keep any home-run ball from hitting pedestrians, cars or a plate-glass auto showroom across the street, as Babe Ruth's did once.

My fifth home run that day went even higher over the back screen of the right field roof, even farther out toward right-center. I'm especially proud that it was hit off a knuckleball. Not just any old knuckleball—and they're all pretty tough—but a great knuckler's, Wilhelm's.

The drive came with one on in the seventh inning of another wild game that had been delayed 18 minutes by rain. Despite my hitting, the Giants held the upper hand much of 9-7 second game, which didn't end until 7:55 P.M. I never saw so many fans stay so long, though. They were waiting for one MORE.

When I came up in the ninth, facing righthander Larry Jansen, I, too, had "home run" on my mind. Over-eager, I bit on a bad pitch, a fast ball high and inside. I got under the ball and hit it high, but only to the first baseman. The crowd groaned, then cheered and rushed for the exits, without waiting for the last two outs.

In the clubhouse afterward, Stanky, who had been coaching third base, told reporters I not only had smiled, but actually had laughed as I trotted around the bases after that fifth homer. You know, I just couldn't believe I'd hit five homers in one day—and that no one else ever had.

Never again did I hit home runs with the frequency of the early part of the 1954 season. By the time I hit a three-run triple and a homer off Brooklyn's Carl Erskine in early June, I owned 20 home runs in just 50 games, two games ahead of Babe Ruth's pace.

"I'm still only a singles hitter," I insisted. "The homers are coming to me. I'm not going after them, but just getting out in front of the pitch at times with good wood on a lively ball. There have been a lot of home-run sluggers, but only one Babe Ruth."

(How was I to know that a 1954 rookie named Henry Aaron would hit more career homers than the Babe?)

I believe that—and still do—but I wish I always could have remembered it when, as in 1954, I tried too often to go for the fences. Like many another hitter before and since, I fell under the spell of the magic 60-home-run pace, the barrier Roger Maris finally broke with the help of an extended schedule.

The 1954 season became grim for the Cardinals after Harvey Haddix, our best pitcher, was hurt. Haddix, en route to a second 20-game season early in July, already had 13 victories. He had put together 10 wins in a row, the finest stretch of pitching I ever saw.

Haddix yielded only 15 hits over 36 innings. He pitched successive three-hit shutouts, over Brooklyn and Pittsburgh, white-washed New York on four hits, then followed with a five-hitter at Pittsburgh. There, he missed a record-tying fourth straight shutout only because of a crazy carom and was soon hurt.

The All-Star game Haddix missed could have used a sharp pitcher. Al Rosen hit two homers and other home-town Cleveland players starred as the American League won a wild one, 11-9, before a tremendous 68,751 crowd. Playing left and right fields that day, I had two hits in five tries, but I remember the game mostly because of a balk Bill Stewart, veteran National League umpire, failed to call on Dean Stone when Schoendienst tried to steal home against the young Washington lefthander.

Umpires, though unappreciated and still underpaid, aren't infallible. A couple of weeks later—for one of the rare times in major league history—a game was forfeited when Babe Pinelli judged that Stanky and the Cardinals were stalling excessively to avoid defeat.

The Phillies, sweeping a rain-delayed St. Louis Sunday double-header, led in the second game, 8-1, when darkness made it evident that play could not continue much longer. With two out in the visitors' fifth, after interminable delays, including a fight, Pinelli decided that pitcher Cot Deal of the Cardinals was deliberately pitching wide, low and wild to consume time. The umpire stopped the game and gave it to the Phillies.

At a hearing later in St. Louis, National League president Warren Giles suspended Stanky five days and fined him $100. Giles notified all parties, however, that umpire Pinelli, though undoubtedly right in believing the Cardinals stalled to the point of justifiable forfeiture, was wrong originally in declaring that lights could not be turned on to complete a Sunday game that began later than 6 o'clock. (The second game started at 6:45.) He pointed out, therefore, that the whole mess had been unnecessary. In fact, Giles said, if the Cardinals had protested a misinterpretation of the rules, he would have had to uphold the protest, void the forfeit and order the game resumed.

The "farce," which Giles aptly called it, stung Stanky, who takes his baseball as devoutly as he does his religion. Eddie had already been stunned to hear the St. Louis crowd cheer the umpire for giving the game to the visiting team. The Phillies were managed by a Redbird favorite, Terry Moore, who had been fired by Stanky as a coach. Eddie apologized publicly—humbly and honestly—but the episode didn't help him. Particularly not the way his good-hit, no-pitch ball club was settling deep in the second division.

Defeat can make baseball a grim game, but even a losing season has its lighter sides. We played a late July exhibition for the benefit of the Cleveland sandlot fund before a crowd of nearly 34,000. Having just seen Rosen and Larry Doby show their muscles in the All-Star game there, I wanted to be certain I wasn't embarrassed in a pre-game distance-hitting contest, the first I'd ever entered.

"If I win," I told Greg Masson, the Cardinals' batting practice catcher who was going to pitch to Rip Repulski and me, "there's a $100 suit of clothes in it for you."

Doby hit one out of 10 fair balls over the outfield fence, Rip Repulski and Rosen two each. With Masson laying the ball over the plate, I hit seven "home runs" in 10 tries and hit the right-center field fence with another drive.

After receiving a small trophy from the mayor of Cleveland, I peeled off $100 for a pleased Masson in the clubhouse. "You're a great hitter," Greg chided, "but a helluva economist, paying 100 bucks to win a 10-buck trophy."

Twice during the 1954 season, I was foiled by an unorthodox four-man outfield defense devised by Birdie Tebbetts, imaginative Cincinnati manager. When I came up with two out late in one game, representing the tying run, Tebbetts dropped shortstop Roy McMillan back among the outfielders so that only third baseman Bobby Adams remained on the left side of the infield.

With a yawning hole at shortstop, Birdie was baiting me to go for a basehit rather than the long ball we needed. I went for the long one and Art Fowler struck me out.

"I couldn't put anyone up there on the right field roof," Tebbetts quipped later, "so I was determined Musial wouldn't hit one between my outfielders for two or three bases."

The second time I ran into that four-man outfield, I called time and walked down to talk to Stanky at third base. Did he want me to go for the long one or just to try to get on? I knew that Eddie would ordinarily want me to go for the downs. He knew that customarily I played the team game to the point I wouldn't even ask. But, he knew, I was in a three-way battle with Duke

Snider and Willie Mays for the batting championship.

So with the boss's blessing I went for the basehit and with only Adams available to cover a 90-foot infield strip, I hit the ball right to him!

It was that kind of year and when it was over the Cardinals had finished sixth, the club's poorest showing since 1938. We had led the major leagues in runs scored, but we had also given up the most runs.

Although my batting average dropped to .330 and, after that smashing home-run start, I finished with 35 homers, I'd had a robust season, in many respects my best since 1949. I'd driven in 126 runs, scored 120 and collected 359 total bases out of 195 hits. I believe I got the most satisfaction out of having batted .357 against lefthanders to .312 against righthanders.

Other than the unpleasantness of having played for a sixth-place ball club, I really felt dissatisfied only in having lost ground in a head-to-head battle for the batting title. Down the stretch, I'd always found my second wind, but not in 1954.

The truth is, we'd had a particularly hot summer—St. Louis recorded its hottest day ever, 113 degrees—and I'd tired badly. But it had been hot all over that summer.

As coach Bob Zuppke used to say at Illinois when someone tried to excuse away a football defeat in bad weather, "It always rains on both teams."

Or shines.

17

Down Frank's Lane

The shadows had deepened at Milwaukee's County Stadium except for a deceptive streak of light halfway between the pitcher's mound and home plate. I started out of the first-base dugout to lead off the home team's twelfth inning in the 1955 All-Star game.

Frank Thomas, young Pittsburgh outfielder, called out to me, grinning, "Don't hit like me, hit like Musial. You've been pulling your head, Stan, trying to kill the ball."

I had failed feebly in a game in which, shut out 5-0 for six innings, the National League had rallied to tie. Then we were completely stopped in relief by rangy Frank Sullivan, sidearm sinkerball righthander of the Boston Red Sox.

Determined to get on, I found Yogi Berra, catching for the

American League, unusually quiet for a guy who tried to distract a hitter with lighthearted nonsense. Now, my friend from The Hill in St. Louis merely grumbled.

"What's the matter, Yog?" I inquired.

"It's these extra innings, tough on a guy catching every day," Berra beefed.

Bull-voiced, beet-red Bill Summers, the veteran American League umpire, complained, too, "It's getting just as tough back here."

I nodded. I'd had trouble seeing all day, even before that streak of light caused tricky late-afternoon shadows. "Yeah," I agreed, just before stepping in to face the first pitch, "I'm tired, too."

Sullivan pitched. I swung. The ball sailed high and far toward the right field fence. Even before it fell among leaping spectators, I knew it was gone. So, like Babe Ruth, I didn't bother to sprint. Jogging joyfully around the bases, listening to that partisan National League crowd of 45,000, I wanted to have a wisecrack for Berra when I reached home plate. But as I came around to be met by an escort of fellow National League All-Stars, Yogi already was gone. I guess he'd hit enough home runs himself to know one when he saw one.

The happiest National Leaguer after our 6-5 victory was Leo Durocher, our manager. Even though I wasn't hitting .300 at the All-Star break in 1955 and hadn't been voted into the starting lineup, Durocher had put me into the game as early as the law allowed. In the fourth inning I'd batted for Del Ennis and then gone to left field.

Beaming, Lippy Leo shouted repeatedly in his lusty voice, "He owed me that one . . . he owed me that one . . . after hitting so many against me, including five in one day."

That game-winning All-Star home run was, by far, the high spot of a low season. I called it the Year of the Big Minus because so many of us on the Cardinals were below par.

The club had committed itself to "force feeding," rushing young players into the majors, hopeful they would mature rapidly. Stanky asked me to move back to first base. He wanted to play rookie Bill Virdon, obtained the year before in the Enos Slaughter deal, as the center fielder. Another rookie, Ken Boyer, played third. And Stanky bid for more power production by removing from the front of the right field pavilion a screen that, put up in 1930, had raised the home-run height by more than 25 feet. In '54, Stanky's survey showed, we'd hit the screen 35 times to 15 for the visiting clubs.

When we opened in Chicago, Red Schoendienst and I were not only the sole regulars over 30, but the dean of our pitching staff was Harvey Haddix, who hadn't joined us until late 1952. Our opening-day pitcher, Brooks Lawrence, was beginning his first full season in the majors. I had two hits and drove in a run, but the Cubs once again clobbered us, 13-4.

In late May, we lost a dear friend, our colorful and beloved trainer, Doc Weaver. Before several of us headed to St. Louis for Bucko's funeral, we lost a bitter one-run game in the ninth at Cincinnati. There, cocky Dick Bartell, coaching third for the Reds, taunted Stanky as Eddie steamed across the field for the clubhouse. In the dressing room, Eddie slammed condiment jars which had been placed on an equipment trunk for sandwiches

Stan Musial (right) receives from Bob Feller, longtime Cleveland Indians pitcher, the first Player-of-the-Decade award. The award was established in 1956 by J. G. Taylor Spink, late publisher of *The Sporting News,* for the most outstanding player of the period after World War II. The decision was made by a vote of players, managers, umpires and writers.

between doubleheader games. The mustard ricocheted off the mayonnaise, the jars broke, cutting Eddie's hand ketchup red.

Stanky had a right to be upset then. But such hot-tempered action had piled up against him. And, unfortunately, Eddie wasn't popular in St. Louis. So Gussie Busch, tough he was, and is, fond of Stanky, relieved him as manager and brought in old teammate Harry Walker.

The Hat, as they called the nervous, cap-tugging, talkative former outfielder, was handicapped in the majors because he no longer could lead by forceful example as he had when a playing manager in the minors. Like Stanky, Walker, who inherited a 17-19 record, was also hampered because younger players weren't ready and the older ones were having big seasons.

Not picking up until August when I returned to the outfield as Wally Moon took over at first base, I hit only .319, my lowest average since I'd been ill in 1947. My power production had been good—30 doubles, 33 homers and 108 RBIs—but, reflecting our strange offense, I fell below 100 runs scored for the first time since my rookie season, 1942.

The 1955 Cardinals could hit homers, setting the team record of 155, but we really couldn't score consistently. We finished with 68 victories and wound up seventh, the Cardinals' lowest estate since 1919. It was small consolation that observers—not in St. Louis either—called the '55 Redbirds "the best seventh-place club in history." Somebody must have forgotten the '25 Yankees, pennant winners in 1926.

Unfortunately, when Busch restlessly changed command again, he changed policy, too, bringing in as full-fledged general manager dynamic Frank Lane, who had wheeled and dealed the Chicago White Sox into respectability.

With the Cardinals, however, Frantic Frank said he recognized a "difference." What he meant was that St. Louis had had a farm system, but this was mere lip-service. The first thing he did was to fire Walker and bring in his own manager, Fred Hutchinson of Detroit. Hutch and Lane revived one Redbird tradition by bringing back Terry Moore and Johnny Hopp as coaches, but then the iconoclastic Lane killed another. He removed the time-honored redbird-and-bat insignia from the Cardinal uniform and changed the baseball stockings' basic color from red to blue.

To "stabilize" the young ball club, as he logically put it, Lane acquired a veteran battery on waivers, Ellis Kinder and our old teammate, Walker Cooper. For power, he picked up another high-salaried greybeard, Hank Sauer. And he began to deal doubtfully when he sent righthander Brooks Lawrence to Cincinnati for southpaw Jackie Collum.

Lane decided to reinstall the screen in front of the right field pavilion and, though the decision wouldn't help me, I couldn't blame him. We'd hit just 28 to the opposition's 24. I'd hit the most into unscreened seats—seven—but I can testify that pitchers were more determined than ever not to let me pull the ball.

I was pleased when Hutchinson decided to play me in the outfield—figures showed I'd always hit better there.

The 1956 ball club picked up momentum late in spring training and continued the fast pace during the regular season. I hit a two-run homer off Joe Nuxhall for a 4-2 opening-game victory over Cincinnati and by near mid-May we were in a virtual tie with Milwaukee for first place.

Then Lane began to wheel and deal recklessly. He said that he figured six players were "untradable"—Schoendienst, Boyer, Virdon, Moon, Haddix and me. But soon Haddix, Virdon and even Schoendienst were gone. Except for business partner Biggie Garagnani, I might have been swapped, too, for the Phillies' Robin Roberts.

The trading-deadline deal that sent Schoendienst to the New York Giants in exchange for shortstop Alvin Dark made sense only because Lane previously had unloaded his one steady shortstop, Alex Grammas. But it angered the St. Louis populace. They reacted both to the ball club and to the brewery, which has long, sensitive antennae.

A year later, traded to Milwaukee, Schoendienst beat us out of a pennant. I was heartsick at losing my close friend and roomie. Then Biggie came to me and said that, after checking out a tip with bloodhound J. G. Taylor Spink, knowledgeable publisher of *The Sporting News,* he had learned I was next. Wondering whether he had done all right, Garagnani said he had told the brewery that I wouldn't report to Philadelphia.

Honestly, if pressed, I would undoubtedly have gone. I wasn't ready to quit, but, fed up with rumors as well as watching our clubhouse fill with a steady stream of strange faces, I told Biggie he'd been right. Suddenly, at Busch's insistence, Lane denied I would be traded.

From then on, the brewery withdrew Frank's carte blanche privilege. Under the restraint of checking with Dick Meyer and Busch before dealing, he was a better and wiser trader in 1957.

Meanwhile, I had my moments, but not enough of them. At Pittsburgh, facing Vernon Law, I beat the Deacon, 3-1, with one of the longest home runs of my career. It was a line drive over the seldom-cleared brick wall in dead center field at former Forbes Field—436 feet from the plate.

At mid-season, I received an honor I deeply appreciated. *The*

Sporting News had completed a poll of 10-year players, managers, scouts, umpires, clubowners, baseball writers and broadcasters to determine its first Player-of-the-Decade award. I was flattered to be selected over Joe DiMaggio, Ted Williams, Bob Feller, Jackie Robinson and others.

At an awards' luncheon the day before the All-Star game, I received Spink's handsome grandfather's clock that is exhibited now in the St. Louis Sports Hall of Fame at Busch Memorial Stadium. I meant it that day, when I said:

"I can't hit like Williams, field like DiMaggio or throw like Feller."

But I did enjoy competition, as I believe I proved again in the All-Star game we won 7-3 at Griffith Stadium. My young St. Louis teammate, Ken Boyer, collected three hits and made two dazzling diving stops at third base there. An amusing thing happened, too.

In the sixth inning Ted Williams hit a tremendous home run into the right-center bullpen off Warren Spahn. Pressbox historians thumbed through their records and, by sheer coincidence, just as I came to bat in the visitors' seventh, a voice announced over the intercom:

"Ted Williams' home run was his fourth in All-Star competition and tied Stan Musial . . ."

Just then I hit the first pitch from Boston righthander Mel Brewer into the left-center field stands.

"Sorry," said the pressbox voice, to laughter, "Mr. Musial has just untied the record."

Slumping in August, I did some thing really rare for me. That game I fouled up afield, fumbling a ground ball at first and then throwing past second another time with a doubleplay chance. As I went to bat, I heard the loudest boos and juiciest oral razzberries of my career.

The next day Musial loyalists took out paid advertisements of apology in the St. Louis newspapers. That was nice, certainly, but there's no getting around the fact that I played my worst ball game on Aug. 22, 1956. That first lusty booing in St. Louis had been a long time coming, but, as Frank Lane said, the fans wouldn't forget 15 years in 15 minutes.

I—we—didn't do too well that uncertain season of '56. My average, .310, was the lowest even though I led the league in RBIs, 100. With Henry Aaron leading in batting with only .328, the hitting title would have been an easy one to win.

Players traded away in 1956 hit more or pitched better than players we'd obtained. But the greatest sacrifice—youth and speed—couldn't be measured. For a club that tailed off from a 13-7 record when Lane made his first trade, to 28-25 when he made his last one, then down to a distance fourth with 76-78 at the finish, we still played a part in a hot three-way pennant race.

Early in September, we swept a three-game series from Cincinnati to knock the Reds three games behind league-leading Milwaukee. By the time the Braves came to St. Louis for the last series of the lead, they were ahead of Brooklyn by one game.

The first night we knocked out Bob Buhl to win, 5-4. Aware that Milwaukee's park was bigger than Brooklyn's, Terry Moore quipped that "We play like heck to lose money (Series shares), but I'm glad to see someone else sweating for a pennant. That's how we had to do it."

After the Dodgers had swept a Saturday afternoon doubleheader from Pittsburgh, the next night's climactic contest, was truly a classic. Time and again, Bobby Del Greco, the small-sized large disappointment Lane had acquired from Pittsburgh for Virdon, robbed the Braves with the inspirational center fielding of a Tee Moore or Curt Flood, Joe DiMaggio or Willie Mays.

In the twelfth inning I doubled to right-center off Spahn. And when Rip Repulski's grounder glanced off Eddie Mathews' glove for a scratch single, I scored to beat the Braves, 2-1, in a game that cost them the pennant.

Spahnie, beaten despite a masterful performance by his arm and Del Greco's glove, strode off the mound, head down, tears of frustration in his eyes. Angrily, he fired his glove at a photographer who had leaped out to catch the noble warrior in an unguarded moment of grief.

Spahn missed, but, to the Braves' haunting dismay, so did Del Greco on the first ball Milwaukee hit to him on opening day in '57. The Braves really let Bobby have it, and good, then. But, as Spahn has said more than once, the Cardinals' series victory over the Braves at the end of the 1956 season, which cost each member of the Redbirds a few bucks out of the World Series financial pool, proved an expensive, yet noble example of professional pride and integrity.

18

The Seventh Crown

I had a secret in 1957, one of the best and most exciting years in my career, one of the most satisfying, and yet frustrating.

The secret had begun to mull in the off-season as I settled into the pleasant pace of family life. I experienced that fall the exhausting, vicarious joy of a father watching a son in high school football. Dick, blond and good-looking like his mother, didn't have my size, but he had my speed—my FORMER speed—as a breakaway halfback. Dick attended Christian Brothers College, a military high school operated by a Catholic teaching order. He loved the school, the brothers, football and track, too. He liked baseball, but the uncomfortable comparison with a big league father always had made the game difficult for him.

If subconsciously Dick envied my baseball ability, certainly I

When Stan Musial was honored in St. Louis early in 1957, five of the first six big league managers for whom he had played were present. From the left, Eddie Dyer, Eddie Stanky, Harry (The Hat) Walker, Musial, Fred Hutchinson and Marty Marion. Only Billy Southworth could not make it.

wished many times, cheering him on a long run for C.B.C., that I'd been able to play his game—and play it as well as he did.

During the winter before the 1957 season, I decided—with Lil's encouragement—to give up smoking. For years I had smoked occasionally, but in 1956 I really had picked up the nicotine habit. I think heavy cigarette smoking affected my nervous system, my concentration and my vision. I know I felt better, stronger, after I quit.

In January, I was guest of honor at a fund-raising dinner given by the St. Louis branch of the Denver American Cancer Hospital. I mention it only because it brought together five of the six managers I had played for. Only Billy Southworth hadn't been able to come. I appreciated very much the presence of Eddie Dyer, Marty Marion, Eddie Stanky, Harry Walker and Fred Hutchinson. I appreciated most what Stanky and Walker had to

say because they touched on my whole philosophy of playing:

I don't believe in star-system special privileges in a team game—whether practicing, playing or traveling. I do believe that going all-out brings its individual rewards as well as its team benefits. For instance, if a batter breaks away from the plate at full speed, he'll often get the extra base that eludes him if he waits until rounding first base to shift into high gear. It's too late at that point to realize that a long single might have been a short double.

The highlight of that dinner, with my mother, Dick Kerr and Ki Duda there as guests, came when the boss, Gussie Busch, announced that no other Cardinal player ever would wear my number—"6." The Cardinals never had retired a number.

A couple of days later I sat down for the annual contract ceremonies with Mr. Busch. I had agreed beforehand with Frank Lane to take what amounted to my first salary cut. After dropping from .337 to .330, then .319 and finally .310, I saw no reason to quibble over $5000 even though I had led the National League in RBIs. Despite my steady decline, Mr. Busch told me he thought I would win "another silver bat," symbolic of the batting championship. At 37, five years after having won my sixth hitting title, I could have felt that Gussie was too optimistic, but I honestly didn't.

"I believe I've got a chance to match my lifetime average," I told reporters, then smiled. "That used to mean .350. Now it means .340."

I felt good about the ball club, too. Under restraint, Frank Lane had proved that he could trade well. Off-season deals for pitcher Sam Jones and outfielder Del Ennis, both in disfavor elsewhere, made sense. Jones, a righthander with a good fast ball and as wicked a curve as anyone ever saw, had been wild enough that the Cubs had lost patience with him. Ennis, a constant run-producer in his home town, Philadelphia, had outlived his welcome there because, of what I guess, seemed to be defensive nonchalance.

Despite those trades, the bad ones still rankled Mr. Busch. At the annual pre-spring-training dinner of the Knights of the Cauliflower Ear, a St. Louis sportsmen's group which he and I belong to, he said:

"I expect the Cardinals to come close to winning a pennant in 1957—and 1958 is going to have to be a sure thing—or Frank Lane will be out on his rump."

Just before spring training, Lil and I spent two weeks in the Bahamas, so I was strong and rested when I reached camp, eager to work on my "secret."

To amplify what I said at the outset, I thought it most important for a hitter to concentrate mentally, to relax physically and to avoid hitting the fly ball to the deepest part of the park, center field.

When fatigue set in over a 154-game schedule, wiggling my fanny to unlock the hips and flexing my fingers to make certain my hands and wrists weren't petrified in over-eagerness, I found carelessness and lack of concentration the hardest thing to fight. Then along came the slider, which I had first seen Ray Starr throw to complicate hitting at Cincinnati in 1943.

The slider, used wisely and well by a pitcher with control, can trouble a good hitter. That happens no matter what any older, old-timer might sneeringly say about the sophisticated pitch that looks like a fast ball, yet breaks like a curve.

I could detect the spin of a curve ball, but I couldn't tell until late that a slider wasn't a fast ball. Therefore, striding into the ball as I did, I had found myself fooled just enough to miss getting the fat part of the bat on the ball. And remember, please, that I swung a light, thin-handled bat, at times as light as 30 ounces. My bat, with a thick barrel modeled after Jimmy Foxx's bat at the butt end, had a slender Babe Ruth handle because I didn't have large hands. And though I prided myself on breaking few bats and repeatedly smudging the bat out there on the big business end of the wood, I didn't like that pitch darting unexpectedly in on my fists.

That was the righthander's slider, which seemed a fast ball inside to pull until it moved abruptly toward the hands three or four inches, just enough to jam me. Ted Williams, also troubled, began to hit off the slider rather than the fast ball, relying on his trigger-quick hands to recover if the pitch were the fast one. Me? I came up with my own "secret" for attacking the pitch that has trimmed points off ALL batters' averages.

To try to join the slider, if I couldn't beat it, I decided not to stride directly toward the plate. By cutting down the degree of my stride, I'd leave the outside part of the plate unprotected for a well-controlled fast ball, but how many pitchers can thread three straight strikes across the outside corner? Besides, if I didn't make the change too obvious, maybe I could get by, at least for a while. Maybe during that time, pitchers would continue to move the ball in and out on me, trying with the pitch inside to dart that slider toward my bat handle.

The change proved an immediate success. I had the best opening day of my career in an easy victory at Cincinnati—"4 for 4," including two doubles.

If rain hadn't prevented the second game of the 1957 season at Crosley Field, my consecutive-game streak would have ended at 775, short of Gus Suhr's record 822. Swinging the last time up on opening day, I'd suffered a deep muscle injury and massive internal hemorrhages in the lower back. The muscles spasmed, bunched up as hard as ridged wood. I remember that both Fred Hutchinson and Frank Lane were pale as they watched trainer Bob Bauman treat the injury.

Bauman's expert treatment—and the rain—kept me in the lineup. Doc sprayed my back with a thin stream of freezing ethyl chloride to shock and relax the hardened tissues, then taped me like a mummy and advised that I fly to St. Louis that evening rather than take a long overnight train ride. Back home, I used the portable whirlpool I had bought as a concession to athletic old age. The next day, an open date in St. Louis, Bauman used an ultra-sonic appliance on my back so long that he must have felt like an overworked shirt-presser in a Chinese laundry. Thanks to good ol' Bo, I was back at first base in the Cardinals' home opener the following night.

Despite the injury, the secret was holding, and I got off to my finest start since 1950. I was hitting better than .400 at the end of April when I homered in the thirteenth for Hit No. 2801 to beat Roy Face at Pittsburgh.

Our infield defense was poor through the opening weeks. Even an excellent third baseman, young Ken Boyer, was caught up in the ragged play. At New York, the old Gas House Gang foreman, Frank Frisch, advised Lane, "Tell the players they're not going to be traded, so they can settle down. The whole team is jittery."

With the club floundering in May, Gussie Busch made one of his infrequent playing-field suggestions. Why, he wondered, with center field still our biggest problem, didn't Hutchinson move versatile Boyer to center and play rookie Eddie Kasko at third base? Hutch made the switch and it helped considerably.

We went into June just under .500 and hardly resembling a pennant contender. Our pitching was the poorest in the league. Not only did we have a third baseman playing center field and a shortstop at third base, but a first baseman, clutch-hitting Joe Cunningham, was playing the outfield part-time. Pitching help came from the most unexpected sources—from babes.

At Milwaukee, Lindy McDaniel beat the Braves, 4-3, and I called Bob Broeg over to listen to what the 21-year-old righthander, less than two years off his family's Oklahoma farm, had told me when I congratulated him. "If you won't give any walks or any home runs, it's going to take a lot of singles to beat you," Lindy said.

That's as pithy a description of the art of pitching as I've ever heard.

Listening, too, was Lindy's 18-year-old brother, Von, a 6-foot-3, 190-pound bonus pitcher we had just signed as a June high school graduate. Astonishingly, a few days later, the younger farm boy made a near-perfect four-inning relief appearance in a game already lost at Philadelphia.

Von's debut came just after I tied and then broke the National League endurance record. I missed only 16 games my first 13 full years in the major leagues and none over a five-year period, that could have been considerably longer if Marty Marion hadn't urged me to take off the final game of the 1951 season. But I'm not as proud of the consecutive-game record as I would like to be. It was, unfortunately, tainted, and I was relieved to see Billy Williams break it with Chicago.

Back in August, 1955, just after I had been hit on the back of the hand, manager Harry Walker had circumvented at least the spirit of the consecutive-game streak merely by listing me in the batting order of a game at Pittsburgh. Then he had Pete Whisenant bat for me when my turn came up in the first inning. Technically I had been in the ball game, but actually I hadn't. Although I couldn't swing properly, I could have played and frankly would have preferred to, so I was sensitive to criticism about the "phoney" record.

Until the last couple of seasons before I was credited with

breaking Suhr's consecutive-game record, I played because I loved to be in the lineup, because the ball club needed me, and because I didn't bruise easily. When I did get hurt, I healed quickly. My only selfish consideration in being in there, if it's selfish to want to hit, had been the determined quest of the 3000 hits.

The night I broke Suhr's record, getting a single and double that boosted my average to .385 as we beat the Phillies, Frank Lane wheeled out a big cake with three large numbers—"823." I was particularly pleased by a wire from Millbrae, Calif., from a man I had rooted for as a kid at Pittsburgh. Gus Suhr's telegram read, "Congratulations on breaking the National League record for consecutive games played. Rooting for you to get 3000 hits—sincerely."

Best of all, our eighth straight victory put us back in the race.

A spectacular swing through the east was climaxed with our first doubleheader victory at Brooklyn since 1945. In it, Von McDaniel pitched four more scoreless innings and was rewarded with a big league victory—in only his second professional game. After Von had allowed his only hit to the Dodgers, who trailed by a run, menacing Duke Snider strode to the plate. Alvin Dark trotted in from shortstop and inquired, helpfully, "Do you know who's batting, Von?"

"Oh, sure," said the polite 4-H boy. "It's Mr. Snider."

As Hutchinson said, Von McDaniel was the most remarkable, the most poised, young pitcher he—or any of us—had ever seen. And Hutch had been a schoolboy wonder himself.

A week later Von made his first start at St. Louis against the champion Dodgers before nearly a capacity crowd. The kid said I was his idol, but I'm afraid that night I proved I had feet of clay. I not only ended a 20-game hitting streak, but after Junior Gilliam's looping liner in the sixth inning became Brooklyn's first hit, I fumbled a bunt by Pee Wee Reese. When Snider also bunted and reached base safely, the Dodgers had the bases loaded with none out.

Even an experienced pitcher might have quavered in that spot, but Von McDaniel, only two weeks off the farm in the forlorn southwest corner of Oklahoma, acted as if he was still pitching on that red-clay high school field, which ran uphill. He induced Elmer Valo to tap to him for a double play by way of home plate, then threw out Gino Cimoli and walked off the field to one of the greatest ovations I've ever heard. He won a two-hitter that night, 2-0.

Von's string of four straight victories provided both an actual and a psychological lift to our club. From a point eight and a half games out on May 25, we stormed into first place, knocking out Cincinnati with a four-game series sweep, and opened a two-and-a-half-length lead at the All-Star break.

St. Louis, host to the All-Star game that year, was more excited over the pennant race, although a full house turned out to see the American League beat us, 6-5, in a game in which I had one hit, a double, in three trips.

Tiring, I agreed heartily with Fred Hutchinson that the wise thing was to begin to sit out the second games of doubleheaders in hot weather. On a scorcher in Pittsburgh July 22, my consecutive-game streak probably would have ended, except that the second contest was suspended by the Pennsylvania curfew after eight innings. If I played the ninth inning when the game was resumed at a later date, I would be considered to have played on the date of the original game. Frankly, I didn't care. Slumping, all I could think of now was to help the Cardinals hold the league lead and maybe regain the batting lead myself. Pitchers had wised up to my changed batting stance.

I remember that just after Von McDaniel pitched a one-hit victory over the Pirates, I had a big day that regained the league lead for us at the beginning of August. I had 4 for 4 against the Giants, including two home runs. When I arrived home that evening, daughter Gerry, 13, was extremely happy—the autographed picture of Elvis Presley I'd promised her had just arrived from Memphis.

Deflating? That's nothing. "Daddy," Gerry tried to sweet-talk me, "why don't you bring my favorite player home to dinner?"

Her favorite player?

"Sure, Von McDaniel. He's so cute."

My second daughter, Janet, just 8, had to get into the act.

"Bring home my favorite, too, Daddy, Don Blasingame. He's cuter."

Blasingame couldn't wait for Janet to grow up. He married beautiful blonde Miss Missouri, Sara Cooper, daughter of our veteran teammate, Walker Cooper.

"If you have boys," big Coop told the little Blazer, "you can make a fortune if they hit like me and run like you, but they'll probably run like me and hit like you."

Just after we came up with Billy Muffett, a relief pitcher who worked brilliantly the rest of the season, our momentum ground to a halt. Baseball is a game of momentum—good and bad.

Clinging to first place in a close five-club race, we had won eight in a row into the first week in August before the Phillies' Harry Anderson stopped us with a two-out ninth-inning home run. As Bob Bauman has said after nearly 40 years as trainer for the Browns and Cardinals, a three-week home stand is too much in St. Louis in the summer. Bat-weary, we dropped nine straight, the Cardinals' longest losing streak in 10 years. Coincidentally, three other contenders also cooled off. The other one, Milwaukee, got as hot as the weather, won 10 in a row and—just like that—opened a nine-length lead.

By the time we moved from Chicago to Milwaukee for a return series with the Braves, the race seemed over. Hutchinson, trying to relax a tense, tired team that had scored only 13 runs during the nine straight defeats, let the word get around as we reached Milwaukee that he had suspended the 12 o'clock curfew that night.

"The McDaniel boys," Hutch said, forcing a smile, "might even indulge with a double-thick malted milk."

The Big Bear carried his managerial psychology a bit further the following night when we opened the four-game series at County Stadium. The batting-order card he posted in the dugout had none of the regulars in the lineup. It listed our equipment manager, Butch Yatkeman; the visiting clubhouse attendant, Tommy Ferguson; coaches Terry Moore, Stan Hack and Al Hollingsworth; my son, Dick; Hollingsworth's boy, John; 42-year-old catcher Walker Cooper and our 18-year-old bonus righthander, seldom-seen Bob Miller.

The gag was good for a laugh, which is what Hutch wanted. It relaxed everyone except the Braves, who suddenly discovered that the race wasn't over, after all. We won three out of four and missed a series sweep only because Ennis wasn't able to hold a low line drive in left field.

We were still in the race, five and a half games out, as we went east for the last time. I'd had a good series at Milwaukee, winning one game with a tenth-inning homer off Juan Pizarro. At New York, I was even luckier. I hit home runs off Curt Barclay and Johnny Antonelli to give us one-run victories in both games of a low-score doubleheader, 4-3 and 3-2. With the Giants already having announced they would move to San Francisco, I played what seemed likely to be my last game in the Polo Grounds and went "2 for 2," with a homer off Stu Miller, in a one-sided Redbird victory.

I had good personal reason to be sorry to see the Giants leave New York, after having hit nine of my 29 homers off their pitchers, six at the Polo Grounds. But there was more than selfishness involved. As I said then, I'd always regarded New York fans as the fairest and the smartest I'd ever seen. And I've certainly seen many assorted crowds, all of whom really have been kind to me.

I looked forward to one more visit to my happy hunting grounds, Ebbets Field, but I never got there. Before going to

Brooklyn, we moved over to Philadelphia. And there, Aug. 23, with Wally Moon breaking on a hit-and-run play, I swung at a high, outside pitch, difficult to pull, and tried to jerk it around behind the runner. The swing was awkward and exerted tremendous unnatural pressure. I yanked the left arm out of joint, fractured the bone of the shoulder socket and tore most of the heavy muscles over both the collarbone and shoulder blade. Unaware I was severely hurt, I finished the time at bat, grounding out, but when I tried to throw the ball around the infield, I couldn't raise my arm.

Hitting .340, I hated to leave the lineup when the ball club had a pennant chance, but I couldn't agree with medical opinions that the chipped fracture and accompanying shoulder injuries would keep me out the final five weeks of the season. I really didn't care that the consecutive-game streak ended at 895.

The important thing was that while I was out, the Cardinals hung in the race. Sixteen days after I'd been hurt, I managed to take batting practice and returned to the game as a pinch-hitter against Joe Nuxhall, Cincinnati southpaw. The shoulder still hurt, but, punching the ball, I singled to start a winning rally.

A week later, though I really couldn't throw, I convinced Hutch that I could play without risk. After all, I pointed out, Cunningham hadn't had to make a tough throw at first base. We swept a doubleheader that day at Pittsburgh and I poked three hits, two of them doubles. We were only two and a half games behind.

Every day someone else came through in the clutch as we won time and again by coming from behind, giving us 13 victories in 17 games since Labor Day. But then, just before we went into Milwaukee to begin the final week's play, Jerry Lynch homered off Herm Wehmeier at Cincinnati to tie us in the ninth and Roy McMillan's first home run of the season beat Wehmeier in the tenth.

That one, a body blow, took pressure off the Braves, who clinched the pennant on Sept. 23. We battled them into the eleventh inning of a game in which I'd singled and doubled off Lew Burdette at County Stadium, but then Henry Aaron hit the home run that did it. There was dancing in the streets of Milwaukee even before Hutch walked across the field to congratulate Fred Haney, a little twinkle-eyed baseball veteran who had waited a long time for that moment of triumph.

Frank Lane, often critical when worked up in the heat of a game, paid tribute to the 1957 Cardinals. "This is a heroic ball club, a bunch of guys who wouldn't quit and I admire 'em for their magnificent battle," he said.

You need kind words when you've lost baseball's great prize, a pennant, but I knew in my heart we didn't have the better team. Hutch had done a masterful job and the players had "picked one another up," as we say in the dugout—except for that unforgettable nine-game spell at the plate in the dog days of early August.

I, of course, had the best consolation prize of all the Cardinals, most of whom welcomed the $1200 second-place money far more than I. At nearly 37, after a five-year wait, I'd hit .351 to win a seventh batting championship and had driven in 102 runs out of 171 in scoring position. And I'd been named National League Player of the Year by *The Sporting News*.

From the time I returned to the lineup after my injury, just stroking the ball because of my shoulder, I'd collected 16 hits in 31 times at bat. The last one was a pinch single that helped us clinch second place.

Afterward, Hutchinson came to me in the Milwaukee clubhouse, stuck out his hand and said:

"You're my Most Valuable Player candidate, Stan. Take off the last three days while I look at some kids. Those other guys couldn't catch you in the batting race if they tried all winter."

19

"3000"

Ever hear of a ball player getting more money than he expected—or asked—for anytime before the free agent bonanza of 1976?

I did in 1958.

By the time contract-negotiating came around, a new general manager sat in the swivel chair at Busch Stadium. In November, Frank Lane, with a year still to go on his Cardinal contract, had left for Cleveland. He never had gotten over the public win-or-else rebuke, just as Mr. Busch never got over Lane's early irresponsible deals. Lane's latest miff: Management wouldn't let him trade Ken Boyer to Pittsburgh.

Boyer, a third baseman used in center field, had been just about the only regular who hadn't played up to par or better in

Stan Musial and one of his biggest boosters, Bing Devine, the Cardinals' general manager from 1958-64, and again since 1968, when "Der Bingle" succeeded The Man as G.M.

1957. Even so, the new general manager, Bing Devine, gambled that the Boyer who had hit over .300 and with power in 1956 was the true Boyer, rather than the one who had hit just over .260 as a rookie in 1955 and again in '57. The first thing Devine did when he took over was to turn his back on the Pittsburgh offer. He also rejected Philadelphia's bid of Richie Ashburn, to fill our center field vacancy, and pitcher Harvey Haddix. Philadelphia's offer was fair, but Devine's decision was one of his best. Boyer stayed with the Cardinals to become one of the best and highest-salaried players in the National League.

Devine, 40 when he became general manager, was a career organization man, a Washington University graduate who had grown up in the Cardinals' Knothole Gang, watching the championship club of the mid-20's and early 30's. He had spent nearly 20 years working up through the front-office ranks after a brief Class D playing career.

I've had many pleasant moments with this quiet, unassuming, deep-thinking man of ability and integrity, and one of the earliest was most surprising.

I'd had a big year in 1957 and the Cardinals had drawn nearly 1,200,000 home attendance, their best since 1949. I looked forward to my first pay increase in several seasons, but, at 37, I didn't intend to be unreasonable. Devine wanted to know what I had in mind.

"I'd like," I said, "to be the highest-salaried player the National League has had. I believe Pittsburgh paid Ralph Kiner about $90,000."

Devine stuck out his hand and we agreed on $91,000. Before the formal signing at the brewery, though, Bing called me back into his office.

"I've got pleasant news for you, Stan," he said. "Mr. Busch wants you not only to become the highest-salaried player in National League history, but the first to receive $100,000."

When I signed gratefully in the big bosses' office, I winked at Mary Murphy. The little old Irish lady with the rosy cheeks chuckled merrily when I said, "Did you think, Miss Murphy, when I signed for $4250 in 1942 that I'd ever be in this position?"

There was a pleasant preview of 1958 for me at Key West. In that February meeting of player representatives, Bob Feller suggested a benefit game, and we raised $10,000 for baseball's old-timers. We played without benefit of spring training, so I made certain not to reinjure the left shoulder. I just stroked the ball, as I had the final month of 1957, and hit safely three times.

That shoulder injury had emphasized how quickly a career might be ended. Although certain by now that I could play another year or two beyond 1958, I had a burning desire to get the 3000 hits, only 43 away.

"I'm going out to get them in a hurry," I said the night before the season started, "because—who knows?—I might get hit by a cab."

I estimated late May as the target date, but I had a disappointing first effort in as frustrating an opener as I ever played. We got seven hits and eight walks off Jim Brosnan and three other Chicago pitchers, but left 15 men on base in a 4-0 loss. I not only singled just once in five trips, but I struck out twice.

That game symbolized the season for the Cardinals. Alvin Dark, a fine leader, had slowed at shortstop, and Fred Hutchinson found himself wishing that he could play Boyer both in center field and at third base. The pitching also had suffered. The McDaniel boys, the babes who had contributed so much in 1957, encountered trouble.

Lindy had to be farmed out to Omaha for a time in '58, but returned to become one of the best relief pitchers I ever saw. Young Von couldn't make it and gamely returned to the infield in the minors. Had he just been lucky? An accident? No one will ever know, definitely.

I think this: At 18, the kid was doing instinctively what polished, older pitchers learn only through experience. He started college in the winter and failed for the first time to play basketball. So, at 19, he felt the weakness and weariness that all ball players do, particularly pitchers, in spring training. Puzzled that he couldn't throw hard, Von tried harder. He lost rhythm and control. When he lost control, he lost an even more precious commodity—confidence.

The McDaniels weren't the only problems in 1958. The ball club had forgotten over the winter how to win in a league in which it needed new directions. The National League had changed face in 1958, with San Francisco replacing New York and Los Angeles taking over for Brooklyn. And that brought the air age to baseball.

Even though hitting hard and often early, I knew I'd lost two favorite hitting targets, Ebbets Field and Polo Grounds, and had picked up two ball parks reputedly tough for lefthanded hitters. Sure enough, on a raw, chilly night at San Francisco's roofless Seals Stadium, the park the Giants temporarily had taken over, I found that the trade winds made it tough for a lefthander. The fences were at equitable distances, but the brisk breeze gave wings to anything hit to left field and served as an anchor on drives smashed to right.

Although not a righthanded hitter, at least I could try to hit like one. Given a wonderful reception by San Francisco fans and just punching the ball to the opposite field, I doubled once and singled twice as we won a night game. In our only other victory in six games I'd hit two homers at Chicago.

A spectator at San Francisco said something that interested me. "Musial still runs good," Ty Cobb told Jack McDonald of the *Call-Bulletin.* "His legs are holding up. There's no reason he couldn't play as long as I did."

Old Tyrus had played until he was 42, when he still hit .324.

That first trip to San Francisco was good for me, but bad for the club. So that really meant bad for me, too. Not even the most delightful restaurants in a city of so many good ones can take away the bitterness of the horrible late-inning games we lost on that first trip west in 1958.

In one game the Giants got two runs on homers by veteran Hank Sauer, my former roommate, who credited me with having helped his comeback by urging him to swing a lighter bat. It's just common sense, as a player gets older and his reflexes slower, to try to compensate for nature's toll by going to a more easily handled bat.

At Los Angeles, experiencing the contrasts of tempo between northern and southern California, we found another good hitter in trouble. Before a night game which attracted more than 60,000, Duke Snider pointed out the inequities of the Coliseum, the famous football and track stadium converted into a temporary baseball park. The high left field screen was only 250 feet from home plate and left-center a mere 310, but the distance to right-center, 440 feet, actually was even deeper than to dead center.

The Duke, a great home-run hitter at Brooklyn, was bitter about the disadvantage of the lopsided field to lefthanded hitters. At the batting cage, where we talked briefly, I tried to console him.

"You can't let this thing throw you," I told him. "You can't beat a park like this, so join it."

The night I tried to prove my point, I lined four singles in four times at bat. But we lost again. Afterward, the Dodgers' general manager, Buzzy Bavasi, gently needled his old friend, Bing Devine:

"What are you going to do when Musial goes back to hitting like Musial, which is enough, and quits acting as if he's afraid there's going to be no tomorrow?"

I finished that first trip to the West Coast with the same figures in San Francisco as Los Angeles—seven for 11. I wasn't always so successful out there, but I believe I did prove that a lefthanded hitter could beat the unfavorable wind in Seals Stadium, the distant fences in the Coliseum.

Although I was hitting exceptionally well, I'd been leading off too many innings, and we lost 14 of our first 17 games. Then on the Sunday, May 11, that partner Biggie Garagnani and I closed down our restaurant and threw a private party in anticipation of my 3000th hit, the Cardinals and I had a big day. We came from behind twice in the ninth inning to beat the Cubs, and I had five hits. Even though I was batting .484, I was still two hits short of the golden goal. So when Lil and I left the dinner party to catch a midnight train for a two-game series in Chicago, several of our friends came along. They knew just how much the 3000-hit goal meant to me.

I had hoped very much to reach the goal in my adopted home, St. Louis. We won the first game at Chicago and I added a double. That left me just one hit away. I said almost idly to coach Terry Moore, "You know, Tee, I hope we win tomorrow, but I'd like to walk every time up—and save the big one for St. Louis."

Moore mentioned my wistful thought to manager Hutchinson,

who huddled over a beer with his coaches at the hotel and then phoned me in my suite. He told me that, unless he needed me to pinch-hit the next afternoon, I wouldn't play.

"That way, you'll get the big one at home," he said.

"Thanks, Hutch," I told him. "I'll do anything you say, you know, but I am grateful."

Hutchinson, forthright as usual, called St. Louis writers traveling with the Cardinals and explained his decision. "I could say Stan has a bellyache and nobody would question this, but I'm not going to lie," the Big Bear said bluntly. "We'll use him if we need him, but I just hate to see the guy get the big one before three or four thousand when his closest fans, the ones back home, can have the chance a day later."

Lil and I looked forward to a relaxed evening with our friends, particularly to the treat of watching Frank Pizzica enjoying himself. My old Monongahela basketball sponsor is a fun-loving, effervescent man. His wife, Molly, a kind, home-loving woman who seldom tries to keep up with him, had gone up to their hotel room to rest before dinner while the others had a drink or two.

By the time our party gathered in the lobby for dinner out, I had Hutch's permission to shade the midnight curfew. I counted heads. "Where's Molly?" I asked.

That was to become our cry into the night—"Where's Molly?"

Pizzica called the room. No answer. He went up to the room. No Molly. We tried rooms and suites occupied by others in the party. No Molly. The lobby again. The bar. The dining room. Michigan Boulevard. Three nearby movie houses. No Molly.

We called the police, who checked all the hospitals. By then, we were as frightened as we were puzzled. Hours later, at a quarter to 3, I finally gave up and went to bed. Still no Molly.

At 9 A.M. our phone rang. Sleepy-eyed, I answered. It was Molly!

"Where have you been?" she demanded, "and where's Frank?"

"Where have WE been, Molly! Where have YOU been? Frank is in your room."

"No, he isn't," came the puzzled, frightened reply. "He has stayed out all night and I'm worried."

It was my turn to be bewildered, but, step by step, though it took time to convince Molly that she, not we, had been lost, we pieced together a story that became funnier the more we thought about it.

When Molly decided to take a nap after the ball game the previous afternoon, she had stepped off the hotel elevator at the wrong floor. She had the right key, but the wrong room and couldn't open the door. The elevator man came to her aid with a pass key and Molly went in.

Tired, she dozed off, napped longer than she intended, waiting for our call. Finally, convinced we had gone on, still weary, a bit miffed and more than just a little timid in the big city, too, Molly had spent the night in a room that she thought was her own. And she hadn't phoned me earlier because she didn't want to interfere with my rest!

I was still a little tired at Wrigley Field that afternoon, even after trainer Bob Bauman, laughing all the while at my account of the Case of the Missing Woman, rubbed my legs with oil of wintergreen. Since I wasn't playing, I decided to sit down in the right field bullpen and soak up the mid-May sunshine. But in the sixth inning when we trailed, 3-1, with a runner on second base and one out, pitching coach Boots Hollingsworth nudged me.

"Hey, Stan," he said, motioning to the dugout, "Hutch wants you."

A sound began to rise as I walked toward the bench. There were fewer than 6000 persons in Wrigley Field on May 13, 1958, but when I picked up a bat and started toward the plate, they made tremendous noise. Field announcer Pat Pieper, who went back almost as far as Tinker-to-Evers-to-Chance, said in his clipped, clear style:

"Attenshun . . . number 6 . . . Stan Mus-i-al . . . batting for Sam Jones."

The pitcher was a young Pole, Moe Drabowsky, who had me beat on at least one point. He'd actually been born in Poland. When the count reached "2 and 2," Moe fired a curve ball for the outside corner. I picked up the spin of the pitch, strode into the ball and drove it on a deep line into left field. I knew as soon as it left my bat that it would go between the left fielder, Moose Moryn, and the foul line.

When I pulled into second base with my 3000th hit, which scored a run, I heard a deafening roar. The third base umpire, Frank Dascoli, who claimed the ball when it was returned to the infield, came hurrying over, smiling. He handed it to me and offered congratulations.

As I turned toward first base, there was a sight that must have reminded spectators of an old Keystone cop comedy. Fred Hutchinson was lumbering toward me, followed by a swarm of photographers, who ordinarily are not permitted on the field.

Hutch grinned, stuck out his hand and said, "Congratulations, Stan. I'm sorry. I know you wanted to do it in St. Louis, but I needed you today."

I think the Big Bear was as excited as I was. He must have been because, forgetting that the reason for keeping me sidelined

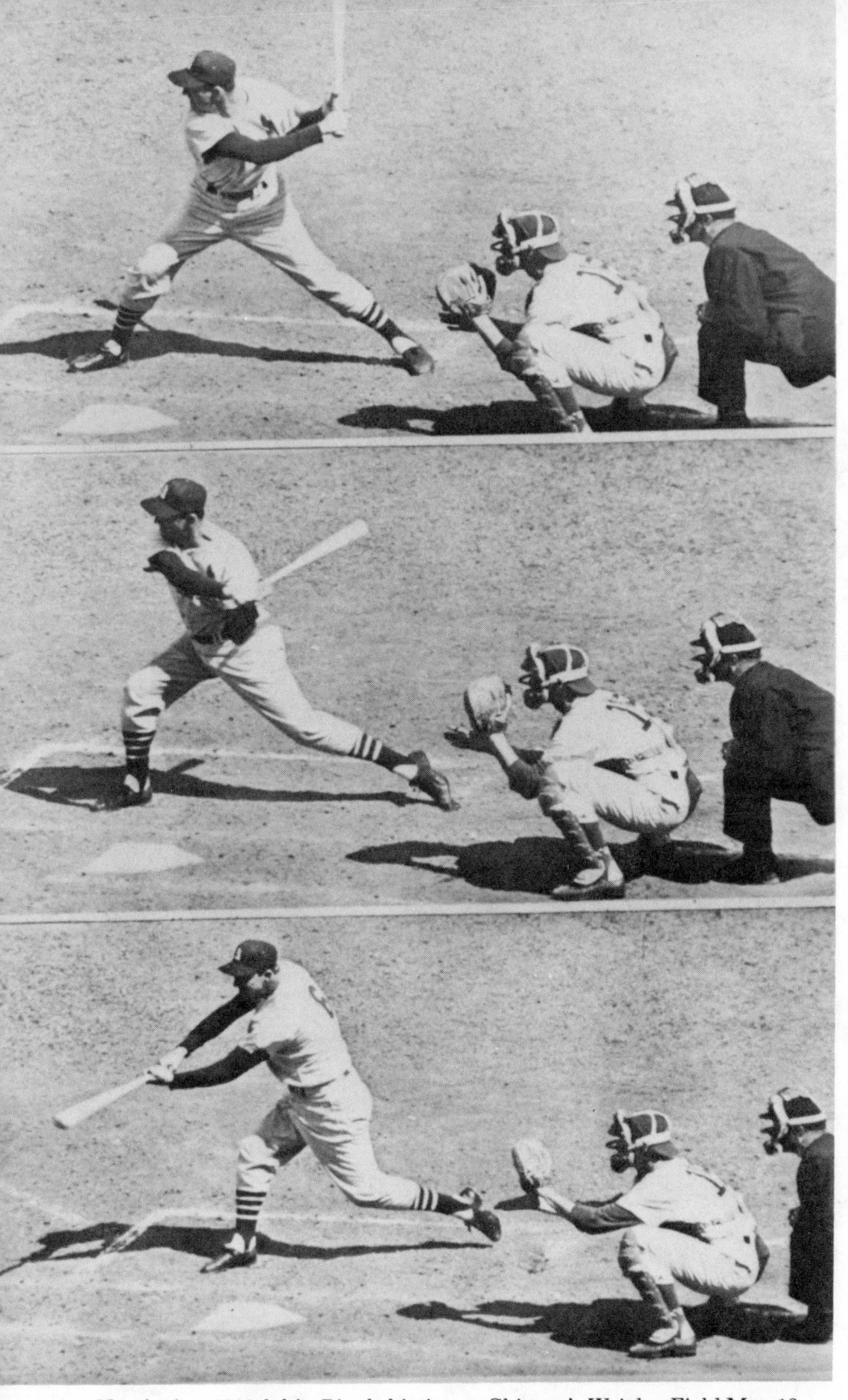

Here's that 3000th hit. Pinch-hitting at Chicago's Wrigley Field May 13, 1958. The Man stroked an outside curve ball into left field corner for a double. The catcher is Sammy Taylor, the umpire, Augie Donatelli.

After the big 3000th hit at Wrigley Field, Stan impulsively trotted over to wife Lil for a congratulations kiss.

had been eliminated, he took me out for a pinch-runner. As I trotted off, the photographers in pursuit, I thought first of Lil, seated in a box next to the first-base dugout. We hugged and kissed.

As I started down the runway through the dugout, a photographer asked, "Say, Stan, did you know that blonde?"

I laughed. "I'd better," I told him. "That's my wife."

Any other time, I would have stayed on the bench. But to accommodate so many photographers who spilled into the dugout after me, I had no choice except to go to the clubhouse. By the time I reached it, I learned that the Cardinals had continued the rally and taken a 5-3 lead. If this really was to be my biggest day, we just had to win. And we did—our sixth straight.

Afterward, because there wasn't enough room in the clubhouse, I returned to the field to appear on television, newsreels and radio. Then followed a joyful bus ride to the Illinois Central Depot on Michigan Avenue. The train trip back to St. Louis that evening with friends and teammates was one of the best experiences of my major league career. In the private club car, a steward brought out a big cake with "3000" in red frosting. And the Cardinals' long-time play-by-play broadcaster, Harry Caray, surprised me with a pair of diamond-set cuff links commemorating my batting milestone.

That noisy, happy trip back to St. Louis was like a championship celebration. I bought Sam Jones, the winning pitcher, a bottle of champagne and Sam acted as if he had been given a week off to visit his wife and children.

By the time Lil and I finished dinner, it was dark. The train slowed down to a stop at Clinton, Ill., where a crowd of about 50 had gathered on the platform, chanting, "We want Musial! We want Musial!"

I was happy to go out on the steps, to shake hands and autograph whatever they handed up to me. Fifty minutes later at Springfield, Ill., there were 100 or more well-wishers waiting. Again I shook hands and gave autographs. The crowd sang, "For he's a jolly good fellow . . ." The warm feeling was wonderful.

When the train started again, I returned to the parlor car and sat down. Suddenly, though the others were talking and laughing, I fell asleep. Lil later told me that one of our party, Bill Heinz, who had been commissioned by *Life* magazine to follow my efforts to get 3000 hits, wondered if I ever showed any nerves.

"Never," Lil told him. "You know, sometimes if the children do something wrong and he raises his voice just a little, they stand there with their mouths open, as if to say, 'Look at Daddy. What's the matter with Daddy?' "

About half an hour later, I awakened, refreshed, and winked

at Molly Pizzica. "Where's Molly?" I said, laughing, taking her hand.

When the train pulled into St. Louis' Union Station, late, about 1000 people were jammed behind the welcoming committee that included Dick Meyer and Bing Devine. I was led through the cheering crowd to a spotlighted platform to say a few words.

"I never realized," I told those smiling, friendly faces below me, "that batting a little ball around could cause so much commotion. I know now how Lindbergh must have felt when he returned to St. Louis."

Somebody in the crowd yelled, "What did *he* hit?"

Everybody laughed and, carried away, I turned to the eager small fry present and said, "No school tomorrow, kids."

The 3000-hit occasion had two pleasant postscripts. The next night, playing at Busch Stadium where I had hoped to get the big one, I came up in the first inning to a standing ovation—and made No. 3001 a home run.

In June, the Cardinals threw a 3000-hit party. First, they had a private dinner at my restaurant on a Saturday night, then a public celebration between games of a Sunday doubleheader. They honored all eight 3000-hit players, including the memory of the three who were dead—Honus Wagner, Eddie Collins and Cap Anson.

Illness kept 83-year-old Napoleon Lajoie from making the trip from Florida and 70-year-old Ty Cobb from Georgia, but plaques were sent to them by the Cardinals. On hand to receive theirs were Tris Speaker, the ruddy, silver-haired 70-year-old dean of center fielders, and my old Pittsburgh idol, little Paul Waner, wizened at 54.

Lil and I received commemorative gifts from the ball club, from my teammates, from manager Fred Hutchinson and from National League president Warren Giles. My mother was honored, too. My good friend, James T. Blair, Jr., governor of Missouri, presented me with new state automobile license plates—"3000."

I enjoyed most the chance at dinner to talk with Waner and Speaker. I'd known Paul, of course, just as I did Cobb. I never did get to meet Lajoie, I'm sorry to say. And even though I'd been in the big leagues 17 years, I'd never before had the chance to talk to Speaker, a gracious gentleman.

"That's nothing, Stan," the great Grey Eagle told me. "I had to introduce Honus Wagner and Eddie Collins to each other after their playing days. Honus had played 21 years in the National League, Eddie 25 years in the American League—and they'd never met."

I wish the honeymoon in 1958 could have lasted, but it didn't. After overcoming that horrible start, we surged to second place and by the end of June were only a game and a half behind Milwaukee. But the pitching didn't hold up, our hitting fell off, and we slumped to fifth place.

I couldn't maintain that stratospheric batting average, either. I think I may have experienced a letdown after chasing that 3000-hit rainbow so long. Maybe, too, there were too many festive occasions I couldn't turn down that summer. I do know that when I slumped wearily after playing doubleheaders, Hutch and I agreed in July that I couldn't play two games a day any longer.

Going to bat only 472 times, just five more than in my rookie season, 1942, I batted .337. I'd had 35 doubles, but only 17 homers and just 62 RBIs. I was completely tired at the end of the season, physically whipped. And I was mentally beat by the club's poor season and Mr. Busch's decision in September to dismiss Hutchinson as manager. I always felt, as he subsequently proved at Cincinnati, that the Big Bear was a helluva good manager.

Hutch's successor came as a surprise to the players and to the fans. He was Solly Hemus, a utility infielder for the Phillies for two years after having been one of the pawns in Frank Lane's trades. Hemus, 35, had been a hustling, humorous holler guy with us, a player who made the most of limited ability. I'd helped him learn to pull the ball better by suggesting a thin-handled bat. He'd impressed me as a keen student of the game, but I'd never thought of him as manager of the Cardinals, certainly not without previous managerial experience.

Hemus had the immediate advantage of a fall practice. The Cardinals played a post-season series of games in Japan. As far back as May, I had said I opposed the trip because I knew I'd be worn out, but I was persuaded to change my mind. The Japanese said that if I wouldn't come, they didn't want the Cardinals. I wasn't about to disappoint teammates who wanted to go.

I'm mighty glad now that I went. So is Lil. She was nearly six months pregnant, so I persuaded the tour promoter, Yetsuo Higa, to let us miss the stops at Guam, Manila and Okinawa. After the Cardinals played a couple of games in Hawaii, Lil and I enjoyed a few days at Waikiki before flying directly to Japan. I rejoined the Redbirds in time for a one-game trip to Seoul, South Korea.

My recollection of the Japanese trip is one unending whirl of parades, ball games, receptions, conducted tours, cocktail parties, dinners and entertainment. From the prime minister to the countless kids we saw playing ball every day on their way to school, the Japanese were gracious, kind and courteous.

Our hosts intended to be generous everywhere except on the ball field. They had beat the Brooklyn Dodgers four times in 1956. Now, by pooling the top talent of their major leagues to create an All-Star team, the Japanese expected to win at least five of their 16 games with us. Hemus, on the other hand, was determined we wouldn't lost any.

Although impressed with the control of Japanese pitchers, wide strike-zone interpretation and a rock-like dead ball that makes power-hitting difficult, we lost only two games. But we showed the Japanese something more by out-hustling them. We took the extra base, used the double-steal, the delayed steal, the hit-and-run, constantly putting pressure on them.

They don't run out routine grounders or pop flies over there. When they do take off, it's in a flight of fancy. For instance, an attempted steal when they're several runs behind. Basically built for speed more than power, the Japanese weren't nearly as aggressive or imaginative as I had expected they would be in baseball. But they dearly love the game. As spectators, Lil noted, they're so silent, even when 50,000 of them are in a ball park, that it's weird. They've begun to lose their respect for the umpire, but they're still too polite to boo a bad play and apparently too reserved to go all-out in applause of a good one.

Before every game, firecrackers popped, pigeons flew skyward and colored balloons soared. A band played martial music and each team lined up on the field. While cameras clicked, kimono-clad cuties ran out with armloads of flowers and gifts for every player. The U.S. was never like this. We took as many pre-game snapshots and movie films as the camera-conscious Japanese did. Once the game began, the fun was over. We had come to play and win.

We left with rich memories of Japan, but I value most the tribute paid us by our host, Yetsuo Higa:

"Of all the major league teams that have come to Japan, the Cardinals hustled the most, taught the Japanese more about baseball and made the best impression on the Japanese fans, on and off the field. Above all they have done, the Cardinals have set a precedent that all American baseball clubs should follow when they come to Japan in the future:

"Go all the way—or don't go at all."

As the ichiban star, I'm afraid Musial-san was a disappointment to the wonderful Japanese fans. I tried awfully hard to please them, on the field as well as off it, but I was tired. I hit over .300, but I had only two home runs, and home runs were what they had expected from me. I'm sorry they couldn't have seen me earlier.

Still, there were many good laughs. At one of the countless interviews I had with press, radio and TV people in Japan I mentioned that I was in the restaurant business.

"Ah-so, Musial-san," one writer said, "are you then a waiter?"

Stan (The 100 Grand) Man in 1959, the year after his 3000-hit achievement when he became the National League's first $100,000 player.

20

. . . The Other Half

I made a terrible mistake in 1959 and paid for it. I learned how the other half lived, as Joe Garagiola put it. And I didn't like it—the unpleasant experience, I mean, not Joe's crack.

After tiring badly the second half of the 1958 season, I felt that if I conserved my energy through the spring, I might have more left for the hot summer. Furthermore, Solly Hemus, the new manager, felt that I'd played too much in exhibition seasons as a concession to spectators in Florida. Looking back at it now, I don't remember that there was any dissenting voice, though it's not likely anything short of a majority vote would have changed the feeling shared by the front-office and field management that, nearing 39, I could afford to train my own way.

We were wrong, it developed, dead wrong.

Although I'd pushed myself away from the dinner plate during the off-seasons, I never had made an effort to retain physical condition. Now, with age, I had gone up several pounds to 187, but, more pertinent, I'd become thicker at the waist, heavier at the hips.

With permission, I reported late for spring training after the birth of our fourth child in February. For a time chubby, blonde Jeanie was a cross baby who kept us awake a good bit that summer. I've heard it said that the lack of sleep contributed to the terrible season which followed. That's unfair to Lil, who was up with the baby considerably more than I was, and to Jeanie, too. No, let's not blame our bundle of joy because too many times that summer I looked like an infant at the plate.

Playing less, I ran less during spring training, even though Hemus had decided to return me to the outfield, which I hadn't played since mid-season, 1956. Solly figured, correctly, that Joe Cunningham played first base better than I did and that I played the outfield better than Cunningham.

The Cardinals had unloaded their two most disappointing hitters of 1958, Del Ennis and Wally Moon. Moon recovered immediately at Los Angeles to help the Dodgers to a pennant. Gino Cimoli, obtained from the Dodgers, couldn't fill the long-vexing center field vacancy.

In spring training general manager Bing Devine dealt righthander Sam Jones to San Francisco for another first baseman, Bill White. With Cunningham, White, me, and George Crowe, who had come from Cincinnati in the Ennis deal, there was considerable hooting about the number of first basemen on the roster. White, of course, became one of the better all-round players in the National League.

By opening night, after we'd had a poor exhibition record, White was at first base and both Cunningham and I were in the outfield, flanking Cimoli. That outfield, I'm sorry to say, wouldn't have made anyone forget the Boston Red Sox's Duffy Lewis, Tris Speaker and Harry Hooper, or even the Cardinals' Enos Slaughter, Terry Moore and a younger, faster Stan Musial.

Our opening-night loss to San Francisco at St. Louis by one run seemed typical of the 1959 season. Faulty base-running, poor fielding, power failure and ineffective relief pitching cost us the game. I went hitless in three official trips and, chasing a fly ball, bumped hard into the left field wall.

The next night I ran back on another drive and again crashed into the concrete, this time bruising myself even more. Hemus decided the safest place for me was first base and I couldn't blame him. A ball player can't see himself, and I didn't realize then just how uncoordinated my old legs seemed when they

An attractive woman and her handsome son—Mom Musial, and Stan. He was always her favorite player, no matter what she said!

weren't in the best shape.

White, as a result, was forced out of position so that we had two first basemen in the outfield. After a miserable start, we reached the All-Star break in sixth place. Starting slowly, too, I'd reached .270, hardly All-Star caliber. But, sentimentally, Fred Haney, manager of Milwaukee's National League champions, had picked me for his squad, just as the Yankees' Casey Stengel had selected Ted Williams, who also was having his first bad season.

For the first time, two All-Star games were scheduled as players sought more revenue for the pension plan. (I never did like taking the glitter off the one game.) At the first one in Pittsburgh, the baseball writers held a dinner honoring Williams and me. Pinch-batting in a game won by the National League, 5-4, I popped out feebly.

An amusing thing happened before that game. My mother was

Ted Williams, then 40 years old, and Stan Musial, 38, meet at the 1958 All-Star game at Baltimore with Ted hitting .315, Stan .341. A year later, both slumping and prematurely regarded as through, neither man was smiling.

standing next to her box seat, getting autographs with friends, when Williams passed. She asked Ted to sign and said, admiringly, "You're my favorite player."

"And that," someone told him, "is Stan Musial's mother."

Ted, delighted, needled me when we had a minute to ourselves at the batting cage. He didn't know that Mom meant he was her favorite next to me—I think.

After talking to Ted, I told reporters, "We'll both hit .300."

For a brief time it seemed that I would. By mid-July, after rapping two home runs in one game off a favorite victim, Don Newcombe, my average climbed from .246 to .305. Then I began to fall back, even though Hemus rested me more than I'd ever rested before.

I was going down by the time the second All-Star game was played in early August at the Los Angeles Coliseum, where the American League beat us, 5-3. Pinch-batting, I drew a walk and went in to play first base in the seventh inning.

On Aug. 14, Bing Devine called me into his office. He wanted to know whether I intended to play in 1959, assuring me that the ball club would like to have me back. He thought it would be a good idea to reach a decision early to avoid repeated embarrassing questions in every town during the last swing around the National League.

I know many people thought I was washed up, but I didn't. Devine immediately called a conference in the pressbox during the game. Afterward, reporters poured into the clubhouse to talk to me.

"I'm confident I'll do better next year," I told them. "I feel that this just has been a bad year, not one in which old age caught up with me. It's a mechanical rather than physical problem. If I were full of aches and pains and if pitchers were getting the fast ball by me, because I'd slowed up . . . well, then I'd know it was time to quit. I can hit the fast ball. It's the other stuff that has been giving me trouble.

"I've struggled to find out what I'm doing wrong, but I just haven't been able to figure it out."

I expected the big question and it came. "You're hitting only .270 and deciding to return, not retire," a reporter pointed out, "when more than once you said that you wouldn't play ball if you couldn't hit .300."

"That was when batting .300 was easy," I said, trying frankly to explain my different standards. "When you're batting .330 or .340, you think a lot differently about having 'only' a .300 average. I want to play as long as I feel I can do the Cardinals some good. I know I can't be this bad next season."

I was asked about former manager Eddie Dyer's thought that I'd have been better off with a more rigorous spring training.

"It's only common sense to wonder if a change might help," I said, "but I'd like to make it clear that all my trouble this season is entirely my own fault. Solly has rested me when I thought I needed it and he has played me when we felt it was best. Whatever the trouble is, nobody else is to blame."

I knew, en route to seventh place, the club's lowest finish since 1919, that Hemus wanted to look at some rookies in September. I was a bit surprised, though, after the mid-August announcement that I wouldn't retire, when I was immediately benched for the season, except for pinch-hitting appearances.

Starting in 92 of the 1959 games—I appeared in 23 others as a pinch-batter—I wound up with a sorry .255 average, which, coincidentally, was practically the same as Ted Williams' (.254). In just 341 times at bat, I had only 87 hits, of which 13 were doubles, two triples and 14 home runs.

I batted in only 44 runs and fell down in two key categories. I was second-from-last among Redbird regulars in RBIs in relation to my opportunities and third-from-last in advancing base-runners. I batted just .196 against my long-time Dodger "cousins," and hit only .240 at home, .234 at night and .221 against lefthanders.

I had a miserable season, all right, but I'm afraid two pitchers wouldn't agree. I had the Cards' only hit in games that spoiled no-hitters for the Cubs' Glen Hobbie and the Giants' Jack Sanford.

21

Vindication

In late May, 1960, I was benched, regarded as washed up when I was certain I could still hit. Few realize how close I came to finishing my career with Pittsburgh. Instead, I almost finished Pittsburgh's chances of winning its first pennant in 33 years.

I look back on 1960 as a season of frustration and vindication, of sadness and success. It was the most emotional season I ever experienced because, as always, I felt obliged to guard my feelings.

I came back to play that year, nearing 40, not because I needed the money—I took a pretty good cut without complaint—but because I still had the old desire to play. I wanted the chance to prove that my bad 1959 season had been a result of poor judgment and improper physical conditioning. If I had quit on that first bad season, after having altered my training habits, I would have been bugged by doubt the rest of my life. I had to bow out more gracefully.

I began a stiff training program after the holidays. At Bob Bauman's suggestion, I put myself in the hands of Walter Eberhardt, St. Louis University's veteran director of physical education. Three and four days a week, I went through an advanced course in modern muscle-toning exercises. Not until I returned to the gymnasium for the first time since I'd quit playing off-season basketball back at Donora, nearly 20 years earlier, did I realize how much I had relied on diet and baseball to keep in shape. I had aged as an athlete, played less and then short-changed my conditioning in 1959. I had lost the muscle firmness of youth.

By the time the Cardinals' management decided to have Doc Eberhardt bring his quips and body-strengthening, muscle-toning program to spring training—ever hear a guy speak German with a New England accent?—I already had lost an inch or two at the waistline. In camp, I again played more often in the exhibitions and I did more running. Weak at first, I gained strength and felt good during a spring in which the Cardinals won the Grapefruit League title. And I hit well, too.

As a result of winter trades, we opened with more power, potentially. Daryl Spencer was at shortstop and Leon Wagner in left field. Wagner, obtained from the Giants, broke in with a home run against his old teammates, but that was the only run—and one of just three hits—we got off Sam Jones. The opener, the first game played at San Francisco's new, windswept Candlestick Park, went to the Giants, 3-1. I was hitless in three trips.

Once again, the Cardinals were troubled by a slow start. We lost our first five games on the West Coast and were plagued by losses on the road. By the time we dropped one to the Cubs at Chicago in mid-May, we hadn't won on the road in 12 tries and were in seventh place with a 10-16 record. I'd sat out day games after night games and the second half of doubleheaders, but on May 14 I was benched for not hitting. I was batting .260.

The next noon before the opener of a Sunday doubleheader at Wrigley Field, manager Solly Hemus told me, "Be ready to play the second game, Stan."

In the first game we scored our first road victory. So Solly decided to stick with a righthanded-hitting lineup in the second game even though sidearming righthander Don Cardwell of the Cubs was tough on righthanded hitters. The Hemus hunch, and it couldn't have been anything else, didn't make sense to me. For the first time I questioned a manager's judgment, though I did it

For years the Cardinals used the talents of Walter Eberhardt, director of physical education at St. Louis University, to condition the club in spring training. "Doc" and Stan, two old turnverein tumblers, couldn't resist this trick after a 1960 workout.

Stan (The Man) Musial and colorful Joe Cunningham, also a first baseman-outfielder, who hit .345 for the Cardinals in 1959.

quietly. When Hemus told me he had changed his mind and wouldn't play me, I was skeptical. "You were just kidding about playing me, Solly," I said.

Call it mere coincidence, if you will, but, facing that righthanded-hitting lineup, Cardwell pitched a no-hit, no-run game, the first against the Cardinals since 1919. Late in the game, when the shadows were deep around Wrigley Field and Don's fast ball was humming, I pinched-hit and struck out.

If ever a manager panicked, I'm afraid Hemus did. In the first 29 games he started 15 players and nine pitchers, including Lindy McDaniel, already a good relief man who became great before the year was out. There wasn't too much logic to some of Solly's other moves, either. For instance, we had picked up hard-hitting, slow-fielding Bob Nieman to give us a righthanded hitter against lefthanded pitching, but Nieman faced only five of the first 13 southpaws we saw.

After Cardwell's no-hitter, I started only four of the next 12 games and got three hits in one of them. According to figures published at the time, the club was driving in 41 per cent of the runners in scoring position—on second or third base—but I had 70 per cent efficiency. I wasn't hitting for average, though, and apparently Hemus was convinced I was through. I know he had lost confidence in me. At Philadelphia, for instance, when we trailed by a run in the ninth, another lefthanded hitter, Carl Sawatski, waited in the on-deck circle to bat for Curt Flood. Just then Spencer hit a game-tying triple with one out.

An intentional pass was the likely strategy, to set up a possible inning-ending double play. Hemus called back Sawatski and sent me up there to take the walk. Sawatski then went up for our pitcher and lifted a fly ball that drove in the winning run. Hemus was delighted with his successful strategy and spelled out his reasoning: He had figured Sawatski would be more likely to hit the fly ball than I would.

We came off the road to find both St. Louis sports editors, Bob Burnes of the *Globe-Democrat* and Bob Broeg of the *Post-Dispatch,* neither ordinarily critical, taking exception to what they regarded as unfair treatment. It was uncomfortable to be the center of such commotion, but nice to have friends who still believed in me.

A week later, May 28, after I'd been in and out of the lineup, the Cardinals swung a deal with Pittsburgh. They sent lefthander Wilmer (Vinegar Bend) Mizell and utility infielder Dick Gray to the Pirates for a promising second baseman from their Columbus farm club, Julian Javier, and future rights to another Columbus player, pitcher Ed Bauta. The Pirates felt that one more experienced pitcher like Mizell could help them to a pennant. He did. The Cardinals felt that Javier's speed and glove ability would help plug a weakness at second base. They did. And I think I'm honest enough to realize that when Hemus decided Bill White couldn't play center field—he put young ballhawk Curt Flood out there—he also helped the defense considerably. White was better defensively at his normal position, first base, than I had come to be.

I felt I could help the ball club in my old position, left field, because a team has to score runs as well as keep from giving them up, but I always had prided myself on playing the good soldier.

Asked to Grant's Farm, Mr. Busch's handsome estate, I found the big boss waiting with executive vice-president Dick Meyer, general manager Bing Devine and manager Solly Hemus. They tried to break it to me gently that Solly preferred to go with a different, younger lineup.

"Whatever you want is all right with me," I said, "though I think I can still help the ball club."

I didn't say so, but I was hurt most because I saw no young star on the horizon. Not, anyway, since Frank Lane's tradeaway program a few years earlier.

I wasn't used, even though a medley relay of players went to left field. Leon Wagner, who later became a home-run hitter with the Los Angeles Angels, was benched. Another rookie, Ellis Burton, was found wanting. He and Wagner were optioned out as the club got Walt Moryn from the Chicago Cubs, then John Glenn from St. Paul. No, not the astronaut, but a well-traveled veteran of the Dodgers' farm system.

Finally, another veteran, Bob Nieman, began to hit. The Cardinals obviously didn't need me.

Near the trading deadline, the Pirates, leading the league, came to town. Before the game, Bob Broeg was talking to Danny Murtaugh, the Pittsburgh manager.

"What's the matter with the Polack?" Murtaugh asked.

Nothing, he was told. Danny, an old friendly rival, shook his head. Bob, aware the Pirates were having first-base trouble, wondered how much I might mean to Pittsburgh.

Murtaugh grinned. "Plenty," he said, "but, heck, Stan never would leave the Cardinals."

Broeg wasn't so sure. "Until now," he told Murtaugh, "you would have been right. But Hemus is convinced Stan is through, and the guy wants a chance to prove he isn't. He might be interested in going to his old home-town area and getting the chance at one more World Series."

So Bob asked me. I didn't think I'd ever say what I did, but I said it—"Yes."

Broeg relayed the information to a surprised Murtaugh. Danny's eyes widened. He wondered aloud whether the Cardinals, if they weren't going to play me, would give me my unconditional release and, therefore, escape my $75,000-plus salary. The Pirates, he said, certainly couldn't afford to give up a promising young player for one nearly 40. But he'd definitely advise his general manager, Joe L. Brown, to try to get me.

"Musial," Murtaugh said, "could mean the difference for us in the race."

At least until Murtaugh could talk to Brown, Broeg was asked not to write the story. The Pittsburgh general manager later phoned Broeg with what he insisted had to be an off-the-record explanation of his stand.

"As much as we'd like to have Musial," Brown said, "I just can't do it to Bing Devine. Sure, if Musial were released, we would grab him in a minute. As Murtaugh said, we couldn't give up one of our better younger players for him. And to offer too little would be taking advantage of the public sentiment, which is sure to be strongly behind Musial, not the ball club. Devine would be on a spot where I don't care to put him."

Although hurt and disappointed, I wouldn't ask for my release. I had my pride and ethics. I probably missed a chance to play in another World Series, but I'm glad now that I didn't ask for my release. I've been treated fairly by the St. Louis management, and royally by the Cardinals' fans.

If injury-prone Bob Nieman hadn't been hurt, I might have continued planning to quit at the All-Star interlude in July. Four weeks after I had been benched, presumably for good, I played left field at Philadelphia, on June 24. Although I'd been unhappy during the long spell on the sidelines, I hadn't been idle. The year before, I'd watched big George Crowe, our reserve first baseman and powerful pinch-hitter, drive himself hard in practice.

"The more time you spend on the bench, the harder you've got to work to be ready when you're called," Crowe had explained.

Coach Johnny Keane fungoed ground balls and fly balls to me endlessly, and I did daily wind sprints in the outfield, so the month on the bench hadn't hurt me as it would have earlier. I still had the physical edge I'd regained in Florida.

The first day back, playing the outfield for the first time since the second game of the 1959 season, I proved to Hemus' satisfaction that my legs were stronger than they had been the previous year. I covered more ground and threw out a runner at the plate.

At bat, I contributed only one hit in four trips as we lost to Robin Roberts, but old No. 6 felt good getting back into the lineup. My average, .250 when I was benched, had dipped to .238

during unsuccessful pinch-hitting appearances. During the next three weeks, leading the Cardinals' surge into the first division, I hit so hard and often (20 for 41) that my average at the time of the first All-Star game was .300.

Hemus was grateful. "Musial," he told the press, "has delivered the last two or three weeks the most big hits I've seen any player get in years."

I was on the National League All-Star squad in 1960, thanks to Dave Grote, publicity director for the league. I'd just begun to pick up at the plate when the All-Star team was selected by Walter Alston, manager of the 1959 pennant-winning Dodgers. When Alston hesitated over his last player choice, Grote urged him to take me. The heat was intense at Kansas City, July 11. Some of us arrived in the wee hours of the morning after a delayed flight from Los Angeles. I was tired, but extremely happy to be picked again and to have an average—.300—worthy of an All-Star choice.

In the game, I pinch-singled off Frank Lary, excellent righthander. And the National League won, 5-3, on the strength of three hits by Willie Mays and a two-run homer by Ernie Banks.

Two days later at New York's Yankee Stadium, the National League again won, 6-0, behind the pitching of Vernon Law, Johnny Podres, Stan Williams, Larry Jackson, Bill Henry and Lindy McDaniel. Ken Boyer, Ed Mathews, Mays and I hit home runs.

I'll never forget my return to Yankee Stadium for the first time since the 1943 World Series. When I went up in the sixth inning to face Gerry Staley, a former teammate who had become the bullpen ace of the White Sox's pennant-winning club, I received a warm greeting. I had a feeling I'd hit one. I sure did. I drove Staley's sinker high into the third deck of the right field stands, and there was a roar from the crowd.

After the game, Casey Stengel, who had managed the American League team, told the writers, "I shoulda known." He remembered an episode back in 1942, my rookie season.

"I told one of my men to throw 'im the dead fish," Stengel said, "because I never saw a kid who could hit the change-up. My gawd, he almost took the leg offa my first baseman."

Mayo Smith, now scouting for the Yankees, told me later that when the home run went into the stands, he'd found himself on his feet, applauding, tears in his eyes. When you touch the professionals, you've struck pay dirt.

Another old friend, Larry Goetz, was in the stands that day. He had been one of my strongest boosters since a day early in my career. As plate umpire, he watched with annoyance as Van Lingle Mungo, colorful, hard-throwing Brooklyn righthander, twice knocked me down with pitches. Twice I got up and brushed myself off. Then I lined the third pitch into left center for a triple.

As I charged around the bases, Goetz said he couldn't resist yelling at Mungo, "Hey, Van, you sure scared hell out of that kid!"

The 1960 Cardinals certainly scared hell out of Pittsburgh in the pennant race. I hit productively, despite tailing off to .275, and had 17 homers and 63 RBIs, though I wasn't an everyday starter. The big jobs were done by Ernie Broglio, our first 20-game winner since Harvey Haddix in 1953, and by Lindy McDaniel, positively the best single-season relief pitcher I ever saw. Lindy won 12 games in relief, saved more than 20 others and had a 2.09 earned-run average, even counting two ill-advised starting assignments early in the season. In 65 games over 116 innings he allowed only 85 hits, walked just 24 and struck out 105.

My most telling contributions came against Pittsburgh. I think there was a little coolness among my old friends around Donora as I threatened to keep the Pirates from a pennant they had waited for since I was seven years old.

Three times I beat them with home runs, all in August when the race narrowed and the Pirates' lead was shaky. In St. Louis, I beat Bob Friend one night with a late two-run homer, 3-1, and Roy Face the next night with a home run in the ninth, 5-4. But the one I remember best came at Pittsburgh on a mid-August night in one of the greatest games I ever saw.

We had moved into second place, five games out, when we opened a four-game series at Forbes Field. Broglio, who beat the Pirates five times, hooked up in a brilliant pitching duel with Friend, and it was 1-1 as we went into extra innings. There was only one walk, issued by Friend. Each pitcher struck out nine, and four times Broglio fanned the Pirates' captain, Dick Groat, the National League batting champion. In the twelfth inning, I hit a two-run homer and Broglio hung on in the home half for a 3-2 victory.

We won the next day and were only two games behind going into a Sunday doubleheader. The Pirates won the opener, but in the seventh inning of the second game, tied 1-1, we put the first two men on base and had the middle of our batting order coming up, Here, the Pirates' infielders huddled around the mound as Murtaugh replaced righthander Tom Cheney with southpaw Joe Gibbon, to face lefthanded-hitting Joe Cunningham. Cunningham squared around to bunt and dropped the ball perfectly along the third base line. Perfectly, that is, if, as customary, the pitcher had to break over to field the ball while the third baseman retreated to cover his bag. You know the standard bunt defense. The shortstop, holding the runner on second, covers that base. The first baseman breaks in to handle a bunt his way. The second baseman rushes over to take an in-coming throw to first.

But on this play, Don Hoak, the Pirate third baseman, charged just as the first baseman did. Groat, after bluffing the runner toward second, took off from his shortstop position for third, outracing the leading runner to the bag. So when Hoak fielded Cunningham's bunt, the third baseman's throw to third was grabbed by the shortstop for a surprise force-out.

Surprise, all right. So surprising, in fact, that Cunningham, mesmerized, stood in the batter's box to watch the play and, as a result, broke belatedly for first base and was doubled by Groat's peg there. That unorthodox bunt defense took us out of a promising inning and when the Pirates beat our relief artist, Lindy McDaniel, in the eleventh, 3-2, their hold on first place was secure.

We fell back a bit and finished third, nine games out, with 86 victories. That was an unexpected development in a year of personal frustration and vindication, a season that could have been better only if we had gone all the way from seventh place.

The irony of it all was that when the race became close back in August, the Pirates broke our backs with a seldom-seen bunt defense that Groat and Hoak had decided on during the pitching-change delay.

Where had they picked up the idea?

From Harry Walker, a Cardinals coach who had brought back the novel anti-sacrifice defense in 1955—while managing our club.

22

Like Old Times

Why didn't I hang up the glove after that bittersweet experience in 1960? Friends urged me to quit while I was ahead, but still I decided to risk a repetition of the previous season's unpleasantness. For one thing, to be frank, I liked my baseball salary, even though it had to be trimmed a trifle. But since I had a generous income from our new restaurant and a thriving bowling alley, I played mainly because I still liked to—and because, this time, the management asked me to return.

I was confident I could help and believed we would be a pennant factor in '61. It's a good thing I haven't been paid for my predictions on the pennant races. Although I was right about having a better season myself—I batted .288, hit 15 homers, 22 doubles and drove in 70 runs starting just about two-thirds of our games—I was terribly wrong about the ball club. The pitching staff, which had been our strongest department in 1960, had a letdown. Larry Jackson, the steadiest pitcher, suffered a broken jaw when he was hit with a broken bat in spring training. Ernie Broglio and Lindy McDaniel were far off their previous year's form.

A manager is no better than his material, and Solly Hemus was unfortunate that his didn't hold up. In the desperation of inexperience he made some hurried moves and lineup changes that were questionable. So when we sank to sixth place in early July, Solly was fired and replaced by coach Johnny Keane.

The managerial change, made in Los Angeles, came just before the first All-Star game at San Francisco, where I pinch-batted and flied out to left field. The National League won. I was more disappointed over my failure as a pinch-hitter at the second All-Star game, a tie played on a raw, rainy day in Boston. I hadn't been there since the Braves moved to Milwaukee in 1953 and hadn't played at Fenway Park since the 1946 World Series. And even though I received a welcome second only to Warren Spahn's, I struck out trying to swing for the close left field fence.

Our new manager, Keane, was a wiry little infielder who never played big league ball. He had managed for years in the Cardinals' organization. And now he made a couple of moves that helped immediately. He re-established Jackson's confidence by starting him—Larry had been demoted to the bullpen—and letting him stay in to win even though he was hit hard. Larry finished the season strongly. So did Curt Flood, reinstated in center field. The kid hit over .320. Keane settled down the ball club and we won 47 out of 80 games for him, winding up fifth with an 80-74 record.

I remember one game in 1961 because it proved a theory of mine that a performer can concentrate better when he isn't feeling up to par. I was troubled by a pulled leg muscle and a cold which had kept me from sleeping. Then I developed a miserable abscessed tooth. Doc Bauman thought I'd roll off his trainer's table because of the pain. I played against the Giants, anyway, and hit two home runs, one a grand-slam, and accounted for the highest single-game RBI total of my career—seven.

Then I rushed out of the ball park to keep a midnight date with my dentist.

Otherwise, I really didn't do too well for Keane, hitting just .272, with little power production. Still, he called me aside at Philadelphia, where we finished the '61 season, and said:

"Stan, I want you back, not to play less next year, but to play more. I've watched you and I'm convinced that you could have played more. What do you think?"

I welcomed the challenge.

"Good," Keane said. "Get yourself in the best possible shape. If next year is going to be your last one, make it one to be remembered. You can do it."

I looked forward to playing in 1962 because the League's expansion would mean a return to New York, a favorite stop for me. I really thrived on travel, seeing old friends and making new ones and I guess, like any show-business ham, I enjoyed the applause.

The old ham had a big year in 1962, and I'm certain that Keane's confidence in me, his reliance on me, were big factors. I also worked harder in the off-season to keep in shape and pushed myself away from the table more determinedly than before. I even got down, at one point in 1962, to my rookie weight, 12 pounds lighter than the 187 I'd carried in recent times. But at 175 pounds I was a little drawn and weak. So I leveled off at 180.

I felt the benefit of the weight loss most in my sliding. The previous two years I'd been jarred increasingly when I had to hit the dirt. That's the true sign of athletic old age, the physical impact on bones and tissue. But when I slid in 1962, I didn't feel the shock nearly so much. I even stole three bases out of three tries. That left me only 101 behind the amazing Maury Wills.

From the time I got "3 for 3" at bat opening night at St. Louis in a victory over the Mets, I felt the season would be something special for me and, I hoped, it would for the Cardinals, too. We won our first seven games, but we flattened out and finished sixth, six games over .500.

We missed the hustle and RBI potential of Minnie Minoso, a grand old campaigner we obtained from the Chicago White Sox. Minnie suffered skull and wrist fractures when he ran into an outfield wall early in the season. Our young shortstop, Julio Gotay, wasn't ready to play the key position, and another important newcomer, catcher Gene Oliver, had a lot to learn, too. Our pitching was good, but not good enough, especially in the bullpen, and, as a club, we didn't deliver the hit or the late-inning fly ball that would drive in a big run.

I know I tried awfully hard to justify Johnny Keane's belief that a man going on 42 could play regularly and help a young ball club. Keane went out of his way to help, too. I remember a Sunday doubleheader early in May at Cincinnati. In the ninth inning of the first game, I came up with a great chance to help our floundering club. We trailed by a run, 5-4, but had the bases loaded and only one out when I faced Dave Sisler, rangy righthander whose best pitch is a sinking fast ball. With the infield back for a double play, I didn't want to hit the ball on the ground. But when Sisler came right down the middle with a fast ball, I got under it too much and popped it up, nice and easy.

Ken Boyer then hit the long fly that, one play sooner, would have tied the score. Instead, it ended the game and we dragged into the old wooden visitors' clubhouse at Crosley Field, where I jerked off my uniform shirt and sweat shirt. I plopped onto my locker stool, head down, depressed and frustrated. Because I wouldn't play again until we returned home Tuesday night, that failure in the clutch would eat into me for a good part of those 48 hours.

Just then I felt an arm on my bare shoulder. It was Keane. He slapped me on the back. "You're playing the second game, Stan," he said, "and you'll get four hits."

I was surprised and delighted. I hadn't played a doubleheader in nearly four years, but the weather was cool, the season was young (even if Musial wasn't), and I was eager to make up for my failure.

I didn't get four hits, as Keane had predicted, but I did get three. The third one came in the ninth inning of a scoreless duel. It was a line drive into the right field stands off Moe Drabowsky for a home run that gave us a 3-0 victory.

If anyone had told me when I reached the 3000-hit mark in May, 1958, that I would need four years to reach Honus Wagner's National League record for career hits, 3430, I frankly would have said I wouldn't be around that long. But a month after the season opened, having played more major league games than old Honus, I closed in on his hit record. Just one hit short and batting .402, I went into a slump.

So the tension was prolonged. Finally, a week after getting No. 3429, I tied the record at San Francisco with my first hit in 15 trips, a single off Juan Marichal.

By coincidence, one of the spectators was Jim Tobin, the pitcher off whom I'd got my first big league hit 21 years earlier. Old Ironsides, as they called him when he played with the Braves, is the only pitcher ever to hit three home runs in a game. When I heard he was in the crowd, I asked someone to locate him.

"What are you looking for," the 49-year-old bartender ribbed, "another hit?"

I laughed. "I still can't hit the knuckleball, Jim."

Tobin told me something I hadn't guessed when I was a kid. The Braves' pitchers took long windups hoping to tire me while I was in my crouched batting stance, my weight braced on my left leg. Heck, when I was 21 my legs never got tired.

Three nights later my inglorious streak reached one-for-25 after eight more hitless times at bat. I was facing Dodger lefthander Ron Perranoski in the ninth inning of a lopsided game won by the Cardinals at Los Angeles. I took a curve for a strike, then lined the next pitch, another curve, into right field for a basehit.

When I reached first base, a crowd of more than 50,000 roared, and I suddenly went limp, my legs rubbery. I'd wanted the record even more than I had realized. When the throw came in from the outfield, my former St. Louis teammate, Wally Moon, playing first base for the Dodgers, gave me the ball. He started to shake my hand, then pulled it back. Wally's last minute thought of the non-fraternization rule made me laugh. It reminded me of the time I went up to the plate for the 10,000th time, a milestone announced over the Dodgers' public-address system. As I stepped up to the plate, umpire Al Barlick surprised me by sticking out his hand.

I hesitated, a bit embarrassed, I suppose, at the public gesture on the part of a man so obviously neutral.

"Aren't you worried about the non-fraternization rule, Al?" I stammered.

"To heck with that now," he said, grabbing my hand with all the forcefulness that helped make Barlick a great umpire.

After my hit at Los Angeles, I looked around for the expected pinch-runner. I wanted out of there. I was a weary old man. Finally, long after the manager ordinarily would send out a replacement, Don Landrum ran out to take my place and I wobbled to the dugout, where happy teammates gave me a warm greeting. Johnny Keane grinned. "I kept you waiting," he said, "because the fans were giving you such a big hand that I didn't want to spoil their fun."

Afterward, I was having a midnight steak sandwich in the Dodgers' fashionable stadium club. Jack Buck, the broadcaster, mentioned that Jack Hogan, Associated Press photographer in St. Louis, had died of a heart attack. I never had anything spoil a celebration for me so quickly. In fact, I had to be excused for several minutes. Just the previous week, Hogan had sat out there at Busch Stadium, night after night, patiently awaiting the record hit. Now that I finally had gotten it, he was gone. . . .

There was one other postscript to the record—a crack my wife made. After trying to stay awake to listen to the Saturday night game, which ended past midnight, St. Louis time, she had fallen asleep and missed the big moment. "I guess I'm too old for this game," Lil told a reporter the next evening at the airport when the ball club came in from Los Angeles. "It's for young people like Stan."

If 1962 seems to have been one record after another, please understand that I was just lucky enough to be reaping the harvest of so many bountiful seasons, so many healthy years in a big league lineup.

My wife wasn't with me in June at Philadelphia when I passed Ty Cobb's major league record of total bases, 5863, by getting two hits in one inning—a single and a homer—but, happily, she and I were able to share our other big moments of 1962.

Together, we attended Gerry's graduation from high school and, though I again had to leave the ball club on the road, I was able to be with Lil for Dick's commencement at Notre Dame, where the first college man in the Musial family had lettered on the track team. The following Thanksgiving weekend he married a pretty little St. Louis girl, Sharon Edgar. Then he went on active duty as a reserve officer in the Army.

I wasn't able to give Dick the close relationship many fathers and sons enjoy, and, in an old-fashioned way, I expected more of him than I did his sisters. (I guess girls do wrap their fathers around their little fingers.) Dick really came through, and he and his mother deserve great credit. He's a quiet, level-headed kid who survived extremely well the handicap of having a well-known father. Lil and I have reason to be proud of our first-born who, like an old-time actor's son, practically was born in a trunk. Just so Dick doesn't let his sheepskin go to his head, he's not the only Musial with a degree. Monmouth (Ill.) College made the old man an honorary Doctor of Humanities in 1962—and I was tickled pink.

The family seldom traveled with me during my career, but in '62 the Musials—part of them, anyway—made two trips east. Lil and Janet were with me, en route to the All-Star game at Washington, when I hit the four consecutive home runs at the Polo Grounds. The third one in succession that Sunday afternoon made me smile to myself—for two reasons.

Bill Hunter, a young lefthander who had taken over after I homered twice off Jay Hook, threw me a "2-2" fast ball high and inside in the seventh inning. The pitch was too far inside, and Hunter seemed surprised I didn't take it. But I didn't believe in letting an inside pitch get away at the Polo Grounds. I got out in front of the high, tight delivery and tomahawked it against the right field roof.

Circling the bases, I thought of Lil's having missed those other three-home-run performances because she had been, first of all, the dutiful mother. Now, as I stepped on home plate and turned toward the visitors' dugout, I could see Lil and Janet in their first-row box, standing and clapping. The warm glow I felt had nothing to do with the high thermometer reading.

In late July, I broke the National League RBI record (1860) held by my old favorite, Mel Ott, with a two-run homer, off Don

Drysdale, the sidewheeling giant righthander of the Dodgers, in a game at St. Louis. The Cardinals didn't win, but I'm glad I teed off on a tough one like Drysdale, who says I was his boyhood idol. We form a mutual admiration society.

In August, Lil and the three girls joined me in New York—Dick couldn't get away from a job he'd just taken (and from his lovely Sharon)—to help me share quite an occasion. New York was honoring a St. Louis ball player with a night at the Polo Grounds.

The Mets' management arranged it, assisted by good friends like Toots Shor, Ed Mosler, Fred Corcoran, Arthur Godfrey and Horace McMahon. Several years ago, before McMahon became Lt. Mike Parker in the television series, "Naked City," he called me in Milwaukee from Chicago, where his son, Tommy, was to be christened. I agreed to serve as proxy godfather because Tommy's godfather, Eddie Foy, Jr., was tied up in "Pajama Game."

"Best stand-in I ever had," quipped Foy.

When New York friends said they wanted to have the night for me, I emphasized that I wanted no expensive gift. They suggested instead a scholarship fund at Columbia College, which I always think of as Lou Gehrig's alma matter. There were token gifts, the kind that represented personal warmth. For instance, New York baseball writers, who always have been most considerate of me, gave me a small portable typewriter.

One of the nicest touches of the New York ceremonies came when Casey Stengel, presented me a king-sized plaque from the Mets, leaned over and whispered:

". . . And if those fellas in St. Louis decide they don't want you, we want you with the Mets. You'd be a great asset to our organization."

I don't like to speak publicly because I'm enough of a perfectionist not to want to do anything I don't do well, but I can speak better than I did that evening. I hadn't expected to play again in New York after I hit a home run there my last time up in 1957, and I'm afraid I choked with emotion in my acceptance remarks.

I'd had a hectic time getting my brood together for New York's handsome gesture. The Cardinals, flying from Houston after a Thursday night game, had been delayed and we hadn't reached our hotel until 7 A.M. Friday, the morning of my "night." I was up at noon to have lunch with my mother, who had come over from Donora. Then I went out to Idlewild Airport to meet Lil, Gerry and Janet and little Jeanie. There was a delay because Lil's luggage was lost. Back at the hotel, I couldn't find suite accommodations for my family and had to make arrangements elsewhere. I went to my room to pack my bag and it was missing, too.

I hurried through a late-afternoon meal and stepped outside the hotel to take a cab to the Polo Grounds. There was a driving rainstorm and not a taxi to be flagged down. In desperation, I tried the subway, which I hadn't ridden in about 15 years, and would have been lost completely if an old acquaintance hadn't recognized me and directed me.

Meanwhile, when my mother, Lil and the girls finally did get a cab, their trip through the rush-hour traffic in the heavy rain took so long that they would have missed the ceremonies if the game hadn't been called off.

I really needed the stiff drink I was handed at Toots Shor's, where a party had been scheduled. Mayor Raymond R. Tucker was among St. Louis friends who joined with New York and Pennsylvania friends to make it a delightful affair. A gift I particularly enjoyed receiving was a mounted photostat of Page One of the New York *Times* for Nov. 21, 1920, the day I was born.

The next evening—a few hours after a Saturday afternoon game in which I played—the belated ceremonies were held before the hastily rescheduled rain-out. When the fans found out I wasn't in the starting lineup, they began booing loudly, but I think Johnny Keane wasn't certain whether I'd hold up under the 48-hour strain. By the eighth inning, the Cardinals were far ahead. The growing chant, "We want Musial," prompted Keane to send me up to pinch-hit. I dearly would have loved to hit one for those nice folks, but the pitcher couldn't get the ball over the plate and walked me. The crowd jeered the poor guy, then gave me a tremendous hand as I went out for a pinch-runner and ran to the clubhouse in distant center field.

Although I had played more often than in the three previous seasons, I was handled carefully until early August. The Cardinals had dropped out of the race, but I still was leading the league in hitting, though I wasn't playing enough to qualify officially for the batting title. Twenty years earlier, it was possible to win a batting championship by playing in 100 games, a requirement that obviously was not severe enough. The long-standing rule next adopted—400 official times at bat—came under fire as too strict in Ted Williams' later years. Ted, playing part-time, was handicapped further by the numerous bases on balls he drew.

So a new formula was established, one which required an average of 3.1 plate appearances a game, official and unofficial. In the new 162-game schedule, a player had to go to bat 502 times to qualify.

By the time the Cardinals had played 100 games in late July, when I was hitting .347, publicity director Jim Toomey figured I would have needed 310 appearances to meet the 3.1-a-game minimum. I'd been up only 285 times. Johnny Keane decided to talk it over with me.

"I know how much an eighth batting championship would mean, the opportunity to become the oldest player ever to win a title," he said. "If you think you can stand the extra try, Stan, I'm willing to play you more—until either you or I decide it's not in your best interest or the club's."

Sure, I wanted to try. I didn't figure to get this close again and I did feel strong. I knew that the stepped up playing schedule probably would cut my average, but that had been true even at my peak when I never missed a game. I wanted to go down swinging.

Thanks to Keane's clever manipulation, resting me as much as he could while keeping an eye on that formula, I held up quite well. Not enough to keep Tommy Davis from passing me with his truly fine season or to withstand the typical late-season surge of Frank Robinson. But I was in the batting race until the final week, and then I couldn't sit out any games because the Cardinals could affect the pennant race—and did.

Even after we'd taken two out of three from the Dodgers in our final home series, the next-to-last weekend, Los Angeles still seemed to have a firm hold on first place. The second-place Giants had recently lost six straight, then had given away one of two games in St. Louis. When they blew one at Houston, they trailed by three with only six to go. To begin the final week, we went to San Francisco while Houston moved into Los Angeles. The Giants picked up one game out of the next two by winning two straight from us, taking the second even though I drove in three runs with a homer in the ninth.

That evening I was the guest of Horace Stoneham, the sportsman who operated the Giants. Horace was a part of that vanishing breed, a baseball clubowner who ran his own store. As I was breaking away to take in a show with Red Schoendienst and Joe Garagiola, Stoneham said, "I'd ask you to take it easy on us tomorrow, Stan, except that the last time I did that was at your restaurant the night before you hit those five home runs against us."

I laughed. "That's right, Horace, don't ask."

The next day I collected "5 for 5." When we beat the Giants that day on Gene Oliver's three-run homer, 7-4, I was certain they were done.

Baseball just isn't that predictable. The Dodgers, momentarily three up again, lost that night to Houston. Still, they needed only one victory in the three-game season-ending series with us to clinch at least a tie for the pennant. Just one L.A. victory and one San Francisco defeat and it would be all over. The

Giants lost one of their last three with Houston, but the Dodgers never got that one more victory.

On Friday night, Larry Jackson beat them in 10 innings, 3-2. We were playing our best ball in months, charged up by the exhilaration of playing before packed crowds with someone else' pennant at stake. The young Dodgers undoubtedly were tense under the blue-chip pressure.

Saturday night, Ernie Broglio pitched a great ball game, a two-hitter, and we won again, 2-0, when Frank Howard, the youthful giant, dropped a fly ball that let in the game's only runs. And the regular-season race ended in a tie and ultimately in disaster for the Dodgers when Curt Simmons also shut them out, 1-0. Gene Oliver tagged Johnny Podres for an eighth-inning home run they'll never forget in Los Angeles—or in San Francisco.

I got real professional satisfaction out of our performing so well the last two weeks. A ball club can be down, yet still have pride. Neither contending club had been able to use us as a springboard. In fact, the way we saw it, the Giants hadn't won the pennant; the Dodgers had lost it. Somehow, there wasn't quite the thrill in beating the Dodgers that there would have been in the knockdown, dragout past. Except for Duke Snider, none of these kids in Dodger uniforms had been out of high school when St. Louis and Brooklyn last battled for supremacy in the National League.

I'd been so keyed up those last couple of weeks that I didn't realize until the season was over just how tired I'd become, playing frequently enough to qualify for the batting title. I had 505 plate appearances and finished third to Tommy Davis and Frank Robinson.

I set some career records that I'm sure I'll cherish even more as I get older, but what gave me my greatest thrill in 1962 was the year I had at bat. I averaged .330, with 19 homers and drove in 82 runs while starting 116 games. Pinch-batting, I went to the plate 19 times and reached base 14 times. Included were eight hits for a .615 pinch-hitting average. And I hit .325 against righthanders, .345 against lefthanders.

I walked out there, day after day, certain I would play, confident I would hit. It was like old times.

23

The Last Go-Around

Maybe I should have to quit at 42 with a .330 batting average, but, heck, I was having too much fun hitting to want to quit. And Bing Devine, Johnny Keane—the Cardinals—wanted me back. For a moment, though, there was embarrassment and unpleasantness when 81-year-old Branch Rickey, returning to the Cardinals as senior consultant, was quoted as having told Devine that I ought to retire. Devine, who felt the Cardinals were considerably closer to pennant contention, disagreed.

About to take off for the Florida winter league at the club's request, to watch and possibly advise young Cardinal hitters at St. Petersburg, I was ready to chuck the whole thing. I had hesitated about going, anyway, because our little one, Jeanie, was not feeling too well—and now this! But I took the plane because I'd promised to help. And in the midst of the furor that followed, Mr. Rickey explained that he'd heard me mention retirement and believed I'd flatly made up my mind not to return in 1963.

When Gussie Busch was asked for comment by the press, he said, "Since when do you ask a .330 hitter to retire?" I wasn't a .330 hitter by 75 points in 1963, but I'm very glad I played one more year, my twenty-first full season in the majors. I had the thrill of going through an exciting pennant race, one that just failed to produce the greatest stretch drive of them all. And I had the satisfaction of reaching that point where, without anyone else having to tell me, I realized my liabilities were about to outweigh my assets as a ball player.

I secretly felt in the spring that the Cardinals had better than an outside pennant chance. I was sure, for one thing, that we had been better than a sixth-place team the year before. I believed, mainly, that Devine had dealt excellently to obtain George Altman from Chicago for the outfield and Dick Groat from Pittsburgh to play shortstop.

Devine and Keane were gambling, to give up an established starting pitcher, Larry Jackson, and a reliever, Lindy McDaniel. To me, the risk was worth while. Our young pitching seemed pretty substantial, and we needed another good bat in the outfield. Above all, we needed a shortstop who could hold his own at bat, give us steadiness at a key position and help settle brilliant, erratic Julian Javier at second base.

Groat did all these things and more. The former Pittsburgh captain, who won a batting title and the Most Valuable Player award in the Pirates' championship year, 1960, proved to be a field leader who could inspire. Dick did a tremendous job, and I'm sorry he just missed a second batting championship the final week. He deserved to win it.

The Cardinals led the league in team batting and runs scored, but our pitching wasn't quite good enough, especially when Los Angeles' pitching could be so outstanding, as the Yankees learned in the World Series. If young Ray Washburn hadn't hurt his arm—he was positively great when he completed and won his first five starts—we might have had enough.

My final opening-day game, in the old Polo Grounds, wasn't especially distinguished. I had one hit in three trips as Ernie Broglio shut out the Mets on two hits, 7-0. Although it naturally was too good to last, we won our next two games on shutouts, too, behind Washburn and Curt Simmons. Early in May, as we took first place, I tied Babe Ruth's career record for extra-base hits with a three-run double off Don Elston to beat the Cubs, 4-3. Then on May 8, at a time the Dodgers began to find out how to

The Man signed for the last time with Gussie Busch early in 1963 and, as a nice sentimental touch, the long-time secretary to Cardinal presidents, Miss Mary Murphy, came out of retirement to fill in the contract.

beat us, I broke the Babe's record at St. Louis with a homer off former teammate Bob Miller. Of course I'm proud to have more extra-base hits than any player other than Henry Aaron, 1377—but, to me, Ruth is still champ. After all, let's face it, I went to bat some 2500 more times than the No. 1 slugger. Hank had even more at-bats than I did.

I was amused late in May after I got one hit the first game and three the second game of a doubleheader against the Mets on a gloomy, misty Sunday in St. Louis. Someone figured that I had become the oldest player, other than a pitcher, to appear in a doubleheader since Adrian (Cap) Anson in 1897. Not counting men who played one last game as a lark, or Satchel Paige, who's so old his first sandlot batterymate could have been Dred Scott, the oldest big leaguer must have been John Picus Quinn. Jack Quinn pitched 14 games for Cincinnati in 1933 when he was 49.

By the time I next played a doubleheader, we were in trouble. After leading the league through most of June, we fell into a batting slump in Houston, where the lights are poor, the nights extremely hot and the pitching very good. We lost two games there at the beginning of July and went west to lose eight in a row. The Dodgers, whom we had defeated so royally the year before, unseated us from first place.

When we moved over to San Francisco, we were still skidding. The Sunday before the All-Star interlude, I hit a two-run triple in the ninth inning to tie the first game, but we lost it in the fifteenth, 4-3. In the second game that day, I hit a two-run homer in the seventh inning of a scoreless duel between Juan Marichal and Bob Gibson, and we broke the long losing streak with a final score of 5-0.

We were down in fourth place as we headed for Cleveland with our own All-Star infield. Because Pittsburgh's Bill Mazeroski was injured, Julian Javier was named. Bill White, Ken Boyer and Groat had been voted as starters by their fellow National League players. That infield was the strength of the 1963 Cardinals, all right. Branch Rickey, thumbing back through more than 60 years of major league memories, said that this was the finest he could recall. Marty Marion, in mild dissent, said the Cardinals' 1946 infield was a bit better. I'm not so sure, though we did have a good one in '46. I played first base then, Red Schoendienst second, Marion short and George Kurowski third. That far back, Red hadn't yet come into his own as a hitter.

In the Cleveland All-Star game, won for us by wonderful Willie Mays, 5-3, I went up as a pinch-hitter against Jim Bunning in the fifth inning. I knew, in my heart, that this would be my last All-Star appearance. I hit a line drive on the nose to Al Kaline in right field. I got out in front of that pitch just a fraction too much. Looking back, I had great satisfaction out of my six All-Star homers, naturally, and I enjoyed very much seeing the National League wipe out the wide American League advantage. But I enjoyed most the thrill and excitement of the spectacle. And that's why I told a writer that I certainly hated to think this would be my last All-Star appearance. He interpreted the remark to mean that I intended to play in 1964.

I really didn't think seriously about playing another year. Our younger outfielders were beginning to come along, and manager Johnny Keane was getting to use them more often. Although my RBI production was good, my average wasn't, and I found that I just wasn't able to concentrate at bat as completely as I had previously. I was taking called third strikes, something I'd rarely done.

Friends have suggested that too many outside interests created distraction. Some doctors believe dulled vision or rusty reflexes were factors. Others talk about the effect of the pressure on an aging athletic nervous system. I reject the suggestion of outside interests or vision, but I really don't know the answer, as I told St. Louis medical men when I spoke before them at the request of the Cardinals' team surgeon, Dr. I. C. Middleman.

Even though I was no longer able to hit with proper singleness of purpose, I felt my age more defensively. I knew, of course, that I had slowed over the years on the bases and in the outfield, but now I noticed that I really had difficulty untracking to get started after a fly ball. And, as I've always said and tried to show, there's a lot more to baseball than just swinging a bat.

By coincidence, I reached a firm decision just after I had beaten Spahn with a basehit on Senior Citizens' Day at Milwaukee. General manager Bing Devine joined the ball club and suggested we have breakfast together in his hotel suite. Every year, we'd had a preliminary talk about my plans, and this, I suspected, was it. Sure enough, after pleasant small talk, Bing wanted to know what I had in mind.

The words came hard because it's not easy to quit. "After this year, Bing," I said finally, "I'll have had it."

Devine seemed relieved, as relieved as I was when I got the words out. Maybe now I wouldn't be asked the same question in every town. Bing and I talked about how and when to announce the decision. I wanted to make the announcement in St. Louis, not on the road, and to my teammates first. Bing suggested the ball players' annual family picnic, scheduled a few days later at Gussie Busch's farm.

I liked the idea. I don't know if I would have liked it so much, though, if I had guessed how tearful the rainy, steamy Aug. 12 picnic would be. When I made my announcement, friends of the press, radio and ball club put in their sentimental few cents' worth, too. In the course of my halting, emotional remarks, I tried to rally a ball club that seemed hopelessly far behind in third place, but I'll admit I was indulging in wishful thinking when I said:

". . . I'd like nothing more than to go out on a winner. Our 1942 club was farther behind and won. We still have a chance."

My wife, even though she had known my decision, seemed more shaken up than anyone. When I returned to the table where she sat, moist-eyed, with our three girls, I tried to kid her.

"I don't suppose you want to kiss an old retired ball player," I said.

"And you don't want to kiss an old grandmother," Lil said, smiling through her tears.

The fact is, sweating out the arrival of our first grandchild, we were having almost as rough a time as daughter-in-law Sharon. And in the emotion-packed final six weeks of my playing career, concern that everything would go well for the junior Musials was foremost in our minds.

Every town the Cardinals visited that last time around, the fans and ball clubs treated me wonderfully, with a warmth and hospitality that stopped short of just the foul lines. Whenever there was a ceremony bidding me good-bye, I didn't hit a lick. By the end of August, we had fallen seven and a half games behind, and the rampaging Phillies were only a game behind us as we moved into Philadelphia after a last unsuccessful trip to the West Coast. It was there that we began our incredible drive by sweeping a three-game series. We returned to St. Louis with confidence. I'm sure the other players could feel it. I know I could.

We ripped off nine in a row, lost one and found an old ally suddenly back in our clubhouse. Baseball writers, seeking a copy of our old victory song of 1942 and 1946 to play at a retirement dinner for me in October, appealed to Bob Hyland of radio station KMOX. Bob began the same search for "Pass the Biscuits, Mirandy" that his distinguished father, the late Dr. Hyland, had made 17 years earlier. Only now the number was even harder to find. In fact, the dauntless Hyland had to run down Spike Jones himself in Beverly Hills, Calif., before he could get a copy of the bush league ballad about a hillbilly biscuit maker named Mirandy.

I did a delighted double-take when I walked into the clubhouse and heard our new hi-fi clanging with the claptrap of an era when Doc Weaver twanged his mandolin and I played a slide whistle, when Harry Walker beat time with coat hangers and Johnny Beazley raised his voice in an off-key tenor. Bob

Bauman, like Doc Weaver before him, was playing Bob Hyland's hunch—and off we went on another long winning streak.

After we'd won from the Cubs the night of Sept. 10, Lil and I awakened with a start at exactly the same time—4:40 A.M.—and got up, troubled. As she brewed coffee, I paced the floor. Suddenly the phone rang. Son Dick was calling from Ft. Riley, Kansas. Sharon had given birth to a boy. When? Just two minutes after Lil and I woke up.

I was a tired, but happy grandfather as I passed the cigars in the clubhouse that night. I took a ribbing, of course, particularly from former St. Louis-area major leaguers who were being honored by the Cardinals that night and were playing a brief game before we met the Cubs.

"Hey, Gramp, you belong with us," sang out Joe Medwick and an overstuffed Terry Moore.

"Next year," I said, laughing.

That night I hit the first pitch Glen Hobbie threw me for a two-run homer. That one was for Jeffrey Stanton Musial.

With Mirandy passing the bisuits every night in the clubhouse, the Cardinals were suddenly so hot that we even beat two tough 20-game lefthanders, the Cubs' young Dick Ellsworth and the Braves' ancient Warren Spahn. Facing Spahnie for the last time in our 17-year rivalry, I doubled off the right field screen. Ken Boyer immediately homered and we ended Warren's eight-game winning streak. That night Joe Reichler, Associated Press statistical buff, told me that against Spahn over the years I had batted .314 and had hit 14 home runs. Uh-huh, but I hit only one of those homers the last nine years I faced him. I could hit the crafty cuss much of the time, but not for distance.

The Cardinals' streak was the most incredible of my 22 years in the majors, not for sustained play as in 1942, but for spectacular results over a three-week period. Day after day, game after game, we'd rock the opposition at the outset so that they had to try to play catch-up. Young Tim McCarver, catching his first full season, starred and so, too, did our pitchers, especially Curt Simmons, Bob Gibson and Ernie Broglio, starting, and young Ron Taylor and veteran Bobby Shantz, relieving. And when Lew Burdette, who had been obtained from Milwaukee in a June trading-deadline deal, teamed with Ray Sadecki to beat the Braves in a mid-September Sunday doubleheader, we had won 10 in a row, 19 of 20—and were only one game out as the Dodgers came to town.

St. Louis was pennant happy, and I know I felt like a kid. But the Dodgers, though they naturally had lost ground during our torrid spell, had refused to crack. And they met our head-to-head challenge with championship class. The first game, played before a capacity 32,442 crowd, was a scoreless duel between Broglio and Johnny Podres until the sixth inning. Then Curt Flood, our great little center fielder, was fooled by a fly ball Tommy Davis hit off the fists. Curt broke back a step, just enough to prevent his catching Davis' short, looping RBI single.

In the seventh I hit my last major league home run, No. 475, a line shot to the pavilion roof, tying the score, and I thought the fans would tear down the park with joy. I thought, too, as we put two more men on base that we'd get to Podres, but the stocky southpaw choked us off. After Broglio went out for an eighth-inning pinch-hitter, the Dodgers got to Shantz for two runs in the ninth, and Ron Perranoski protected Podres' 3-1 victory.

Between them, Perranoski, the No. 1 reliever, and Sandy Koufax, the No. 1 starter, accounted for a 41-8 record and innumerable saves. Koufax, one of the most impressive pitchers I (or the Yankees) ever saw, held us hitless the following night until I lined a single to center in the seventh inning. We couldn't have scored all night. The Dodgers, meanwhile, broke a string of 28 consecutive scoreless innings pitched by Simmons. They won, 4-0.

Old Gramps got two more hits the next night when Gibson seemed to have a 5-1 victory locked up, but the Dodgers rallied in the eighth and tied the score in the ninth when Dick Nen, a kid just up from Oklahoma City, hit a home run. Perranoski, shrugging off a leadoff triple by Dick Groat in one overtime inning, finally won in the thirteenth, 6-5.

The race was over. I'd hit .325 against the Dodgers in a .255 season, but the champions had defeated us 12 out of 18 times. My disappointment was great, of course, but I'm still proud to have played with the 1963 Cardinals, a club that wouldn't quit. Besides, we finished with 93 victories, the most since 1949, the year we lost the pennant by one game.

The last day of the season, my final game, seems like a hazy dream. I'd been under great strain from all sides for weeks, and it had reached pressure-cooker proportions that final weekend. Photographers and television cameramen had been practically living with us since daughter Gerry served as a maid of honor two nights previously at the Veiled Prophet ball. And with telephone calls mounting, and reporters, relatives, friends and fans crowding in on me, I didn't have time to think about what I wanted to do most. That is, to say a few words that would be right and also to go out, if possible, with a basehit.

TV had turned our clubhouse into a sound stage that last day and, walking in among so much equipment and so many cameramen, photographers, technicians and reporters, I felt guilty for having created confusion and discomfort for my teammates. I felt a little silly, too.

"I've changed my mind," I shouted. "I'm not going to retire."

But I was laughing and didn't fool anyone—Claude Keefe always did say my sleight of hand was better than my jokes—and finally, to get a few minutes alone to compose my speech, I retreated into the one sanctuary of the clubhouse: the men's room.

I was very pleased that commissioner Ford Frick, National League president Warren Giles and American League president Joe Cronin were there to participate in pre-game ceremonies. I was highly honored, too, a few weeks later when the same men and many top players and officials of the big league clubs came to St. Louis for the testimonial dinner by which the local baseball writers raised $40,000 to build a statue of me at the new riverfront stadium. You know, I always thought you had to be dead to have someone do that for you.

Of all the gifts I've been given at one time or another, I believe I cherish most the ring—number "6" set in diamonds—that was presented by my 1963 teammates. My world championship rings had been stolen from my house several years earlier.

"This is a day I'll always remember," I told the crowd, trying to sum up my gratitude and my feelings. "This is a day of both great joy and sorrow, the sorrow which always comes when we have to say farewell. My heart is filled with thanks for so many who made these 22 years possible.

"I want to thank my wife and children for their strong support for a part-time husband and father . . . I want to thank God for giving me the talent I have and the good health I've been blessed with . . . baseball has taught me the opportunity that America offers to any young men who want to get to the top in anything. I hate to say good-bye. So until we meet again, I want to thank you very much."

And now, after being driven in a convertible around the inside of the jammed park, where I played so many years in left field, center field, right field and at first base, I had to try to hit one of baseball's finest young pitchers, flame-throwing Jim Maloney, Cincinnati's 20-game righthander. Neither Maloney nor the Reds were fooling because, as they started the final game, they were hopeful of finishing third, which would be worth about $1300 apiece, and fearful of finishing fifth, which carried with it no first-division prize money.

My legs were wobbly from emotion and exhaustion as I trotted to the outfield to start my last game. When I batted the first time—the trip to the plate was interrupted so that the ball could be given to baseball Hall of Fame director Sid Keener—I took a

Musial's last time at bat and his last hit, September 29, 1963.

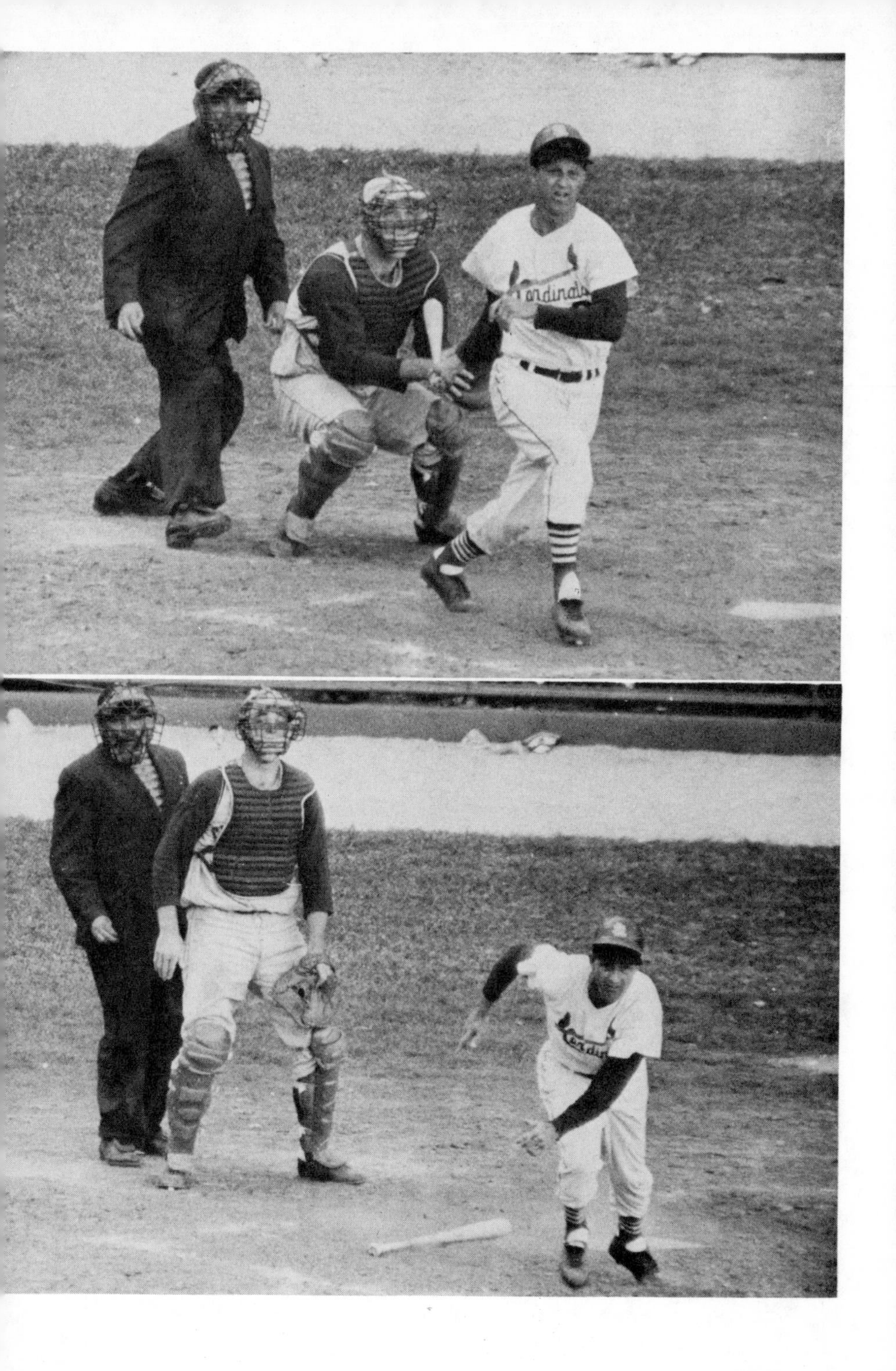

called third strike, a quick overhanded curve.

As I returned to the dugout, trainer Bob Bauman growled, "You weren't bearing down up there."

I smiled at Bauman's out-of-character gruffness. "You're right, boss," I said. If only I could concentrate like the Musial of old, not an old Musial. . . .

When I came up again in the fourth inning, Maloney was pitching no-hit ball in a scoreless battle with Gibson. I crouched low, trying to forget all else except the giant pitcher and the ball he fired so fast. It came low, inside. I swung and grounded the ball to second baseman Pete Rose's right—ah, just beyond his glove into right center—for a basehit.

At least I wouldn't get horsecollared in the final boxscore.

Now it was the sixth inning. The game still was 0-0. Curt Flood was on second base when I came up. The shadows had lengthened on the cool, bright, beautiful day. The batter's box was completely in a darkened area. Sunlight streaked deceptively halfway between home plate and the pitcher's mound.

I fouled off a high fast ball. Maloney threw a curve into the dirt. His next pitch was a fast ball, wide. The "2 and 1" pitch was a sharp-breaking curve, low and inside. I picked up the spin of the ball in time. My wrists whipped the bat down and in. I pulled the ball sharply on the ground and into the hole, just past the first baseman. It bounced into right field for a basehit, No. 3630, a run-scoring single to right.

It was, Johnny Keane felt, as he sent in a pinch-runner, a helluva good time to say good-bye, and I agreed. I was extremely fortunate to have collected two hits in my last big league ball game just as I had in my first one 22 years earlier. And the Cardinals went on to win Sept. 29, 1963, by the same 3-2 score as on Sept. 17, 1941.

I wish I could have gone out in a World Series. I knew I would miss the action, the excitement, the thrill of putting on the uniform, the competition, the travel, the fuss of the fans, and. . . .

They say it's a smart man who quits when he's still ahead. It was a good idea to get out before I actually starting hitting like a ball club vice-president.

24

The Winner's Circle

If, as I said at the time, I had been in left field for the Cardinals in 1964, the Redbirds would not have won that long-awaited pennant. It was the first in 18 years, after the worst drought since the club first hit the winner's circle in 1926.

With the Musial of old, yes, but with an old Musial, no. I could no longer do the things a dashing, daring Lou Brock did when acquired by Bing Devine at the June trading deadline.

Der Bingle has made some good deals, more good ones than bad ones, acquiring through trades such players as Curt Flood, Bill White, Dick Groat, Julian Javier, Richie Allen, Reggie Smith and Lynn McGlothen. But the Brock deal was THE best. Yet it was pretty widely criticized because the Cardinals gave up jut-jawed Ernie Broglio, who had been a 20-game winner.

With Chicago, Broglio quickly faded, but Brock, a kid who had been disappointing at Wrigley Field, trying too hard, relaxed under the thoughtful handling of Johnny Keane and in the kindly atmosphere of St. Louis.

From mid-June on, Lou hit .348 and stole 33 bases for St. Louis. But still the pennant was the uphill kind that has characterized the Cardinals' history, so reminiscent of come-from-behind pennants of 1930, 1934, 1942 and 1946.

I traveled extensively with that '64 ball club because, like an old war horse let out to pasture, I just couldn't seem to cool off too quickly, to learn not to live out of a suitcase. Letting down physically for a time, I sat in pressboxes to drink beer and eat hot dogs, for which I'd had an unsatisfied craving in the no-touch period of 22 summers playing. I wound up with indigestion and exhaustion, and was hospitalized momentarily.

But, taking over as national director of the President's Council on Physical Fitness by appointment from President Johnson, I began again to practice the fitness I'd always preached. I was gratified that the program begun by President Eisenhower with Shane McCarthy as the first director continued to grow and expand so that American school kids, too soft to pass European youth tests, began to toughen up. For their own good, of course, much more than for the country's.

The Cardinals, meanwhile, finishing the first half of the 1964 schedule one game under .500, 40-41, stormed down the stretch, taking 53 of the last 81 to finish with exactly the same record that we'd had my final season in uniform, 93-69. Philadelphia faltered horribly the final fortnight, losing 10 in a row, including three straight in St. Louis. And when skinny Dal Maxvill squeezed a pop fly for the last out the last day of a dramatic season, the Cardinals were No. 1 at long last.

It was a bittersweet moment for those of us, including key players such as Bill White and Ken Boyer, who were aware of how Devine had labored to put together this ball club. Goaded by senior consultant Branch Rickey, Gussie Busch had dismissed Devine as general manager in August, at a time when it looked as if the Cardinals couldn't overtake the Phillies, and when Rickey had advanced a grand plan for calling up minor league kids. It was also the time for setting down such regulars as Javier and Mike Shannon and shipping out veteran reliever Barney Schultz.

Bringing up Shannon to play right field and Schultz to aid the bullpen had been Devine's last moves, the final pieces in the jigsaw. At Rickey's suggestion, Busch brought in Bob Howsam from Denver as general manager. Howsam, out of baseball for a couple of years, had lost heavily when expanding the Denver ball park. At that time Rickey's threatened third major league, the Continental League, had led to expansion in the American and National—and left Denver out in the cold.

Howsam, as he proved at Cincinnati, is an astute baseball man, but he had less to do with winning in '64 than the press-gate ticket taker and other less-important, but long-time employees he fired. The former beekeeper was lucky enough to fall into an aviary and come out clutching a jar of honey.

Rickey had been baseball's most brilliant executive mind, but the old man was in his dotage. If Musial was too old to play ball, B. R. was too old to try to run the show, which he wanted to do with Devine in his way. Rickey figured Howsam would be only a figurehead, but the old man was wrong.

Howsam later did his thing, but not before the Cardinals won an exciting World Series. They beat the Yankees, managed by our old friend, Yogi Berra. The Series went to the seven-game limit, but the key moment came in the fifth contest. The day before, Boyer had hit a grand-slam homer off Al Downing for a 4-3 St. Louis victory at Yankee Stadium. Now, with the Series tied, Bob Gibson had the Yanks shut out into the ninth inning, 2-0.

With a man on base, Joe Pepitone lashed a line smash off Gibson's right hip as the pitcher followed through in his delivery and faced first base. Like a big cat, Gibby leaped back to his right and at the third-base foul line corraled the ball, fired and nipped Pepitone on a brilliant bang-bang play.

Tom Tresh, next up, followed with a game-tying homer that would have won the contest if Pepitone had been on base. In the tenth inning Tim McCarver, the Cardinals' catcher, hit a three-run homer for a 5-2 St. Louis victory.

After the Cardinals won the championship in St. Louis, there was a celebration party at the new Stan Musial and Biggie's restaurant, located on the site of St. Louis University's former Walsh Stadium, just across from Forest Park. We were—and I am—proud of the restaurant. I was proud that Jack Buck, though only second banana on the Cardinals' baseball broadcasts at the time, had the courage to salute the absent Bing Devine.

Gussie Busch, to whom finally winning had meant so much, was shocked the day after the series to find that Johnny Keane, expected routinely to sign a new contract as manager at a pay increase, resigned instead. He succeeded Berra, fired unfairly at New York. Keane's pique was understandable. In August, when Devine was canned, Keane learned that Leo Durocher would succeed him in 1965. And, accustomed to conferring daily with Devine, Keane had found Howsam evasive and unavailable.

To lose the popular St. Louis-born manager of his world champions was a blow to Busch and to the brewery. Howsam wanted to call up his own man, Charley Metro. But the team had to consider public relations. The Cardinals came up with a 10-strike coach, Red Schoendienst.

Sure, I'm prejudiced in Red's behalf because, as I've indicated over these pages, my old road roommate is my friend. He is an excellent all-round player who would be in the baseball Hall of Fame now, in my opinion, if he hadn't walked around for years with tuberculosis. Before the bug finally flattened him after the 1958 World Series with Milwaukee.

Red used to tire in September and his average would sag. He did bounce back once beautifully to pinch hit and help the Cardinals in the early '60's. If only he had been rested properly, Red's career mark would have been at least several points over .300 instead of 11 below it.

As a player, Schoendienst was instinctive, a natural. As a manager, he had one quality which I knew long before I worked with him as his general manager. He knew the game and had the field foreman's greatest virtue—patience. That's why he lasted a club record 12 seasons as manager, twice as long as Richey's previous mark.

Red wore well, was phlegmatic, in that he didn't get too high or too low, and didn't over-manage. He let the players play. And, take it from one who has played under more managers than most, that's the kind of handling that brings out the best in the majority of players. As Eddie Dyer used to say, after both coaching football and managing baseball, you can't steam up baseball players emotionally over an every-day schedule. You can do that in football, a once-a-week sport. In baseball, you need loose wrists, relaxed skills.

I was confident Red could and would last a long time. I felt that even before I became General Manager in 1967 when the Cardinals had finished seventh in '65 and sixth in '66.

With the ball club aging a bit around the edges, Howsam had dealt often and not too wisely before moving over to Cincinnati. He did make a couple of good ones, though, with an assist from others in the organization.

In 1966, just as the Cardinals were preparing to move downtown to beautiful Busch Memorial Stadium, Howsam hedged and vacillated in a deal by which lefthanded pitcher Ray Sadecki would go to San Francisco for first baseman-outfielder Orlando Cepeda.

It was common knowledge that a Cepeda-to-Chicago deal had fallen through because the Cubs, giving up southpaw Dick Ellsworth, wanted something other than the knee-damaged

Prophetically, Stan and long-time road roommate Red Schoendienst laughed in January, 1967, when Musial was named general manager of the Cardinals, for whom Red had been field manager since 1965. The '67 El Birdos breezed to the National League pennant and world championship—and Stan and Red laughed again.

Cepeda to sweeten the pot. Those of us who knew Horace Stoneham were aware you didn't push or prod the long-time sportsman who then owned the Giants. We were fearful Horace would nix the deal with St. Louis, too, but Dick Meyer, always a sound stabilizing influence, urged Howsam to get along with the deal and to forget trying to get more for Sadecki.

So Cepeda joined the Cardinals, and the Baby Bull or Cha-Cha, as he became known, prospered under the care of Dr. I. C. Middleman and associate Dr. Stan London and especially the ever-loving attention of Bob Bauman, the great trainer who had prolonged my career.

Just before I became general manager, the Cardinals had an opportunity to get the veteran Roger Maris from the Yankees. Howsam hemmed and hawed about that one, too. He was mindful of Rog's large salary and concerned because the ailing home-run hitter had had a reputation for a bad temperament. But, even players such as Brock, Cepeda, Dick Allen, Reggie Smith, unhappy elsewhere, had been happy playing in St. Louis. It was the late Mark Eagleton, my old lawyer and the father of

Sen. Thomas Eagleton, who spoke up as a member of the board of directors, urging the acquisition of Maris to play right field. In an unusual autumn exercise at Fairground Park, close by old Sportsman's Park, Schoendienst and coach Joe Schultz, hitting ground balls to Shannon by the hour, had determined that Mike could move in from right field to play third base. Charley Smith, headed for the Yankees in the deal for Maris, absolutely did not fit into our plans at third.

So that's the way it was when I was called in and asked if I'd take over as G.M. while Howsam went on to bigger and better things at Cincinnati. I didn't hesitate. I hadn't wanted to manage. But, though I didn't know the technicalities of baseball waivers and other points of baseball law, I figured I knew the rest of it. I knew the players and had been watching the games as senior vice-president.

In spring training, still putting on the old "6" now and then to work out and offer a pointer on hitting when asked, I liked what I saw. Maybe I helped a little psychologically, too, as some suggested. Chatting and backslapping in the clubhouse, I think I did ease tension there without in any way undermining my man Red's position. (Howsam, you see, was a spit-and-polish, sit-up-straight-in-the-bullpen man. I don't criticize him for that because, after all who can rap the Reds' success?) And just as the long hair, mustaches and beards haven't bothered me in recent times, I was more concerned then with what a player did than how he looked.

The night before the season opened, Bob Hyland and the Knights of the Cauliflower Ear put on their traditional dinner at which not only the Cardinals, but also the opposing San Francisco Giants were present. "Gentlemen," I said when called on to speak, "I have a feeling the National League's 1967 pennant-winning ball club is one of the two in this room."

I should have been so right so often. From the time Gibson shut out Marichal and the Giants opening night, the Cardinals of 1967 were terrific. Cepeda and McCarver ran 1-2 in MVP balloting. Brock and Gibson were super-stars at their peak. Maxvill and Javier formed an excellent second-base combination and Flood was spectacular in center field. So the down-the-middle defense was great when pitching newcomers Nelson Briles, Steve Carlton and, most unexpectedly, Dick Hughes came through. The club breezed in with a 101-60 record and attracted 2,090,145 to our dazzling new stadium.

I'd made one mistake. To help with the front-office detail, I'd brought my right hand physical fitness man, the late Bob Stewart in from Washington. But the former St. Louis University athletic director didn't know baseball law, either. Every department in the front-office seemed to close ranks behind Stan the Man, and when I really was in a quandary, I'd pick up the phone and call my good friend, Bing Devine, then with the New York Mets. Graciously, Der Bingle would straighten out the fine points for me.

If ever a general manager under-general managed, I guess it was me. I made only one roster move, acquiring Jack Lamabe from the Mets after Gibson suffered a broken leg. He was hit with a line shot off Roberto Clemente's bat just after the All-Star game.

A red-letter day for a foursome smiling more on the inside than outside: The National Baseball Hall of Fame induction of Stan Musial and former pitcher Waite Hoyt, standing, and ex-pitcher Stan Coveleski and paralyzed catching star Roy Campanella, seated. Musial went into the baseball shrine at Cooperstown, N.Y., in 1969, the first year he was eligible.

This could have caused a crucial moment because the Cubs were close to us, but Briles came out of the bullpen to take a starting turn and won nine in a row. Gibson returned in September and, talking it over, Red and I figured that with two or three tuneup starts, Gibby would be ready for the Series. We wanted the blue-ribbon man in the blue-ribbon event.

Gibby was just that, a blue-ribbon man. He beat the Boston Red Sox three times to win *Sport Magazine's* award of a new automobile as the top player in the Series. But Brock had been so outstanding, too, hitting .414, stealing a record seven bases and scoring eight runs, that Bob Hyland and his radio station, KMOX, gave Lou a matching car as a pleasant consolation.

Me? I was happy, of course, but sad, too, because in June I'd lost my partner and good friend, Julius (Biggie) Garagnani, a heart attack victim at only 53. Biggie was a shrewd business man, and the one to whom I am most grateful for the success of the operation that his able son, Jack, my boy, Dick, and a capable organization have expanded. It now includes three thriving hotels as well as our restaurant and a bowling alley.

At the time of Biggie's untimely death, I found myself trying to put in a 9-to-5 stint at the ball park and more time at the restaurant, where, naturally, we were in a turmoil. I found that the old Donora graduate who would have had to punch a clock in the mines or mills, if there were any jobs available back home, just wasn't meant to work by the clock or be chained to a desk.

So I let Dick Meyer and Mr. Busch know that I'd be pleased to be relieved of the general manager's job. (After all, it's tough to beat 1-for-1). I was even happier when the only name mentioned as my successor was Bing Devine, by then president of the Mets.

Good ol' Gussie, though a proud and successful tycoon as head of the world's largest brewery, wasn't too proud to ask the hometown boy to come back. And Bing, who had grown up watching Rogers Hornsby, Frank Frisch, Dizzy Dean and the rest of those early heroes, had St. Louis roots that went very deep.

For having put together the guts of the 1964 and '67 teams he'd had to watch win from the outside, Devine was rewarded in '68 with a pennant of his own. Later, however, despite the continued brilliance of Brock and Gibson, the Cardinals were surprisingly upset by Detroit in the World Series, after winning three of the first four games.

The major leagues went to division play in 1969, as the second expansion created unwieldy 12-team leagues. So the Cards do have the distinction of having won the last pennant race played without the new championship series.

The new series is an artificial playoff that creates more pressure, but does reward the players with much more than in my day or previously, $26,000 each to the 1976 champion Reds.

As I mentioned, I don't blame the players for trying to get the most they can individually, but I do question their trying to get the best of BOTH worlds through collective bargaining and as individual contractors. And the free-agent flurry after the '76 season created near-chaos.

Economics have become a factor in baseball. The Cardinals asked me to give up my salary as senior vice-president when they were belt-tightening. It was a couple of years after a disillusioned Busch, who had spoiled his players with lavish raises, petulantly traded off two dissident pitchers, Steve Carlton and Jerry Reuss, young lefthanders who were sorely missed.

Of course, with our businesses flourishing, I didn't miss giving up income from the Cardinals. I was, in fact, relieved to be able to spend less time at the ball games than when I felt it was my duty.

In what amounts to semi-retirement, I take my sitting-up exercises—I'm only three pounds above my playing weight—and I play golf fairly well. I shot a 76 one day at the Los Angeles Country Club for my best round ever. But I just enjoy the game and don't try to beat it.

Lil and I enjoy our family, too. Dick and his wife, the former Sharon Edgar, returned to St. Louis with their three children after operating the Ivanhoe Hotel in Bal Harbour above Miami Beach, and overseeing the Stan Musial and Biggie's Clearwater Beach Hilton. Gerry, a belated journalism graduate of 1976, and her husband, Tom Ashley, righthand man in the radio-television operations of Ted Turner who is the new owner of the Braves, live in Atlanta with their three youngsters. Janet teaches school and her husband, Dr. Martin Schwarze, practices in suburban St. Louis.

The last to fly the nest will be Jeannie, who is crazy about all sports. She went to Houston with Lil to see me in an old-timers' game a couple of years ago. Though I got a couple of hits, which I always do in the Nostalgia League, I kicked a ground ball, threw wildly and Jean said seriously to her mother:

"Oh, I'm so embarrassed."

Jean wondered if I always hit with that crazy batting stance, which National League pitchers wondered for 22 years. She doesn't recall seeing me play officially, but she was there when they dedicated the statue by Carl Mose outside Busch Memorial Stadium. Mom, Lil and the rest of the family were, too.

Frankly, I thought the statue was supposed to be The Man and The Boy, a two-figure autographing symbol of the relationship between ball players and the kids who idolize them and to whom the athletes have the obligation of setting an example. I'll say

The Musials, minus one, in 1967. From left to right in the back are Sharon, and her husband Dick Musial, "The Man," and son-in-law Tom Ashley. In front are daughter Jean Musial, Lil with grandson Jeff, grandaughter Laura Musial, and blonde daughter Janet, who is now

married to Dr. Martin Schwarze. Seated on her lap is twin Kitty Ashley. Little Tommy Ashley snuggles close to mother Gerry, who holds the other unhappy twin, Kit. Born later was Sharon and Dick Musial's daughter, Natalie.

Only a friend as close as Jack Lake would accompany a fellow to Poland in February, but that's what Lake, publisher of the St. Petersburg (Fla.) *Times,* did in 1973, when Musial was honored by Polish sports societies. From the left, the man Stan, wife Lil Musial, sports buff Lake and his dear wife, Catherine Ann, a good sport bundled up for winter in Warsaw.

this, Jeannie, I didn't hit the way that guy in the statue does.

A few years after I'd swung for keeps for the last time, the Cardinals brought together members of the champion Redbirds and Yankees for a weekend reunion in St. Louis. As usual, Casey Stengel and Frank Frisch, both now gone, were the life of the post-game party at the restaurant. In the game I had the pleasure of batting for the first time in new Busch Memorial Stadium.

Allie Reynolds, pitching, wasn't throwing too hard, fortunately, but I got one I liked and rode it over the distant right field wall, bringing a roar and standing ovation from the crowd. I couldn't help laughing for joy as I circled the bases.

"I wanted that one," I said. "I wanted that one—in this park."

I guess you could say I've touched all the bases. I've hunted lion, elephant and leopard in Tanzania as guests of the African government. And Lil and I went to Poland with Jack Lake,

publisher of the St. Petersburg (Fla.) *Times,* to be honored by the Polish Olympic Committee in February, 1973. We liked my father's homeland so well that we went again in '76 with the Piszaks.

Friends will kid that only a Polack would go to Warsaw in February, but we had a delightful time. I met my father's cousin, a spitting image of Dad. We especially enjoyed being carried by horse-drawn troika over the fresh snow on a crisp, clear night. Violinists accompanied us with Polish tunes on the ride, to a mountain resort for a vodka-and-kielbasa version of an American beer-and-weiner roast.

Wherever I go, though, the homing pigeon returns to St. Louis and to my first love, baseball.

In reflection, I'd like to give my personal All-Star teams over a period of 35 years.

For my National League team, I'd give Johnny Mize the edge over Gil Hodges at first base. I know this will be questioned, but I'd take Red Schoendienst over Jackie Robinson at second base. I had the most indecision at shortstop, where I finally chose Pee Wee Reese over Marty Marion and Ernie Banks. At third base, a position that had fewer stars than any other throughout my career, I switched after my playing days to Eddie Mathews over Ken Boyer.

In the outfield, too, where I hated most to leave off Enos Slaughter, I changed my mind over the years and dropped Duke Snider so that I wound up with a threesome of Henry Aaron, Willie Mays and Roberto Clemente.

For catcher, I pick Roy Campanella in a photo finish with Walker Cooper, to catch Warren Spahn, Robin Roberts, Harry Brecheen and Bob Gibson, whom I substituted for Mort Cooper. As a reliever, I'd still want Elroy Face, though aware that Lindy McDaniel has excellent credentials and that Al Hrabosky could, too.

On my major league All-Star team since 1941, I'd still take Face in the bullpen, though I don't suppose he'd get much work behind a starting four of Bob Feller, Spahn, Gibson and Roberts. I don't think Sandy Koufax pitched long enough to qualify.

I'd take that National League infield of Mize, Schoendienst, Reese and Mathews. But I'd put two American Leaguers, Ted Williams and Joe DiMaggio in the outfield with Mays, aware unhappily that I don't have a place for Aaron or Clemente.

And I'd have Yogi Berra as my No. 1 catcher. I remember Yogi back in 1942, I believe it was, working out with the Cardinals at Sportsman's Park. I couldn't forget him because of his squat, fire-plug appearance, his awkward effectiveness and an ability even then to rip the ball against the right field screen.

The Cardinals lost this future Hall of Fame player for $250, the difference between the pittance they offered him and the $500 his pal, Joe Garagiola, had been given. Even earlier, the Redbirds lost another certain Hall of Fame slugger, Ted Williams, because the general manager of their Sacramento, California, farm club didn't think that tall kid from San Diego—or any other boy, for that matter—was worth a $1000 bonus.

It was about that time, Judge Landis made his famous Cedar Rapids ruling of 1938, declaring 91 Cardinal players to be free agents. Among them was Pete Reiser.

To think that in my time the Cardinals sold, not traded, such blockbuster belters as Mize and W. Cooper and a rubber-armed pitcher, Murry Dickson. I honestly believe that if Gussie Busch and the brewery had owned the Cardinals then, in the decade of the '40s when we finished 1-2 every year, we would have won a string of pennants that would have put the old Yankees' dynasty to shame.

Imagine hitting in a batting order that would have included Schoendienst . . . Slaughter . . . Reiser . . . Williams . . . Mize . . . Berra or Cooper! Why, the Cardinals would have had their OWN All-Star team and I'd have had a helluva time making the ball club. But, man, it would have been fun winning.

Ouch! Stan the Man strains his 55-year-old back when taking a swing for charity—and fun—in a softball game between the St. Louis Symphony and the New York Philharmonic in 1976. Musial "managed" the St. Louis team. Umpiring is Dan Dierdorf, All-Pro offensive tackle of the football Cardinals.

STAN MUSIAL CAREER SUMMARY

(Compiled by Lee Allen, Historian,
Baseball Hall of Fame, Cooperstown, N.Y.)

Through a fantastic coincidence, Musial made exactly as many hits on the road, 1815, as he did in St. Louis.

He hit .336 at home, .326 away, batted .340 for 1634 day games to .320 for 1392 night games and hit as follows against National League clubs:

Boston .353, New York .349, Brooklyn .344, Pittsburgh .340, Philadelphia .338, Los Angeles .329, Cincinnati .318, Chicago .317, San Francisco .305, Milwaukee .299 and Houston (only 27 games) .215.

At home, by club, Musial's averages were .360 Boston, .359 Philadelphia, .355 New York, .341 Pittsburgh, .331 Brooklyn, .326 Chicago, .323 Cincinnati, .311 Milwaukee, .311 Los Angeles, .305 San Francisco and .244 Houston.

On the road, Stan's averages were .356 Brooklyn .347 Boston, .343 New York, .339 Pittsburgh, .337 Los Angeles, .318 Philadelphia, .314 Cincinnati, .308 Chicago, .306 San Francisco, .288 Milwaukee and .184 Houston.

Month by month, The Man's figures were:

October .438, September .344, June .344, July .327, August .327, April .325 and May .323.

Position by position, Musial batted .345 for 299 games in center field, .399 for 699 in right field, .330 for 907 in left field and .324 for 1016 games at first base. He hit .263 for 114 official times up as a pinch-batter.

For managers, The Man hit .355 for Marty Marion, 1951; .348 for Eddie Dyer, 1946-50; .344 for Billy Southworth, 1941-44; .322 for Eddie Stanky, 1952-55; .331 for Fred Hutchinson, 1956-58; .323 for Harry Walker, 1955; .321 for Stan Hack, 1958 (7 games); .293 for Johnny Keane, 1961-63 and .273 for Solly Hemus, 1959-61.

Index

— **E** —

— **F** —

— **G** —

— H —

— I —

— J —

— K —

— L —

— Mc —

— M —

— N —

— T —

— V —

— W —

— Y —

— Z —